WARHEAD

THE TRUE STORY
OF ONE TEEN WHO
ALMOST SAVED THE WORLD

JEFF HENIGSON

DELACORTE PRESS

Visit us on the Web! GetUnderlined.com

Educators and librarians, for a variety of teaching tools,
visit us at RHTeachersLibrarians.com

Library of Congress Cataloging-in-Publication Data is available upon request.
ISBN 978-0-525-64790-4 (trade) — ISBN 978-0-525-64792-8 (lib. bdg.) —
ISBN 978-0-525-64791-1 (ebook)

The text of this book is set in 11-point Electra.
Interior design by Ken Crossland

Printed in the United States of America
10 9 8 7 6 5 4 3 2 1
First Edition

Oh, my dear mother, who knew I'd make it?
You, of course. But to be here now,
together—it's a blessing.

•

To Monique:
I'd follow you to any dance floor.

PROLOGUE

One day in the spring of 1981, as I twiddled my thumbs under my desk in Mrs. Hawkins's fourth-grade class while she droned on about adding and subtracting fractions, there was a familiar knock—*tap tada tap tap*—on our classroom door. She went over to answer it, and framed in the background sunlight was my mom. I'd begged Mom that morning—that whole week, in fact—to take me out to the Mojave Desert to watch the space shuttle *Columbia* return from its maiden voyage, but she said Dad would be stuck in the office and the trip would cost my brother and me two days of school, so we'd just have to watch it on the news. All morning in class, I'd been sulking.

But there was my mom, chatting with Mrs. Hawkins, who turned my way and motioned to me to come over. I stuck my tongue out at Jake McCoy, who'd been teasing me all morning about how my plan to see the shuttle land had failed, and I smiled at Chelsea Ashworth, who'd been consoling me, and then I practically skipped to the door. It was the happiest moment in my ten-year-long life so far, because I knew I'd soon be witnessing a miracle.

Mom had the family camper waiting for my brother and me in the school parking lot. Ted, chubby then and two years older than me, claimed the window seat. I didn't complain. Mom wasn't in the best mood, muttering something as she pulled out about how Dad was always working, and I didn't want to push it. I wanted him to be with us, but not if he was all stressed out over a case he was working on. Mom was still talking to herself when we reached the turnoff for Highway 14, the road that would get us to Edwards Air Force Base. "I'm just not going to let you boys miss history being made," she said, shaking her head.

We woke up early the next morning, in the camper, parked on the desert floor. She poured us each a cup of orange juice and set a variety pack of cereals on the pullout dining table. "Are you excited?" she said, looking closely at us.

Ted nodded, eyes wide, as he downed his OJ.

"Heck yeah," I said.

Mom's face broke into a smile.

"Good," she said. "Very good."

After breakfast, we stepped out of the camper onto the dry lake bed. Below us were fire ants, emerging from cracks and disappearing into others, and around us, in every direction, were cars and trucks and motor homes—and people standing or scurrying between them. It was good we didn't need to be anywhere in particular for the landing—just out there on the desert floor with everyone else—because we couldn't have moved fifty feet if we'd wanted to. It was like the whole world was out there waiting with us.

A little after ten o'clock in the morning, twin booms went off as the shuttle pierced the atmosphere. An announcer had already told us it would take a while before we could actually see the shuttle, but still everyone had their necks craned. I scanned the sky the way the famous fighter pilot Chuck Yeager had done when he was going after German fighter planes in World War II. I was the first person in our area to see the space shuttle, and I screamed. Everyone around me was asking, "Where, where is it?" and I just extended a finger. It was a full ten seconds before my brother picked it up—and he had Dad's binoculars.

That was all it took for me. I knew what I wanted, what I would become. From that moment on, I was certain that one day I'd be getting on top of a rocket myself.

•

Not long after the space shuttle landing, I ordered an Alpha III model rocket launch kit from Estes. It arrived during the school week, and Mom handed it to me the moment I got home. She stood there smiling as my eyes lit up, her hands on her waist and her chin held high.

In no time at all, I'd put the rocket together. I couldn't wait to show it to Dad. Mom told me he'd be home late that evening, but I begged her to let me stay up. I sat there by the front door, in my pajamas with my teeth brushed, until his car pulled in at 9:29 p.m., nearly half an hour after my bedtime. The second he walked through the door, I presented my rocket to him, proudly. "I built it all by myself, Dad," I said, sticking out my chest. "We can slide an engine into the tube here and set it up on the launch-pad, and then the two of us can fire it off!"

He set his briefcase down and held his hand out for the rocket, which I eagerly handed over. He ran his fingers over the white nose cone; down the long, checkered cardboard tube; and finally to the black plastic fins. He gently tugged at the metal hook coming out of the base of the rocket, the piece that held one of the insertable rocket engines in place.

"Isn't it the greatest, Dad?"

He nodded but didn't say anything. I thought he'd be impressed. He handed the rocket back to me. I repeated myself, this time scratching my head. "It's great, right?"

"It is well constructed." Dad cleared his throat. "I think it's important, though, that we contemplate why human beings created rockets. Why do you think they exist?"

I frowned. "To launch people into space." I thought it was kind of obvious.

"That is a much more recent application. The original purpose of rockets, and the central one of modern missiles, which are essentially rockets with built-in guidance systems, is to wreak havoc on one's perceived enemy, to cause death and destruction. Armed with nuclear warheads, missiles have the very real potential to bring an end to humanity."

His eyes focused on mine as he waited for me to grasp the gravity of his observation. Since I was a ten-year-old, it went mostly over my head.

I tried to change the subject. He'd definitely be impressed when he saw my rocket take off. "This is just a model, Dad,"

I said. "It can fly for real, though. Would you like to launch it from the back deck with me this weekend?"

He looked instantly irritated. "It may be a model, but launching it in an environment such as ours would be perilous."

I protested. "People launch them all the time."

Dad snorted. "If they in fact do, they're foolish. Rocket engines produce significant amounts of heat," he said. His voice had sharpened. "You may have noted that here in Southern California our hills are covered with dry brush."

"Our backyard isn't. You and Mom planted lots of trees and plants and stuff."

"Can you ensure the rocket will land there? I think not." He sounded annoyed. "It could touch down in the Petersons' backyard, and we nearly lost our home a few years ago to a brush fire that started there."

He seemed to be recalling the near disaster. His nostrils flared.

I stared at him blankly. He was clearly upset with me, but I was too young to understand why. That was when I heard the door to the back deck open, and paws scurrying through the living room. Mom had returned from taking Jezebel and Penelope, our Newfoundlands, out to do their evening business. "There are my girls!" Dad said when he saw them, his voice an octave higher, slowed and soothing. The frustration on his face disappeared. He quickly dropped to one knee, vigorously rubbing Penelope's head. Jezebel nudged him, and after a while he turned to her and scratched her back until she flipped over to expose her belly. He rubbed away, with Penelope eyeing for a round herself. It seemed to go on for ages.

When he finally stood, I realized I hadn't come up with anything to say. Dad looked at his watch. "Isn't it past your bedtime?"

I turned and walked toward my room, running into Ted in the kitchen. He'd been listening to the whole conversation.

"Looks like the doofus just crashed and burned," he said as I passed him. I wanted to turn around and whack him, but my eyes were filling with tears, and the last thing I needed was for my brother to see me cry.

PART 1

CHAPTER ONE

The traffic lights on Colorado Boulevard were timed so well that even on a bike you could get through six or seven of them without stopping. You couldn't do that the first time you rode, of course, but I'd been cruising down that boulevard every single day since ninth grade let out, racing six miles from my home in South Pasadena to C&H Surplus to see if any new parts had come in for my laser project. By then I could practically make it through those intersections with my eyes shut. It was hot out, your typical Southern California summer, but the breeze that formed from me biking so fast was cooling.

My laser project wasn't just me geeking out. There was an actual point to it: to help get me into space. Kids think the only way to become an astronaut is to start out as a pilot, but Dad told me studying science was a much better route. "Pilot astronauts may get you into space," he said, "but once there, it's the science astronauts who do the more substantive work." The project would look good on my applications to Caltech and MIT—

maybe enough to help them ignore how badly I'd blown freshman chemistry.

I was coming up on Allen Avenue, where my buddy Paul lived. His dad, a Caltech scientist, was trying to get one of his experiments brought up on the next space shuttle mission. Paul had been gone most of the summer, which, considering the fact he was my best friend, had made life a little boring.

Lucia popped into my head then. She'd been out of town, too, which was probably good if I was to have any chance of getting my project completed. We'd made out last summer, just after they let us out of eighth grade.

I pedaled harder now, smiling with Lucia on my mind as I soared down the boulevard. As I entered the intersection, I looked across it to see a van quickly approaching from the opposite direction. Its left turn signal was switched on, but it didn't seem to be slowing.

Frantically, I grasped my brake levers, which locked my wheels, causing my tires to lay down a straight black line. I could see the driver now, a middle-aged woman, her eyes elsewhere, as she swung her van into a turn.

There was nowhere for me to go.

Deep in my gut, there was a crushing panic. The last thing I remembered was flying.

●

Something that drove me up the wall was all the people telling me how lucky I was to have survived getting smacked by that van. *Give me a break,* I thought. If I'd actually been lucky, the lady wouldn't have splattered me in the first place.

Huntington Hospital just happened to be the hospital where I was born—exactly fifteen years, four months, and twenty-two days before that lady almost ended my life. After the crash, three people at the hospital told me about my good fortune. The only one I didn't feel like punching was the really cute nurse with the blondish-brown hair who was standing over me when I first woke up. Actually, until she opened her mouth, I thought it was Lucia hovering over me. But then the lady spoke—"It looks like somebody's awake"—and it definitely wasn't Lucia's voice.

"Where am I?" I mumbled.

"You're in an emergency room." I glanced down at my arm, tracing the tube sticking out of it to a bag hanging on a pole next to my bed. An electronic box below the bag was beeping. I kind of instinctively sniffed at the room, but there were plastic tubes in my nostrils. "You were in an accident," the nurse continued. I remembered the van crossing in front of me, but that was it. "Can you tell me your name?"

"Jeff."

"Do you know what year it is?"

"It's 1986."

"And do you know who our president is?"

"He's an actor."

She laughed and told me I was at Huntington Hospital. After several more questions, she asked for my parents' names and their phone numbers. I gave her everything and she said, "You really are lucky, you know?"

"Maybe I would be if you gave me *your* phone number," I said. She was still laughing when I fell back asleep.

The next time I opened my eyes, my father, who happened to be a modern-day replica of Abraham Lincoln, was standing at the foot of my hospital bed. He really did look just like Lincoln, from his wrinkled forehead to his long, broad nose to his scraggly beard. On Halloween five years earlier, my dad had opened the door in the same suit he'd worn to work that morning and a little girl said, "Trick or treat, Mr. Lincoln!"

Dad didn't rush over and hug me. He just stood there, his eyes focused in on mine, as I blinked a few times.

"How are you feeling, son?" he said. My body was aching everywhere.

"Like I just got hit by a van." I kind of wanted a hug. "Where's Mom?"

"They weren't able to reach her. They're going to release you shortly, so you'll see her soon." I nodded. "The good news is you don't have a significant head injury." Just like the nurse, he went on to tell me how lucky I was.

He didn't actually use the word "lucky." He said I was "fortunate." Grandma told me once that my dad never used a two-syllable word when there was a synonym that was longer. The result was that he always sounded professorial—exactly the kind of word he'd use. He was also pedantic, which happened to be one of my favorite words because it described him perfectly. He was so nitpicky about language that you couldn't make it through a story without being interrupted—*and corrected*—at least once. My cousin said that was just the way lawyers were, but half of my friends had lawyers as parents, and none of them spoke like that.

So, Dad said I was fortunate. I said, "How's that, exactly?"

"You have no significant head injury and no broken bones. It could have been considerably worse. Good that you were wearing a helmet."

That told me how much he was listening at dinner two nights before when Mom told him I accidentally left my helmet at McDonald's and it was gone when I went back. "I wasn't," I said, and he just cleared his throat.

The ER head honcho doc strolled in then, which saved me from sitting through more of my dad's weirdness. The doc was with his goons, and he let them poke me and ask all their questions. When Dad mentioned that I hadn't been wearing a helmet, the chief waved away his lackeys and did the exam himself. After a gazillion more taps, pokes, and questions, he shook his head and said, "Remarkable."

I asked him what was so remarkable, and he said something like "You were struck by a moving vehicle, you weren't wearing a helmet, and all you appear to have are lacerations, abrasions, and hematomas." Right after that was when he joined the club the nurse had started, saying, "You're a lucky young man."

•

Fifteen minutes later, Mom saw me hobbling on crutches down the stairs to the house. We lived in Monterey Hills, right smack on top of one of them, at the very end of a long cul-de-sac. There was a flower garden out front. Behind the garden was a hefty stucco wall with openings on two sides, one a glass door for people and the other a sliding glass gate for cars. Whichever way you entered, you'd have to go down a long set of stairs (which passed through another garden). At the bottom of those stairs was our house, made almost entirely of glass. Everybody was amazed the first time they saw it, and while I would agree it was kind of cool, I never liked its location, far away from the rest of the world. Everybody had their thing, though, and the isolated house was my dad's.

As I lurched down the stairs, Mom raced to the front door — which, unsurprisingly, was also glass — and slid it open. She held Amiga back, thank God, because Dad's "puppy," a 130-pound, eight-year-old Brazilian Mastiff that succeeded our two New-foundlands, could have knocked me over with a single enthusiastic nudge. "What happened?" Mom said, gasping. Her face was practically white and her hands were shaking.

There wasn't much you could do when my mom got hysterical except try to appear calm while she frantically swiped her hair away from her eyes. She had tons of hair, thick and brown and cut into a bob, with a little sprout of gray just above the left side of her forehead.

"I'm fine, Mom." She touched my cheek and switched right away to Dad. He was a few feet behind me, carrying the busted pieces of my bike frame. He'd wanted to leave them behind back at the hospital, but I wanted to show them to my friends. When Mom realized what Dad was carrying, she freaked out.

"What happened?" she asked again, the volume shooting up from two to ten.

Dad gave her a quick summary.

She turned to me, speaking very quietly. "You were hit? Are you sure you're okay?" The calm lasted for half a second. She spun back to Dad and started interrogating him. He explained everything as clearly as he could, and almost succeeded in chilling her out until he mentioned that the ER chief said I was quite fortunate.

Mom went ballistic. "Fortunate? How could my son getting hit by a car be fortunate?" It was kind of entertaining to see Dad catch some crap for once, but Mom's voice, which I knew she intended just for Dad, was piercing my ears as well. Plus, she needed to relax.

"Mom, do you think you could tone it down a notch? I'm honestly just fine." She let out a breath and her shoulders dropped. Dad, who was standing behind her, sighed quietly.

•

The next morning, I woke up feeling groggy. The ER chief had told my dad to awaken me every few hours to make sure I was sleeping, not unconscious, and my parents did that in turns all night. The second I swung my legs out from under the sheets, I felt pain surge through every inch of my body.

I slowly extended a sore arm toward the crutches resting on the wall next to my bed, dragging them along the carpet as if they were weights too heavy to lift. I positioned them under my arms and took in a breath. Wincing, I stood.

For several seconds, the pain was more intense, especially in my hands. They were already swollen, but now with blood draining down into them, increasing the pressure. There were stitches all over my fingers and both of my palms were beaten up; I wondered if any of the closed-up holes would pop open. I stood there, motionless, staring at my hands. I didn't start moving until I felt sure they'd been adequately sealed.

I hobbled to the corner of my room. It really was a huge bedroom, as my friends always told me. Nothing made me realize that more than the pain I felt limping across it.

I struggled to pull up the shades, probably looking like my grandma did to me when I was a kid, when she made things that seemed so easy look so hard.

Sunlight poured into the room. It landed on the components of my laser project, which was what I'd limped over to the corner to check out. The rectangular plastic walls that formed the laser tube were there, on top of the wood base I'd cut for it. Glued to the surface were shiny copper plates that would be charged by the power supply on hold for me at C&H Surplus. Along the side was the "spark gap"—the area where the energy pulse was released that would cause the laser beam to form and fire.

I'd shown it all to Dad a few times, telling him how impressed the admissions people at Caltech would be when they read about it, but he never seemed to agree. "You'd be better off improving your grades," he told me once. It pissed me off at the time, but it didn't matter. I couldn't wait to see the look that would appear on his face when he saw the laser working.

There was a soft knock on my door. "Yeah?" I said. The door swung open. I was surprised to see my brother.

"So you're not dead," Ted said, smirking.

"Sorry to have dashed your hopes."

"Seriously, I'm glad you're okay. Mom wants to know if you can make it upstairs for breakfast or should she bring it down."

"Tell her I'll hobble up."

He raised an eyebrow. "You sure about that?" He didn't want to freak her out.

"Walk up, I mean."

Ted rubbed his nose. "Do you need, like, any help?"

I laughed. "Go upstairs. Chill Mom out. I'll be there in a minute."

Ted nodded and disappeared into the hallway. I followed, only slowly, passing the bathroom and making my way to the base of the long staircase that connected my downstairs pad to the rest of the house.

The moment I looked up the stairs, my stomach tightened. I turned back, feeling like I needed to make a run for the bathroom, but just then, my head began to spin. I reached for a wall to steady myself, dropping one of the crutches. I looked at the door in front of me — it was moving. Soon there was a tunnel between me and it, and it kept elongating.

At some point, the spinning and stretching stopped. I stood there, blinking, for several minutes.

That was when I heard Mom calling my name, her footsteps approaching the staircase. The room had stabilized.

"Everything okay down there?"

I wasn't sure what to say. I had no idea what had just happened. But I was certain I didn't want to freak her out.

I turned back and looked up at Mom. "Everything is perfectly fine," I said.

•

Three weeks after the crash, Mom dropped me off at Paul's house. He'd finally gotten back from computer camp. We'd become instant friends in seventh grade, when he called out of the blue to talk about model rockets and outer space and that kind of thing, after a classmate told him a story I'd shared about a rocket I launched at the beach.

Paul welcomed me with his big, toothy smile. "I'm just finishing up *WarGames*," he said. I'd already seen it twice in the theater, a hair-raising movie where this teenage geek hacks his way into a U.S. military supercomputer and unintentionally almost causes World War III. "Come watch the last ten minutes with me."

I sat down on the living room couch as he pressed play on the family VCR. It was at the freakiest part in the film. The supercomputer was about to launch America's entire nuclear arsenal against the Soviet Union, "thinking" America could win, and the teenager was desperately trying to convince it that winning a nuclear war was impossible.

I grabbed a pillow and pulled it to my chest. Paul, who normally lounged on the couch with his feet on the table, was sitting straight up, his left hand covering his lips.

The moment came when the supercomputer got the launch code. A surge went through my gut, because the end of the world was moments away. But then the geek hero won the argument.

Nuclear war "is a strange game," the supercomputer said. "The only winning move is not to play."

Paul and I sat there for a couple of minutes, watching the credits roll, until he got up and switched everything off. "Don't you just love that ending?" he said, slowly shaking his head. He looked over at me.

I shrugged. "Nuclear war just scares the crap out of me."

"You and the rest of the world," Paul said. "My room?"

•

I plopped myself down on his beanbag. "So how was computer camp?" I asked. "Did you score with the ladies?"

He sat on his bed. "Boring, as always. How was your summer?"

I laughed. "Definitely not boring."

Paul's eyebrows shot up. "No way! Did you finally manage to hook up with Lucia?"

I shook my head. "Hardly. She's still out of town, anyway. So no." Paul looked disappointed. "But I did manage to get hit by a van, just a block away from here."

Paul frowned. We yanked each other's chains so often we'd developed a pledge system for swearing something.

"*Truth?*" he asked.

"*Truth,*" I said. His face suddenly looked like mine probably had when the movie ended.

I told him the whole story, from how I was headed to C&H Surplus to pick up the last part for my laser project to thinking about Lucia to the clueless driver who smacked me, and finally to the super-cute nurse at Huntington Hospital.

"That's seriously amazing," Paul said. "Did you get her number?"

"Ha, no. But—*truth*—I asked her for it!"

Paul cracked up.

After catching up in his room, we went outside to bump a volleyball around. I was more into baseball, the first sport I ever played, and one that Dad took us to watch at Dodger Stadium when we were kids. But Paul was a volleyball fanatic—he had the whole vocabulary nailed and wore Sideout Sports clothes 24/7 and pretty much worshipped Karch Kiraly—so that was what we played at his place.

We bumped for a while, with Paul correcting my "technique," which was funny to me because I didn't know I had one. I was thirsty and it was hot out and my head started feeling a little weird, but we kept playing. Paul asked if I wanted to practice spiking, and I told him not really, but then this puppy-dog look appeared on his face and I gave in.

"We really need three people for this," Paul said. "But I'll pretend to receive the ball, and then I'll set for you, and you can try spiking." I rolled my eyes. "I know it's hot. Just try this and we'll go back inside."

"Fine," I said. He really wanted to get me into volleyball.

Paul cupped his hands around the ball and threw it into the air, stretched out his fingers and sort of caught it and tossed it back up at the same time, and then looked to me. The ball hit the ground in front of my feet and bounced away.

"You were, um, supposed to spike the ball just then," Paul said.

"Oh, gotcha," I said. I was feeling a little strange, like my head was lighter than normal.

"Jeff?" Paul said. "Everything cool?"

I drew in a deep breath and blew it out. "Yes. Spike the ball. Let's try again."

Paul smiled. "Cool."

He picked up the ball and got back into position. Once again, he threw it into the air, and I watched it come straight back to him. Then he tossed it with his fingertips. "Now spike it!" he shouted.

Just then, my stomach tightened up. I lost my focus on the ball. Everything around me started spinning. I stumbled and felt Paul's hand grip my arm, but I said I needed to get down. I dropped to my knees first. Paul was saying something loudly, maybe just my name, but I couldn't make it out, and soon it was as if he were standing at the opposite end of an elongating tube.

I flipped onto my back. The trees, the garage, Paul's house, the sun—everything was spinning. The tension deepened in my gut. The only other thing I felt was desperation, like the whole world was coming to an end.

When things finally got still, Paul's face snapped back into focus. I think he'd been talking for a while, but I couldn't understand a word that came out of his mouth. I finally made out "Are you okay?"

I managed to say I needed to go home.

Sometime later, Mom arrived. There was concern on her

face. She questioned me, but I waved her off and slipped into the passenger seat. She interrogated Paul as I fell asleep.

•

Mom took me to see a specialist, a neurologist by the name of Hermann S. Gourevik. He was indeed special. From the graduation certificates on the wall behind him, you could figure out he was in his early forties, but the way he plodded through everything he might as well have been eighty. He was short and chubby and mostly bald with a black beard so scraggly that you'd think he'd missed puberty, and his tiny eyes were set five feet back into his head. Whenever I said anything, he blinked and his nose scrunched up as if he were allergic to me. His pale cheeks were flabby, probably because he never exercised them by doing anything like smiling.

On that first day I saw him, he didn't smile once, and this was after we waited fifty-six minutes for the appointment to start. He just sat there with his hands cupped like a judge while I told him about the accident and all the strange things that happened afterward. He asked a bunch of questions, half of which I'd already given him the answers to, which he would have known if he'd bothered to listen. The ten-minute physical in his exam room was the worst part, because the man desperately needed some mints. Only when we sat back down in his office could I start breathing again.

He asked how long "the incident" at Paul's house had lasted. I said I wasn't sure, maybe thirty seconds.

Mom shook her head. "Seven minutes," she said. She read back the transcript of her conversation with Paul and listed off everything I complained about to her in the weeks after the accident.

"Thank you, Mrs. Henigson." I couldn't tell if he was being sincere or a condescending prick. He cleared his throat and looked at me. Mom had her pen ready. "The episodes you describe may very well be epileptic seizures."

"What is that supposed to mean?" I said.

"Well, are you familiar with epilepsy?" he said.

"You mean like falling down and flipping around and all that stuff? I've seen it in movies. But that's totally not what happened."

"Epilepsy is a group of neurological disorders characterized by abnormal electrical activity in the brain. The episodes during which this abnormal activity is occurring are referred to as seizures. There are many different kinds of seizures, with varying levels of intensity. What you experienced sounds very much like a seizure."

"How exactly do you get epilepsy from a car accident?" I asked.

Mom seemed to have the same question—she was nodding.

"The accident may have caused trauma to your brain that subsequently led to the seizure. But you also could have been predisposed to epilepsy, in which case the accident simply triggered seizures."

Mom stiffened. "What do you mean by 'could have been predisposed'? You can't tell which it was?"

Dr. Gourevik folded his hands, set them on the table, and

smiled curtly at my mom. "It's important we focus our attention on what matters. In this case, it's getting Jeff's seizures under control with medication."

Mom noisily cleared her throat. "Without knowing exactly what the cause is?" she asked. I wanted to high-five her.

"I'll order an EEG—an electroencephalogram, which is a test for abnormal electrical activity in the brain—but if Jeff isn't having a seizure in that moment, it's unlikely to show anything."

"What about those CT scans?" Mom asked. I'd heard of them. They gave them to people they thought might have Alzheimer's disease.

"Mrs. Henigson, while I appreciate that you've done your research, a CT scan is expensive and unnecessary. We should address the seizures first and move on from there."

Mom shook her head. "I do not want to *move on* from there, Dr. Gourevik. I'm not a doctor, but I'm sure it's better to know the cause of a problem before you start treating it."

He started with "Mrs. Henigson—" but she cut him off.

"Would you like to set up my son's CT scan or shall I take him somewhere else?" He considered protesting—you could tell—but everyone in the room knew he'd just had his balls handed to him. He reached over to his intercom and barked at his assistant to set up a scan.

Mom looked satisfied. She dropped her notebook into her purse and said thank you, and we headed to the door.

I was so happy to get out of there and never talk to that blowhard again. I had no clue how many times I'd be coming back.

CHAPTER TWO

We didn't get around to having dinner that evening until nearly eight o'clock, with Dad running late at work, and once again it was plain, overcooked chicken. Mom used to do really fun dinners, like her taco assembly line with homemade salsa and guacamole and Mexican cheese, but after all the news last year about kids dying from food bacteria, things had gotten a little boring. Meat was the worst. She cooked it so dry you couldn't get through a bite without sipping from your water glass.

"How was your appointment with Dr. Gourevik?" Dad asked, rehydrating himself with some red wine after trying Mom's chicken.

"I'd be happy to never see him again for the rest of my life," I said.

Ted snorted. "Exactly how most people feel about *you*, Jeff," he said.

Mom squinted at him.

Dad ignored Ted's jab, pulling the napkin from his lap to

clear droplets of wine from his beard. "Have you received any diagnosis?"

"He said I might have epilepsy, and he was going to put me on medication, but Mom said he shouldn't treat something without knowing exactly what's causing it." I remembered how satisfied I felt when she said that. "It was pretty funny. She put Dr. Gourevik in his place."

Mom smiled, her chin a little higher than usual.

Dad seemed to have missed my comment about her. "The epilepsy diagnosis," he said, pausing for another sip of wine, "is it solely based on what happened at your friend Paul's house?"

I hesitated. "Um, I guess." I hadn't told anyone about the incident at the bottom of the staircase just after the accident, or the three other weird spells since. I'd just been waiting for them to go away.

"You appear uncertain," Dad said. I felt like I was on the witness stand.

I swallowed and looked up at him. "I'm not uncertain, Dad. It's definitely the only thing he based his diagnosis on."

Dad sat there for several seconds, looking at me. "So we'll await the test," he said.

"Speaking of tests," Mom said—she could tell I was uncomfortable—"you have your test for your driver's permit this week."

I'd totally forgotten about it.

Ted pushed back from the table. He always finished eating way before everyone else. "The last thing this world needs is Jeff driving in it," he said as he stood.

"Ted," Mom said sharply. "Could you please ask to be excused?"

Ted sighed and sat back down. "May I be excused?" Mom looked over to Dad. He nodded.

"Please clear your plate," Mom said. Ted did one of his eye rolls and left.

Dad didn't go back to talking about epilepsy or Dr. Gourevik. Mom had successfully changed the subject. He asked if I felt prepared for the driving test, and I reminded him that Mom had been taking me out to practice in an abandoned parking lot in Arcadia, and I added that you'd have to be a moron to fail the California DMV's written questions.

Dad seemed to agree. He then changed the subject to his current case, giving Mom and me an update. Ted never stuck around for them, and I only did to be polite. This one was seriously boring. After listening for a few minutes, I asked to be excused.

"What about *NewsHour*?" Dad said. He was referring to his favorite television program, the *MacNeil/Lehrer NewsHour*, which Mom recorded for him every night on the VCR.

"I already watched it," I said.

Dad raised an eyebrow. He often said how important it was for us to "stay abreast" of the news, and since it was one of the few things I could actually do with Dad, I'd often sit through it with him. Sometimes, like when the topic was politics and Dad got energized, it was even interesting.

"Really," he said.

It seemed like a news quiz was coming, so I cut to the chase. "Yes, really," I said. "What you'll definitely find interesting is that the head of the Soviet Union—"

"Premier Gorbachev," Dad interjected.

"Yeah, Mr. Gorbachev. He said that President Reagan will violate some treaty if he starts testing stuff for his Star Wars program."

Dad seriously disliked that program, the one President Reagan said would defend us against nuclear weapons. Once, when Dad and I were watching *NewsHour* together and President Reagan was talking about the Strategic Defense Initiative—the Star Wars program—Dad flinched. "The notion that we can ever reliably defend ourselves against nuclear weapons is pure fantasy," he said sharply, shaking his head.

Dad didn't like the news I'd just shared. I could tell from his jaw, which was flaring. He was no longer doubting that I'd absorbed the news; he was irritated by the news itself. "So *Mr.* Reagan is considering withdrawing from the Anti-Ballistic Missile Treaty?" Dad used "Mr." instead of "President" when he was really ticked off.

"I think that's the treaty they were talking about."

"Wonderful," Dad said, with sarcasm in his voice. "Just wonderful."

For a second, it seemed like he was going to blow his lid. Mom and I sat there, silent.

Dad drew in a long breath and slowly let it out. "That president of ours is endangering this nation with the increased threat of nuclear war. Not only that, he's going to spend us into the ground."

•

The first time Dad told me about nuclear weapons, when I presented my very first model rocket to him and he responded with a lecture on the danger of missiles, I wasn't all that scared. I'd definitely heard of the atomic bomb—Dad was stationed on a minesweeper in the South Pacific when we dropped two of them on Japan in 1945, and very occasionally he'd talk about the war—but it didn't feel like a major threat to me. That was in total contrast to the Holocaust, for example, because my grandma used to hold me in her lap when I was a little kid and tell me about the gas chambers. I had nightmares about the Nazis for years.

One evening when I was twelve, Dad announced at the dinner table that the whole family was going to watch a movie together over the weekend. We never went to the movies with Dad, so Ted and I were really excited at first, until Dad told us it was going to be on television.

Sunday came and Dad got us all assembled in front of the playroom TV. For the next two hours we watched *The Day After*, a fictional story about some American survivors of an all-out nuclear exchange between the United States and the Soviet Union. I got so scared I almost peed in my pants. Even Ted looked freaked out, and he hardly ever cared about anything.

The second the movie was over, I turned to Dad and said, "Could that happen?" I was so anxious that I stammered when I said it. Mom tried to hug me but I pushed her away. "Dad," I said, pleading with him. "Could that *ever* happen?"

Slowly, he considered my question. "I don't think the film we saw was realistic," he finally said. I felt my stomach lighten a bit. It was good to hear something like that was unlikely. I glanced over at Mom, who nodded at me.

Ted was frowning. "*How* wasn't the film realistic?" he asked.

Dad cleared his throat. "Were there an actual nuclear exchange between our two countries, there would be no survivors. With the number of nuclear weapons in our arsenals, I'm afraid it would be the end of humanity."

My stomach knotted up and I leaned forward. Mom moaned softly before touching my hand. She did the same to Ted, but he was frozen in place, his mouth half open.

Dad, on the other hand, wasn't even with us. His eyes were turned up and to the left, as if he was trying to recall something. For several seconds, he didn't say a word. "Bob," Mom finally said, and then he looked at us.

He shook his head. "Boys, it's impractical to spend your time worrying about nuclear war. What matters is politics—and policy. We have to vote the right leaders into office. And no matter who is there, we must do whatever is in our power to influence policy. Anxiety—in the absence of action—serves no purpose whatsoever."

Dad's words didn't soothe me, but I'd never forget them.

●

I ended up acing my driver's permit test. I nailed the written questions, and the middle-aged guy who graded me said, "Wow, perfect score." Mom high-fived me when I told her the results and she took me straight to Fair Oaks Pharmacy to celebrate with an ice cream.

Test number two, the CT scan of my brain, took place the next day, at nine o'clock in the morning. Like always, Mom drove me there. She kept rubbing her nose on the way, something she did when she was nervous.

"Chill out, Mom," I said. It always made her laugh.

Mom filled out a bunch of paperwork. When she was done, a plump woman in her thirties appeared. "Come with me," she said, smiling. She escorted me to a changing room, where she handed me a gown.

"What do I need a gown for? You're scanning my head, right?"

She smiled again, this time more plasticlike. "It's just our procedure."

A minute later, she walked me down a long hallway, stopping in front of an open metal door. There was a sign above it that had a large, red, three-bladed radiation symbol, along with the words CAUTION: RADIATION AREA. The lady smiled a third time, like I'd arrived at Disneyland or something, and she gestured toward the room.

A guy took over, probably the same age as her, and also pudgy. "Have you ever had a CT scan?" he asked.

I shook my head. "Nope."

"Well, they're pretty easy. We'll have you lie down on the white table there, we hold you in place with some soft straps across your forehead, and then we slide you back into that vertical tubelike structure, which is the CT scanner." I looked over at it, then back at him. "I can assure you, it's absolutely painless."

"Okay," I said. "How long is it gonna take?"

"Probably about twenty minutes." Just like the lady before him, he put on a completely artificial smile. "Shall we get started?"

The scan itself wasn't that bad. I didn't particularly like being strapped down, but it wasn't painful or anything. Just boring. I spent my time trying to count the number of perforations in one of the overhead ceiling panels, but each time they slid the table deeper into the scanner, I had to restart.

The guy returned a while later. It seemed like twenty minutes had passed. I figured I was finished.

"Please don't move," he said. "We're not done yet."

"I thought you said it was gonna be over in twenty minutes."

"Well, the technologist would like to get some additional images, so we're going to use some contrast dye, if that's okay."

I swallowed. "Why does the technologist want extra images?"

"I'm just an assistant, so I can't tell you the reason for it. Sometimes it's just to get a better perspective. Anyway, have you ever had an injection?"

"What, like a vaccination?" He nodded. "Of course."

"Great. We'll inject the dye into a vein in your arm, and then it'll be just a few more minutes in the scanner, okay?"

"Fine," I said. It wasn't like he was really giving me an option.

The whole thing ended up taking twice as long as they said it would. I felt like complaining to someone, like the lady who had walked me in—right up to the point when she returned to escort me out.

Her face looked different—a little pale. Her smile was gone. She didn't make eye contact. She just asked me to follow her, walking me back to the changing area, and then, when I got my shirt back on, to the waiting room.

Mom hopped to her feet the second she saw me. She wrapped me in a hug. It felt so soothing.

The lady who'd dropped me off hadn't left. She was just standing there. She dipped her head toward Mom, who nodded politely. I ignored her and started toward the door. Mom followed. Just as I reached it, the lady said, "Good luck."

•

The next morning, I woke up late. It had taken me ages to fall asleep, with that lady back at the CT lab swirling around in my mind, but around two in the morning I finally nodded off.

I swung out of bed and walked over to the corner window, raising the blinds. No one could see in from there, so it was like my private space, and just a foot back was where I had my laser project set up.

It was so close to being finished. I just needed the power supply. *Maybe Mom could head up to C&H Surplus with me,* I thought.

I took a quick shower, threw on some clothes, and headed upstairs. Ted was sitting at the kitchen counter, flipping through a magazine. "Hey, man," he said, half smiling. I only got a greeting like that when he was in a really good mood. The norm was more like "The doofus has emerged."

I grabbed a bowl from the cabinet and poured myself some cereal. "Where's Mom?"

"On the phone."

From the kitchen you could see all the way down to the other end of the house, where Mom had her office. Probably 99 percent of her time at home—at least while she was awake—was spent either there or in the kitchen. Her office was empty.

I looked back at Ted. "What, like on the phone in their bedroom?"

"Yeah," Ted said, setting down his magazine and stepping off the stool. He looked at the clock. "I'm gonna take a shower."

As I munched on my cereal, I thought about Mom. Maybe something was going on with her mother. She'd had Alzheimer's for years and could no longer speak, and recently she'd had two serious bouts of pneumonia.

Just as I started my second bowl, Mom appeared.

"Everything okay?" I said.

She walked over and gave me a hug. "Good morning, honey."

"Is your mom okay? You can totally tell me."

"She's fine, Jeff. Nothing new, at least."

"Oh, good." I was happy I'd gotten it wrong. Which was also good because maybe we could take that ride together. "How about we head up to C&H Surplus today so I can actually finish my project? And since I've got my permit now, maybe you could let me drive your car."

She rubbed the back of her neck. "Well . . ."

"C'mon, Mom. I'll be super super careful. I promise."

"It's . . . not that."

I jolted my head back. "Well, what is it, then?"

Mom hesitated. "We've got an appointment with Dr. Gourevik today at noon."

I rolled my eyes, then glanced at the clock. That was in less than an hour. I looked back at Mom. She was rubbing her nose. "Wait a second, were you just on the phone with Dr. Gourevik— in your bedroom?"

"Not with him." Mom swallowed. "But yes, with someone from his office."

I tossed my spoon into the cereal bowl. Milk splashed onto the counter. She didn't react. "Mom, just what the heck is going on?"

She sighed. "I honestly don't know, Jeff. They called this morning—you were asleep—and asked if the family could come in today."

"The *family*?"

"I checked with your dad and was just now calling them back. He's going to meet us there." I looked away, squeezing my eyes shut. "Jeff, would you like your brother to come?"

I spun back to her and shook my head. "No, Mom. I *don't* want my brother to come." His hello that morning—the unusually warm one—came to mind. I squinted at Mom. "Did you tell Ted?"

"I did."

I couldn't believe what I was hearing. It was like I'd woken up into an especially weird episode of *The Twilight Zone.*

Thirty minutes later, as Mom and I were heading out the front door, Ted called my name. I stopped and looked back at him. "What's up?" I said.

"I, um, just wanted to wish you good luck."

Unlike our first visit to Dr. Gourevik, this time we didn't have to wait at all to see him. He even stood up to welcome us when we walked into his office. That was all I needed. Dr. Gourevik was a social Neanderthal. The fact that he was being polite could only mean I was in serious trouble.

He started with something right out of a television script. "I'm afraid I've got bad news. The scan revealed a tumor in the left-temporal lobe of your brain. That's in this area," he said, running his finger in a circle above his left ear. He said it had nothing to do with the car crash, though the crash led to the discovery by causing the seizures. He looked at me. "You're going to need surgery right away, Jeff."

I sat there for several seconds, staring back at Dr. Gourevik, slowly shaking my head. I understood what he was saying, but it all seemed crazy. I mean, I felt fine. I hadn't even had one of those weird episodes recently.

A thought popped into my head. "Maybe they gave you someone else's scan by mistake. I feel totally normal."

"They're exceedingly careful about that. And brain tumors often do not present any noticeable symptoms until—" Dr. Gourevik suddenly paused.

"Until what?"

He coughed into his hand, then cleared his throat. "Until they've substantially developed."

I looked at my parents. I wanted them to intervene, but they didn't say a word. Mom had been taking detailed notes, something she'd once done professionally as a stenographer. But now she was underlining a single word—"surgery"—over and over, with her mouth ajar. Dad looked like he was working on a question, his eyes tilting up to one side, but he couldn't manage to ask it.

It didn't feel like either of them was with me. It got me agitated.

"Could we focus for a second?" I barked out. My parents snapped to attention. Dr. Gourevik shut up. "Are you absolutely positively certain I need to have brain surgery?"

"Yes," he said.

Maybe I could delay it. That was it. If we held off for a while, and the tumor didn't get any larger, then maybe I wouldn't need surgery after all. I could even get my project done. I definitely needed to finish that project. It was what would get me into a top science school. And then I could join NASA.

I straightened up in my chair. "I'm working on a very important project, Dr. Gourevik. I need to finish it. It won't take long—I can get the whole project done this summer. Then we can reevaluate the surgery idea—"

Dr. Gourevik interrupted. "I'm afraid there's nothing to reevaluate, Jeff. I understand this is very difficult for you to hear, but you have a tumor growing in your brain. It has to be removed."

I swallowed. "I did hear that. A tumor growing. And surgery. I'm just saying, like, realistically, when would that need to happen? How about a month from now—would that work?"

Dr. Gourevik sighed. "It would not. You should undergo surgery the moment you find a neurosurgeon."

That gave me hope. It would probably take some time to do that.

Dr. Gourevik slid a sheet of paper across the table, with a list of neurosurgeons and their phone numbers typed across it. He focused his eyes tightly on mine. "Those are the best names in Southern California. You should find the first available. Were you to find that person today, my very strong recommendation is that you have the surgery performed tomorrow."

I slumped in my seat then, my shoulders curling forward. I began to rock back and forth. It was like the moment in my childhood when a riptide had pulled me out to sea and I'd given up on trying to make it back to shore. My brother was the one who saved me, swimming out to meet me and then guiding me back. This time it was different. I was back out there at sea, but the shoreline was empty, and, behind me, a massive wave was forming.

Mom had clasped my hand. Dad was clutching my arm. I could barely feel them. It felt like I was falling. Down, down, with nothing below me but darkness.

CHAPTER THREE

I woke to Dad knocking on my bedroom door. "Come in," I said groggily. Lucia had been in my dream, the girl Paul had asked me if I'd hooked up with yet. She was waving to me from the end of a hallway that was lengthening. That was all I remembered.

"Good morning, son," he said. Amiga was next to him, her tail wagging along the carpet. It was unusual for him to wake me up. Mom would, and only if my alarm hadn't done the job. Dad was normally down at the track with Amiga anyway.

He asked me how I'd slept, another thing he didn't usually do. I began wondering what was up. "What time is it, anyway?"

"Seven," Dad said.

I groaned, grabbing a pillow and covering my face. It was like he'd never heard of summer.

Dad tugged the pillow away. "You've got a busy day, son," he said. "And you should get started with a nutritious breakfast." That's when I remembered it was Choose Your Own Brain Surgeon Day.

I followed Dad and Amiga upstairs. The second Mom saw me, she hurried over and gave me a big hug. "Good morning!" she said, much louder than normal, even though Ted's bedroom was ten feet away and he had to be asleep. She pointed eagerly to the counter. "There's your breakfast."

Since I was twelve, it was pretty much understood that I could put together my own breakfast. The only time Mom did it was when I was home sick or when she was making brunch on a weekend. But there it was: scrambled eggs, bacon, and three slices of slightly browned white toast on one of Mom's nice plates with a folded cotton napkin next to it. Nice, but weird.

Just then, I heard the toilet in the bathroom around the corner flush, the sink turn on, and the door open. Ted was actually up. "Morning, dude," he said, plopping himself onto a kitchen stool next to me. "I can come to your appointments, if you want." He grabbed the carton in front of him and motioned toward my cup. "Want some OJ?" It seriously felt like I'd fallen into a *Leave It to Beaver* episode.

The three of them were convinced I was on my way out.

I leaned down and rubbed Amiga's back, my eyes shifting from Mom to Dad to Ted. "Just so you guys know," I said, "I'm not planning on dying."

Mom dropped the pen she was holding, and her jaw fell with it. "No one is saying that," she said with her hand pressed against her chest. I was about to point out everyone's completely abnormal behavior, but I saw Dad's lips press together as he slowly nodded, his jaw slightly flaring the way it did when he was proud of something.

"You're going to fight," he said.

"I'm going to win," I said back.

Dad smiled broadly, like he was proud. I must've smiled back. Mom's shoulders dropped, and she finally bent over to pick up her pen. I turned to Ted, who was still holding the orange juice carton. "Okay for some OJ," I told him, "but you don't need to come to my appointments. You'd die of boredom." Ted instantly looked relieved.

•

One thing I really liked about Dr. Kathleen Egan, the first of three appointments we had scheduled that day, was that she actually started on time. Mom, Dad, and I were sitting in her waiting room for my 11:00 appointment, and she walked in at 10:58 to welcome us. She came straight to me, a smile on her face, and introduced herself. It wasn't one of those plastic smiles some adults pasted on their faces when young people were around, but a real, genuine one. She gave me a solid handshake, too.

She invited us into her office. It didn't have the pastel colors from Dr. Gourevik's that made me want to puke, and she didn't have every degree and award she'd ever received on the wall behind her. Instead, there were some nice pictures of a sailboat in the ocean. Her med school degrees were on a wall off to the side, and I nudged my mom when I saw she'd gone to the University of Southern California—Mom's school. Things were off to a good start.

Dr. Egan said she needed to take a look at my CT scan and the report. Dad handed over everything, including a letter from

Dr. Gourevik. She said she'd need a few minutes to review it all and told us to chat away if we liked. I didn't feel like talking.

While she reviewed my charts, I reviewed her. She used to have completely blond hair, I figured, but whitish-gray had taken over everywhere. Her hair was a little longer than my mom's, but without any curls. Each strand was perfectly straight. Her posture matched. She sat with her shoulders back and her head held high, her hands and forearms planted firmly on her desk, with a posture that communicated confidence. Compared to my parents, she looked like a giraffe. Watching her was calming for me.

It went on so long, I started fantasizing that Dr. Egan was going to finish reading and say, "I'm not sure how this happened, but your scan is perfectly normal."

After the longest few minutes of my whole life, Dr. Egan set everything down and lifted her head. The three of us tensed. "I agree with Dr. Gourevik's recommendation for surgery," she said. Mom and Dad sighed. They'd been stuck in the same fantasy.

Dr. Egan asked me if I knew the difference between a benign tumor and a malignant one. I said a benign tumor was like a golf ball that you could carve out and it wouldn't come back, and a malignant one was more like a weed that could extend roots deep into your brain, which was pretty much how Dr. Gourevik explained it. She said that was a good analogy.

She asked if I had any questions.

I glanced at my parents. They were both looking at me. I definitely had stuff I wanted to ask, but I also didn't want to destroy my mom.

I looked back at Dr. Egan and exhaled. "How do you—you know—get in there?" I tapped the side of my head.

"This might sound unpleasant," Dr. Egan said. I motioned for her to continue. "After shaving the surgical area and cleansing it with alcohol, we make an incision through the muscle and tissue over the skull. It's basically a large upside-down U. That allows us to access the skull."

Mom and Dad swallowed at the same time. Dr. Egan's description was definitely gross to hear, considering we were talking about my *actual* head. I also didn't like the idea of having a scar on the side of my head.

She continued. "Then we use a small saw and remove a rectangular section of bone plate from your skull. We make an incision through the *dura*—a tough membrane that envelops the brain—and from there, guided by the scans, we proceed to the location of the tumor. We remove the tumor, close the lining, replace the bone, and then reconnect all the tissue we had to penetrate. That's it. Did that answer your question?"

I imagined what my head would look like, all cut up and everything. "It mostly did."

"Jeff, I find my patients feel best after they get the things they're concerned about out in the open. Is there something specific that's on your mind?"

It was like she'd seen right through me. "Well, okay. For starters, with you cutting in there," I said, motioning to the left side of my head, "am I going to end up looking like a freak?"

"You won't," Dr. Egan said, without the slightest doubt in her voice. "The procedure will leave a scar, but your hair will ultimately cover it."

That was better than I thought it would be. I didn't want to walk around and have people pointing at me.

"Anything else on your mind?" Dr. Egan asked.

I did have something. It would freak out my mom. Still, I had to ask.

"What are my chances of coming out of this, you know, a vegetable?"

Mom sighed, quietly. Dad cleared his throat. I avoided looking at either of them.

Dr. Egan stayed completely calm. "At this point, we're working off the CT scan. We won't know what we're dealing with until we actually go in. But I feel confident that we're going to get you through this in one piece—that is to say, get the tumor out and minimize any negative effects from the surgery."

That sounded mostly good. "What do you mean by 'negative effects'?"

"Any disruption to your normal brain function. The area where the tumor is located is responsible for language processing. The worst-case scenario would be your losing certain abilities to communicate, whether that's understanding language spoken to you or formulating words. At this point, I just don't anticipate that."

"Why?"

"Because of the tumor's location. My gut feeling is that we'll be able to separate the tumor from any surrounding brain tissue, which would make complete tumor removal possible."

I noticed how she didn't grip her hands together the way Dr. Gourevik did. She didn't wear a fake smile, either. The whole time she spoke, she kept that stable posture, her shoulders completely relaxed.

Dad stepped in with some questions—how long the surgery would take ("four to eight hours"), how quickly I could be out of the hospital ("two to three weeks")—and then Mom, with her hands shaking slightly, asked if I'd feel any pain.

Dr. Egan's face warmed. "The very good news about that is there are no pain receptors in the brain. As strange as it may sound, the brain itself can't hurt."

Mom's shoulders dropped.

I was sort of wondering how Dr. Egan became a neurosurgeon, since everyone on Dr. Gourevik's list with the exception of her was a guy, so I asked. She said she'd started out as a surgical nurse. She worked for a famous neurosurgeon. Once, during a surgery, she watched as one of his residents—they're like junior doctors—was about to make a mistake. She called the resident on it, which really angered her boss, until he realized she was right. After that he said, "Come hell or high water, you're going to become a neurosurgeon."

She sat back in her chair, crossed her arms, and smiled broadly. "I'm really happy I did it."

I decided it was okay not to hold back at all. "Even if some of the people you're performing surgery on die?"

She nodded. "That happens sometimes, in some very complex surgeries. It's extremely hard to bear. But I've also seen patients who started out with a tough diagnosis, and then they came out on top of things, and it's felt great knowing that I was able to help them. That's what keeps me going."

I allowed myself to look at my parents then. Mom, to my surprise, was actually smiling a little. Dad was nodding very slightly—practically his highest form of praise.

We thanked Dr. Egan and headed to the car. Mom looked at her day calendar for the next appointment and then at her watch. She was calculating how much time we had.

"I want to cancel my other appointments," I said.

"Why do you want to do that, Jeff?" Mom asked.

"Well, what do *you* think of Dr. Egan?"

Mom thought for a second. "I really like her confidence."

"Exactly—same for me. Not only that, she worked for a famous neurosurgeon and went to a great school, and she clearly loves saving people. I just know she's the one."

Mom smiled, nodding. We were in agreement.

Dad was standing by the driver's side of the car with his arms crossed. An argument was coming.

"I believe it would be prudent to consult other medical professionals," he said, "and to only make such an important decision after assessing the entirety of their recommendations."

He wasn't hearing me. "I trust her, Dad," I said.

"If she is best suited for this most important of exercises, our trust will be sustained after consulting the other candidates." The more serious a situation got, the more he sounded like a lawyer in the courtroom.

I matched his crossed arms and looked directly at him. "It's *my* brain, Dad," I said. "I want Dr. Egan to do my surgery."

I let that sink in. He looked away, toward the mountains, which for once weren't hidden by smog. After several seconds, he turned back and nodded.

●

The day before I was admitted to the hospital, instead of doing something fun with Paul or finally calling Lucia, who was back in town, I went to Supercuts to get my head shaved. I ended up with Jenna, someone who'd cut my hair a couple of times before. "What are we thinking today?" she asked after sitting me down in the barber chair.

"A buzz cut," I said.

She frowned. "Seriously? You have beautiful hair."

It was probably the most depressing thing she could've said. Lucia had told me the same thing earlier that summer, just before she left on her trip, when we were making out in her bedroom until her mom came home early from work. "I totally love your hair," she had said, running her fingers across my scalp and smiling.

Jenna was looking at me through the mirror in front of us. "Just cut it," I told her. "Super short everywhere. Like this long." I held my fingers an eighth of an inch apart.

Jenna shrugged and reached for the razor.

In the run-up to surgery, I'd gotten fixated on my hair. It wasn't just because Lucia was back in town and I dreaded the thought of her seeing me with a gruesome scar carved into the side of my head—so much so that I didn't even call her back to tell her what was ahead. I also worried about the kids at school, like whether they were going to be pointing at me and whispering and all that kind of thing. But the image I just couldn't shake, whether during the day with people around or alone at night in my bed, was Dr. Egan shaving my head. It was like she was going to strip me of something that was mine.

That's why on that last day before going to the hospital, I decided to take control of things. Dr. Egan might be cutting into my skull with a saw, but she wasn't going to touch my hair.

Jenna finished in half the time it usually took her. "How's that?" she said.

I didn't even look at myself. "Fine," I answered.

Fifteen minutes later, Mom and I got back home. She let me drive, which was cool. As we walked down to the house, I saw Ted crossing toward the front door. He'd make a comment about my head, no doubt.

"So, um," he started as Amiga wiggled her way past him to get some attention.

I knelt down to pet her as Mom slid by to the kitchen. "Yes, Ted, my hair is very short. They call it a buzz cut. Are we done?"

He looked confused. "No, it's not that. It's . . ."

I was getting irritated. I stood. "Can you just spit it out?"

"Lucia. She called. I thought she knew about tomorrow and everything."

I slapped my hands against my cheeks. "No way, Ted. Did you tell her?"

"I didn't know it was supposed to be a secret."

I hadn't even told Paul, let alone Lucia. "Jesus," I said, closing my eyes and moaning.

"There's more. She's on her way over here."

My jaw dropped. I looked back at him. "You've got to be kidding me."

He didn't have to say anything more. The doorbell rang. He looked up the stairs, I spun around, and there, at the outer door, was Lucia.

Mom, who I'm sure had overheard everything, called out to me from the kitchen. "Honey, shall I buzz her in?"

Ted hurried off toward his room.

I walked to the kitchen, throwing up my hands at Mom as she waited for my response. "Fine," I said.

Lucia walked down the steps. Something was in her hands—a big, fluffy white teddy bear. There was something tied around its wrist, a red ribbon that ran up to a helium balloon. As she got closer, I could see it said *Get Well Soon*.

The teddy bear looked like he was being given an IV. It was probably the last thing I ever wanted to receive from a girl I'd been hoping so long to sleep with.

When I appeared behind our glass door, with Lucia just on the other side of it, she raised her hand to cover her mouth.

I didn't want to open the door, but I knew I had to.

"Jeff!" Lucia said. "You cut your hair."

•

Walking into the admissions area of Huntington Hospital felt a little like visiting an old folks' home. That's not to say that every incoming patient was grandparent age, just that all the elderly people in the room seemed to be twiddling their thumbs as a younger family member read through paperwork and filled out forms.

Our last name was called, and Dad and I stood up. Mom had headed off to the bathroom. A lady in her forties invited us to sit down with her, and the first thing she did was smile at me and say, "It's very kind of you to accompany your father."

Dad lifted his glasses and rubbed the bridge of his nose. I rolled my eyes. "You owe *him* the compliment," I said, thumbing in his direction. "I'm the one checking in for brain surgery." The lady gulped. She was lucky Mom wasn't around.

Mom did show up a moment later, when the lady was handing Dad a stack of paperwork. My eyebrows shot up when I saw how thick it was. We were going to be there for a while.

We went back to the seating area and got straight to work. At first I tried to help, but I didn't know a thing about Dad's health insurance policy, or my social security number, or whether I'd been vaccinated against measles, mumps, or rubella. In no time at all I was like the old folks in the room, tapping my foot and glancing at the clock on the wall, as Mom and Dad did all the reading, form filling, and consulting with each other. The only thing I seemed necessary for was offering my brain for surgery.

A couple in their fifties came into the room, the guy on crutches, with a cute girl my age, maybe a little older, just behind them. They ended up sitting down near us but were summoned by the paperwork lady, and then returned with paper and pens in hand. The girl grinned at me. A bit nervously, I grinned back.

Mom and Dad finished my paperwork. Mom asked me to

look after her bag while they turned everything in. Almost like clockwork, the girl's parents got up. That's when the girl turned to me with an even bigger smile on her face. "It's tough when one of your parents has to get surgery, isn't it?" she said. I worried I was turning red, though she didn't seem to notice anything strange. Luckily, Mom and Dad were making their way back. I motioned their way. The girl glanced over at them, then turned back. "Good luck to all of you," she said.

My parents sat down.

"It may take a bit," Mom said. "We're waiting on a wristband and a room assignment, and—"

I cut Mom off. "No worries," I said. The girl was looking straight at us. I didn't want Mom to reveal me as the patient. I could see she was about to say something more, so I jumped in again. "You just let them take their sweet, pleasant time," I said, winking. Mom smiled a little awkwardly.

I started praying that the girl's dad would get called before me. That way I could make a clean exit. But it seemed uncertain—we'd registered first. A better bet would be for me to head off to the bathroom for a while, like Mom had.

I was just about to do exactly that when a nurse who'd briefly spoken with the lady who registered me started walking in our direction.

"Heningson?" she said, mispronouncing our name like everyone always did.

"He*nig*son," Dad said. My back stiffened. I took a glimpse in the girl's direction. She was looking right at me.

The nurse, holding a clipboard in one hand and a wristband

in the other, smiled at Dad. "May I have an arm, Jeff?" she said to him.

Dad sighed. "I certainly wish I were the one undergoing all of this." He motioned toward me. "This is my son," he said. "That's Jeff."

I could feel my face go bright red. I was sure the girl was looking at me, but I didn't look back.

●

Around three in the afternoon of my second day in the hospital, while I was playing cards with Ted and trying to ignore how neurotic Mom and Dad seemed as they paced around in the background, Dr. Egan and her team showed up at my room. We'd seen her that morning, when she'd explained the day's procedure: a cerebral angiogram. Totally calmly, she'd explained how a plastic catheter was going to be inserted into a large artery in my leg and threaded up that blood vessel all the way to the carotid artery in my neck. Dye would be injected into my brain that would reveal in an X-ray any blood flow to the tumor. Mom had winced throughout Dr. Egan's description. Dad clenched his jaw. I told them both to take a chill pill. The thing to worry about wasn't the procedure itself—which ended up going just fine—it was what the procedure might reveal.

The Dr. Egan in front of us with the results that afternoon was completely different from the one we'd seen that morning. Her posture was stiff. Her smile had left. The expression on her face was hard to read, but it reminded me of Dr. Gourevik.

Ted folded his cards and hopped off the bed. Mom and Dad nodded hello to Dr. Egan and huddled close. I tried to straighten up, but that made pain shoot through my bandaged right leg. I grimaced.

"The angiogram has revealed a number of blood vessels going into the tumor," Dr. Egan said. "Frankly, it was something I was hoping not to see."

"Why were you hoping not to see lots of blood vessels?" I asked.

"Because they are a potential indicator of cancer and could also make tomorrow's surgery more complicated."

I frowned. "Why are you telling me this?"

"I know you like to be fully informed, Jeff."

I crossed my arms and stared at her. Even though she was a foot away and talking to me, it took a while for her to actually look back. "Wait a second, are you asking me if I want to go ahead with the surgery?"

She nodded. "I was about to."

"I didn't think I had an option. Dr. Gourevik said the tumor had to come out. You agreed with him. Are you saying there's an option?"

"I'm saying that the surgery may be more dangerous than I thought."

"So what you're actually saying is I need the surgery, but it might kill me. Is that it?"

Dr. Egan slowly nodded. "It's unlikely, but it's a possibility. I just can't give you any guarantees."

Mom moaned. Dad drew in a breath and exhaled slowly. Ted stared at his cards.

A chill went down my spine. I looked at my hands.

Dr. Egan had been standing at the foot of the bed, but now she came around to the side. "May I sit?" she asked. I didn't look at her. I just motioned that she could.

"There is something I can promise you, Jeff. I will do everything that is humanly possible. I will not quit. I'll give you everything I have."

Her words rang in my ears. It felt as if her confidence was back. She was ready.

I decided I was, too. I looked up at her and nodded.

●

Until that afternoon visit from Dr. Egan, I had never once thought of my own death. Sure, I had plenty of nightmares about dying, thanks to Grandma's bedtime Holocaust stories, but I didn't walk around thinking something might actually kill me. Now that death seemed possible, I found myself wanting something I'd been after my whole life: for my dad to tell me he loved me.

I got a nasty blood infection when I was twelve. It gave me an off-the-charts fever and made my liver bulge out above my stomach. I was hoping I'd hear those words then, but Dad just patted my shoulder and told me to hang in there. At the time, it really bummed me out. But I got around to reasoning that my actual life wasn't on the line—that if it had been, he would have said the words I was after.

The evening before surgery, with worry about my own death gnawing at me all afternoon since Dr. Egan's bone-chilling visit,

Dad and I were alone in the hospital room. Ted had just high-fived me and wished me luck and headed home, and Mom had stepped out to have a quick chat with him in the hallway. Dad had been sitting in the recliner, going over papers from work, but he got up and came over to the side of my bed.

I was hoping he'd look at me, but his eyes were tracing the IV lines going in and out of me, and then the pole that held the heart rate monitor.

I was struggling to sum up the courage to ask Dad if he loved me. I could come out of tomorrow's surgery unable to speak or to understand anything he said to me. Worse, I could end up dead. I felt a pit deep in my gut. This could be our last conversation.

He drew in a deep breath and slowly exhaled. "You've got a big day ahead of you," he said, his eyes now on my hand, where a thick tube entered through a vein.

"Dad," I blurted out. He looked into my eyes, but all of a sudden I wasn't sure what to say.

He waited. I stayed silent. "What is it, Jeff?"

I swallowed. "Do you, like, have anything you want to tell me?" My right hand started shaking, but I grabbed it with my left.

Dad's mouth opened, but nothing came out. He abruptly swallowed, the way I did when I got called on to speak in class but had nothing to say.

"I . . . I want to tell you to fight the good fight tomorrow."

"Well, okay, but what if things go wrong? What if there are gazillions of blood vessels and Dr. Egan can't get things under control and I end up dying? If that was the situation, is there anything you'd want to tell me now?"

He tightened his grip on the metal crossbar of my bed. His eyes nervously traversed the space between us, never fixing on anything, never looking directly into mine. I could hear his breathing, light and fast, as if he'd just gotten back from one of his morning runs. His right hand was shaking, too.

My father, someone a fellow World War II vet had once called "a vessel of confidence," was filled with anxiety.

After his silence, I felt that way, too.

•

The next day, after surgery, in the early afternoon, I woke up to my mom's touch. At first, I didn't know where I was. Sounds seemed like they were coming through a muffled speaker. But I could feel a hand resting on top of mine, and I knew it was my mom's. Her thumb was stroking my wrist. Her fingers were wrapped around my palm. I could feel her squeezes, like she was speaking to me in her own Morse code, pulsing out "I'm here" and "I love you."

That's the first thing I clearly heard before finally getting around to opening my eyes. In a crackly voice, I said the same thing back to her.

It took a while to fully register where I was. There was something sticking out of the side of my head that made it uncomfortable to turn. I reached for it, but Mom stopped me. "What is it?" I said.

"It's a drain tube."

"What's it draining?"

"Fluid from your brain."

That's when I realized what I was waking up from.

My eyes were so dry it hurt to move them. I asked Mom to get in front of me so I could see her. Her eyes were full of tears, but she was smiling. I didn't want her to leave, not even for a second.

She stayed for a long time. Her smile was soothing. It looked genuine, too, like she was celebrating. I asked her a few days later what she had been thinking in that moment. "That my son was alive," she told me. "That he could speak. That everything was going to be okay."

From time to time, she glanced to her side and gestured with her head. I realized what she was doing—trying to get Dad to come over. She kept at it, but I could tell from her jaw clenching that she was getting frustrated. "Bob, come here," she finally said, ordering him into position. Even then, it felt like a lot of time passed before he appeared.

He looked like fish do after you catch them and pull them out of the water. Mom had him in position, but it was like he didn't belong there. The muscles around his neck were flexing like gills in need of air. His eyes were blinking rapidly.

He touched my hand after Mom pushed his elbow. He didn't speak until she prodded him again.

He finally managed to say, "Hi, Jeff."

He cleared his throat then. It seemed like he was going to say something, like ask me how I was doing, or congratulate me for making it through surgery. When I saw how much he was struggling, I hoped he might be trying to say something much bigger. Seeing him struggle so much made me nervous, too. I clamped down on his hand and waited.

"Jeff," he said. "When you're discharged from the hospital, and feeling up to it, you may have a party."

I immediately let go of his hand. Weeks before, I'd asked him if I could have a party at our house, just for fun, like my friends did every once in a while. He told me I'd have to earn it, and pulled a list of tasks straight out of the air. "Wash your mom's car. Mow the lawn. Pull the weeds in the garden. Water the trees. Clean the pool. See if it needs chlorine." The list went on. I knew it would keep growing until I gave up, so I did.

He thought a *party* was going to brighten up my life now, in a hospital ICU, after my skull had been sawed open and a tumor had been carved out of my brain.

I pressed my lips tightly together. I was filled with anger, so much of it I couldn't feel the pain in my body or my head.

I glared at my father. "I don't want a party," I said. "I just want you to leave."

CHAPTER FOUR

When I first woke up in the ICU, I didn't want Mom to leave my side. But by the end of my second day there, with her asking me every two seconds if I needed anything, I practically wanted to boot her out. Dad had pissed me off with that crap about how I could have a party, but at least he wasn't stressing me out just by being around.

That evening, I was in the middle of a nap when I was startled awake by a nurse's voice blaring through the speaker above my bed. "Can I help you?" the voice said. My eyes popped open to see Mom, inches away from me, with her finger next to the intercom button.

"Everything all right?" Dad said from the recliner. Mom ignored him.

"One of my son's IV bags is almost empty," Mom said. "No one has been by in the last forty-seven minutes." She sounded irked.

There was a pause. Mom tapped away on the metal frame of

my bed. "I'll have someone stop by," the nurse finally got around to saying. Mom shook her head and exhaled sharply.

A minute passed, and in that time Mom asked me twice how I was doing. I assured her I felt fine. When the nurse showed up a moment later, smiling at us with a fresh bag in her hand, Mom just pointed at the empty one.

With the new bag in place and Mom still right next to me, the nurse maneuvered to adjust something on the wall directly behind my bed. In the process, she accidentally whacked my drain tube, the one coming out of the side of my head. I felt a surge of pain and grimaced, and Mom screeched. Dad jumped to his feet and rushed over to my bed. "What happened?" he said. He'd glanced at me, but his focus was on Mom.

"She slammed Jeff's head, that's what happened!" Mom said, shaking her hands. She turned to me, distraught, but with concern on her face. "Are you okay, Jeff?" The nurse was frozen in place, her lips trembling. She looked pretty freaked out.

Dad was standing just behind Mom. His eyes were drilling into mine, demanding my attention. He motioned toward Mom as she shook and tutted over me, then flicked his head toward me. I got his message.

I labored to make the pain in my head disappear from my face. "I'm totally fine, Mom," I said. She wasn't convinced. Dad nodded, like I was moving in the right direction.

I wrenched myself up in bed. My leg throbbed suddenly, in the area where they'd inserted the catheter for the cerebral angiogram, but I kept the pain buried. Mom turned back toward the nurse, who winced like she was expecting to be slapped, and that's when I extended an arm, perforated with half a dozen IV tubes, and grasped my mom's shoulder. She whirled back.

"Mom," I said, making my voice sound as deep and calm as I could. Her brow was furrowed, her lips slightly separated, as if she was afraid of what I was going to tell her.

I'd already removed my hand from her shoulder. Now I flipped it over, palm up. I motioned toward it with my nose. Mom looked down and clasped it.

Dad stood there, observing. I felt the pain in my head, but I had to ignore it. I placed my other hand on top of Mom's. "Everything's good, you hear me?" I forced a smile.

She let a long breath out and nodded. Dad, almost imperceptibly, nodded his approval.

A minute later, with everything much more relaxed, the nurse left the room. Mom followed her out, I'm sure to deliver a major lecture. That's when Dad turned to me. "You're taking it like a soldier," he said. I was blown away by the comparison, considering he'd actually fought in World War II and he'd never said anything like that before.

He wasn't finished. "It's really helping your mother."

I stuck my hands in my armpits, my thumbs pointing up. I exhaled deeply. I got what he was telling me. It was like right there, in the hospital room, I had an actual job to do. Not only that, but Dad was telling me I was doing it well.

I looked into my father's eyes and grinned. Like a soldier, I said, "Yes, sir!"

●

In the days after that moment in the ICU when I managed to chill Mom out, I found myself getting more stressed. Mom had nothing to do with it—if anything, her newfound calm helped me relax. The problem was Dr. Egan weaning me off the pain pills. They'd kept my mind suspended in a relatively warm daze. Now I was being dropped into a cold reality. I became conscious of everything around me.

The lights in the ICU, which I'd hardly noticed before, were on around the clock. The heart monitor was constantly beeping. The only real distinction between day and night was who was around, and the hushed conversations going on between staff on the slower night shifts—about a new movie, who was sleeping with whom, and so on—were loud enough to keep me awake. Other times, an alarm would fire off, and I'd hear nurses and residents rush to a room down the hall. The more aware I became, the more anxious I felt.

On the morning of my fourth day in the ICU, which was starting to feel like detention, Mom walked in wearing a confident smile. She had a grocery bag in one hand. "I've got something for you, sweetie," she said. My mind was on the code-blue alarm that had gone off fifteen minutes earlier, which meant that someone on my floor had gone into cardiac arrest. But I didn't mention that to Mom.

I reached into the bag she handed over and instantly recognized the contours of my Walkman. I probably smiled genuinely then, because Mom's eyes lit up. "How'd you manage to get this in here?" I asked. The day we checked into the hospital, the lady out front had told me they weren't allowed.

"I said to Dr. Egan that separating a teenager from his music would be an emergency, and she gave it the okay."

I thanked Mom, grabbing her hand and kissing it, then went back to the bag. It had headphones and the Walkman with fresh batteries in it, but nothing else. "How about the tapes?" I asked.

Mom gasped, then touched her lips. "Did I actually forget them?" she said.

I nodded and laughed.

It turned out one was in there, a mixtape my buddy Paul had made for me earlier that summer. When I finally got Mom to stop apologizing, I put on the headphones and pressed play.

The song that came on had an eerie beginning, a deep, dark hum with a clock countdown steadily ticking away and snippets of what sounded to me like radio transmissions between American and Soviet military personnel. It was Sting's "Russians," about the insanity of nuclear war. The moment it stopped, I rewound the tape and listened to it again.

It didn't matter to me that Mom had brought only the one tape. Even that afternoon, after she came by with more, I was still listening to it, and mostly to that one song. When Mom told me Dad would be by shortly, I looked forward to playing it for him, considering how concerned the two of us were about nukes, and I wondered what he'd say.

He showed up in the evening. "How are you feeling, son?" he asked.

"I'm fine." I grabbed my headphones and handed them to him. "Put these on." He hesitated, but I knew I had the advantage of lying in a hospital bed. Mom, observing from the recliner, smiled.

Dad listened to the whole song. When it was over, he set the headphones down around his neck.

"What do you think?" I said.

"Quite interesting, especially considering some news I heard on the drive up here."

"What's that?"

"Two of President Reagan's senior officials are in Moscow right now to discuss a U.S.–Soviet arms control agreement."

"Wow." It was weird, Dad's news lining up perfectly with a song on Paul's mixtape. "What do you think about the Moscow meeting?"

"It's difficult to say. From a political perspective, our countries are locked in conflict. History—in particular, the Cold War—shows us that our systems do no lend themselves to peaceful co-existence. But Mr. Gorbachev is raising a more important concern."

"What is it, Dad?"

"That in this nuclear age, all of humanity is under threat. A button is depressed, and soon after, it's the end."

A chill went through me as the image of a mushroom cloud formed in my head. I jammed my hands into my armpits. The thought of nuclear war always freaked me out. But then I felt my nostrils flaring. My teeth biting down. My lips beginning to curl.

"Why the heck are we doing this, Dad?"

He looked puzzled. "Why are we doing what?"

"Pointing all these missiles at each other. Getting ourselves set to end the world. It just . . . well, it makes me angry."

"I'd say that's a good thing."

"What? It's good that we're getting ready to end humanity?"

"No. We've reached this point because people aren't adequately animated. We've created an extraordinarily dangerous world, and yet people accept it. If you're angry, then perhaps you'll be motivated to bring about change."

Dad let out a slow breath. He pulled the headphones from his neck and handed them to me. "In any case, I share the musician's sentiment."

"Sting's? Which one?"

"I hope the Russians love their children, too."

•

After five days' imprisonment in the ICU, Dr. Egan set me free. I couldn't go home, but she ordered that the big drain tube be taken out of my head, half of the lines be withdrawn from my arms, and the catheter—the one for peeing—be pulled from you know where. My new room was a thousand times better, too. With a big, north-facing window and every surface covered with flowers, chocolates, and teddy bears, it was a major step up from the ICU.

Dad returned to work. Mom, very occasionally, would sneak out to run an errand. That gave me time to do some reading, which I actually enjoyed.

I was in the middle of *The Outsiders* when one of my favorite family members—my mom's first cousin—appeared in the doorway. "Loretta!" I practically shouted, bolting upright in bed. Some cards that had been sitting in my lap went flying.

"Wow," Loretta said, shaking her ultra-blond hair. "If my husband had ever been this happy to see me, we probably wouldn't be getting a divorce."

I busted up laughing. It would've gone on for minutes if I hadn't felt a shooting pain in the side of my head.

She got me caught up on all the family news. She had three daughters, two of whom were the same ages as my brother and me. She was finishing up telling me about her oldest. "Jalee visited some colleges last week. That's why she couldn't make your grandma's funeral."

I frowned. "Excuse me? What are you talking about?"

Loretta closed her eyes and moaned. She crossed her arms and dropped her head. "I wasn't supposed to say anything about that."

I found myself agitated. "About what?" I asked, nudging Loretta's shoulder. She didn't say anything. "C'mon, Loretta, what the heck is going on?"

She grabbed my hand and looked into my eyes. "Your grandma passed away last week. The Alzheimer's finally took her." Grandma had been living in a hospital for years, unable to move or speak. Still, it was shocking to hear she'd died.

"When did it happen?"

"Last Wednesday."

My chest tightened. "What, like the day I got admitted?"

"Yes."

"So when was the funeral?"

"The day of your surgery. Your mom stayed with you."

It was my turn to moan. I pulled my hand back and covered my face.

Loretta sighed. "Please don't tell her I told you this, honey. I was supposed to keep it under wraps."

My mind was squarely on my mom. I'd been so irritated by how neurotic she was acting, asking me millions of questions or going after the nurses or adjusting my sheets—and here her own mom had just died. I felt like a jerk. And Dad, with all his nods of approval when I pretended in front of Mom that nothing hurt at all—he was probably just trying to insulate her.

I dropped my hand and looked back at Loretta. It was time to practice what I knew I had to do in front of my mom.

I smiled at Loretta. I put my hand on her shoulder to reassure her. "This will be our little secret. Thanks for letting me know."

Loretta was biting her lip. I smiled more broadly, reaching toward her and giving her cheek a pinch. "Are we going to pout all afternoon?" I said.

Finally, she let out a deep breath. Soon after that, we were goofing around.

•

A few days later, after lunch, Mom and I were playing gin rummy. She seemed to be enjoying herself—it was her favorite card game—except she kept asking me how I was feeling. After I said I was fine for maybe the seventh time, I told her if she asked me again I'd get a nurse to shoot her up with some Valium. For a few minutes after that, she was mostly normal.

We were in the middle of a game when Ted walked in. I wasn't expecting him. He'd been swamped with a summer college-prep class and get-togethers with friends before the school year began, and Mom hadn't mentioned he was coming by. "How's it going?" he said, crossing his arms. Something about him seemed a little off.

I was about to ask what brought him by when Dad appeared in the doorway. The three of them assembled in my hospital room at the same time, completely unannounced—especially after Dad had returned to work—could mean only one thing: Dr. Egan had received the biopsy results. Why had everyone kept me out of the loop? My lips pinched together as I thought about what to say, but not even a minute passed before Dr. Egan knocked on the door.

"Come in," I said. They'd taken down the metal gate around my bed, so Dr. Egan sat at the end of it and looked straight at me. I swallowed.

There was no small talk. "The tumor cells were cancerous," she said. It felt like something was stuck in my ears, or they were both ringing. I wasn't sure I'd heard her correctly. I looked at my parents, who were standing behind her. The shock on their faces confirmed the news. Dad let out a sigh. Ted's eyes fell to the floor. Mom pressed her hand against her chest, as if her heart would fall out if she didn't.

Dr. Egan let her diagnosis sink in.

"What are my chances?" I said quietly.

"I know you don't like doctors glossing over things, so I won't. It's a very aggressive form of cancer. Statistically speaking—and every patient is unique, Jeff—the five-year survival rate for this cell type and grade is low." She went on to tell us about astrocytomas and said there were treatment options—radiation, chemotherapy, and so on—and that I shouldn't just assume I was going to die.

Dr. Egan left. My parents moved next to me, standing by my bed, silent and uncertain. Ted stayed back, burying himself behind a huge flower arrangement, as if trying to erase himself from the moment. I wanted to scream. I imagined grabbing the IV pole and smashing it through the window. I was flooded with emotions—anger, fear, grief—and I could feel my muscles tightening.

My father was somewhere else. I looked at him, but he didn't look back. Emotionally, he'd departed.

Ted's eyes traced the lines between the black-and-white floor tiles. His arms were crossed, his hands gripping his biceps.

Only Mom was really there, her eyes wide open and focused on mine. Her hands were shaking. Her face was pale, and her mouth hung open. Her whole body seemed unsteady, as if she was about to collapse.

That's when I remembered the moment with Loretta a few days before, when I committed to bracing my mom, shoring her up. I had to support her. She couldn't support herself.

With each breath, I buried my feelings. Fear of what was ahead, the possibility of dying—I refused to acknowledge them. One by one, I hid them away, pushing them deep into dark corners. I reached for my mom's hand, pulled it toward me, and kissed it. It wasn't fake—I loved her so much and knew that would help her—but at the same moment, my heart went numb.

CHAPTER FIVE

Everybody's favorite analogy for cancer, I learned during my time in the hospital, is war. Dr. Egan used that word and several others like it, saying on my last day there that a long, drawn-out fight was ahead. Just before I left the hospital, Dad told me I'd fought my battle admirably. In the stack of get-well cards I carried home, war came up a dozen times.

The analogy never really fit right for me. In real wars, there were combatants, people busy trying to kill each other. Who were the combatants in my war? The cancer cells made up one side, but who was fighting them? It certainly wasn't me. Dr. Egan and the other doctors and nurses were the ones who did all the work. I was just a spectator. Now I'd be moving on to the next phase of the war—chemotherapy and radiation—and again I'd be sitting around, swallowing pills or getting my head zapped, but not plotting and planning and fighting. People seemed so intent on calling the whole thing a war. But I wasn't one of the combatants. I was the battlefield.

•

The day after Dr. Egan dropped the cancer bomb, she said I could go home. Mom's face broke out into a permasmile you couldn't get off with a chisel. Dad called from the office, just after Mom gave him the news, and that's when he told me I'd fought the battle admirably. It was nice to see my parents so enthusiastic, and I was definitely happy to be getting out of that prison. But to me, Dr. Egan saying that I could leave—considering the other news she'd just given me—was more like telling me that home would be a more comfortable place to die.

Mom was folding my dirty clothes and tucking them into a duffel bag when Ted showed up with a couple of cardboard boxes. "Orders from Her Highness," he said, motioning toward Mom. She smiled and pointed at the flower arrangements. Ted looked at me, winked, and rolled his eyes. I chuckled.

Dad showed up. He looked more relaxed than usual, at least until Mom handed him the mile-high stack of paperwork the nurse had dropped off. He plopped himself into the recliner and started a review I expected would end around Christmas.

I didn't have anything to do. I offered to help, but Mom told me to stay in bed. Ted said it was the last time I'd get five-star care like this, so I should live it up. That got me thinking something dark, though thank God I didn't say it out loud: Just how long was I going to live?

Forty-five minutes later, with everything packed up and the papers signed, there was a knock on the door. Ted had been standing in front of it with his arms crossed, but he stepped aside. In walked Dr. Egan, three of her medical residents, and several of the nurses who'd been taking care of me. The room was quickly crowded.

"On behalf of my team," Dr. Egan began, "I wanted to say goodbye. I can honestly say you've been one of the most amazing patients I've ever had."

"*One* of the most?" I said. Several people smiled. Dr. Egan chuckled.

"Okay, *the* most. I know plenty of challenges are ahead, but you've handled this with remarkable maturity."

I glanced at Dad. His jaw was jutting out. Mom instantly teared up. Ted smiled at me.

"Thanks, Dr. Egan," I said. "Thanks to all of you, actually. It's really nice to be leaving this place still able to think and speak and listen. I'm going to tell you something, but I don't want any of you to get offended, okay?" I waited until Dr. Egan, her residents, and the nurses looked at me and nodded. "I honestly hope I never have to see any of you here again."

•

The first thing I did when we got home, after saying hello to Amiga, who couldn't stop wagging her serpentine tail until I gave her a five-minute-long tummy rub, was call Paul. Ever since he'd witnessed my seizure at his place, he'd been checking in, and he was the one person outside my family I allowed Mom to keep in the loop.

He answered after one ring. "Dude, are you home?"

"Yup," I said. "Relaxing downstairs on my couch with half a brain."

"C'mon, man." He didn't think that was funny. "Tell me how you're feeling."

"Overall, pretty good." I hesitated for a second. "Did, um, my mom tell you the diagnosis?"

I heard Paul suck in a breath. "You mean the cancer part?"

"Yeah, that."

"She did." He paused. "But she said the surgery went really, really well."

I sighed. "I guess. It's just that the tumor might, you know, grow back or something."

"Dude, you've got to think positive. And also know your friends totally have your back."

I sat up straight on the couch. "Wait a second, you didn't tell anyone, did you?"

"You made me say 'truth' not to fifteen times."

"So, truth, you didn't say a single word to anybody at all?"

"Jesus, truth."

My shoulders relaxed. "Okay."

Paul sighed. "I don't see why you're so worried about people knowing."

"Dude, have you forgotten freshman year? My knee gave out in front of the football jocks and the whole year they called me Stumpy. If I caught that much crap for a messed-up knee, just imagine what I'll get for a hole in my head."

"Those jocks are a bunch of dickheads. I'm talking about our friends. Which reminds me, everybody's getting together Wednesday evening at Bahama Lanes—you know, our last hurrah before sophomore year begins. Will you come?"

"I don't know." I definitely wanted to see people, but I didn't want people feeling sorry for me. The thought of having to tell people made Lucia pop into my head. I figured I'd better check with Paul. "So, like, is Lucia going?"

"I don't think anyone invited her. You want me to call her?"

"Not unless you absolutely want to guarantee that I won't join you." I was still having nightmares about her surprise visit after I had my head shaved. What a humiliating experience.

"Whoa, dude, time for a chill pill." I was quiet, thinking about Lucia, when the distinctive sound of a fart came through the receiver. "I gotta jet," Paul said.

"You just did."

Paul laughed. "You're hilarious. Look, you absolutely have to come next week. I never have fun without you. But I do have to go now. If I could take you into the bathroom, I would."

I cracked up. "Now you're absolutely full of shit."

"Not for long," Paul said, laughing out loud as he hung up.

•

My first dose of chemo pills began just three days after I was released from the hospital. Each round of chemo would be four days, with pills in the morning and evening. When Dr. Egan mentioned them, I didn't realize I'd be starting right away, and I never imagined they'd be administered at home. Grandma had gone through chemo six years earlier, and she'd stayed at the hospital the whole time.

After breakfast, Mom put on some latex gloves and filled a little paper cup with the morning dose that Dr. Farbstein, my oncologist, had ordered the day before. "Water or orange juice?" she asked. I pointed to the OJ. She poured it and handed me the little cup, and I downed the pills. We sat there together for maybe ten minutes, expecting some of the things the pharmacist had warned us about—nausea, fatigue, and so on—but nothing bad happened. We were pleasantly surprised.

The evening rolled around, and Dad and Ted watched as Mom administered my dose. Dad seemed impressed. He recalled how sick his mother had been when she was on chemo. "You're tough, Jeff," he said, which made Ted cringe and me feel a little proud. Still, I wondered whether the pharmacy had given me the wrong pills.

On day two, there was a little rumbling in my stomach after lunch, though nothing major. I ate dinner along with everybody else. I burped a couple of times while reading *The Outsiders*, but that was it. At ten o'clock, I went to sleep.

The following morning, when I emerged at the top of the staircase, Mom said, "Hello, sleepyhead." I glanced at the clock. It was half past eleven. "How are you feeling?"

I checked in with myself. No nausea. No headaches. None of the side effects Dr. Farbstein had talked about—save fatigue, considering I'd just slept thirteen hours. I told Mom I felt fine.

She was thrilled. She asked what I wanted for breakfast, and then made me one of her perfect omelets. I ate the whole thing, along with two pieces of toast and a glass of orange juice.

I took my dishes to the kitchen. "Unnecessary but appreciated," she said, her hands in latex gloves. "Unfortunately, I have to give you these guys now." She handed me my paper cup of chemo pills and another glass of orange juice. I downed them and headed to the living room.

I plopped myself down on the sofa and opened *The Outsiders* to where I'd left off, where Ponyboy is reading a Robert Frost poem to Johnny, who's blown away by it. It was my favorite part of the book. I was reciting the poem "Nothing Gold Can Stay" from memory when I felt a deep rumbling in my stomach.

I waited for it to go away. It didn't. I changed my position on the couch, sat up a bit, and burped loudly. "Mom," I called.

She appeared at the top of the stairs. "Yes, honey?"

I was breathing rapidly now—quick, shallow breaths—and my head was moving up and down.

"Oh, Jeff, what's wrong?" she said, the pitch of her voice showing panic.

I closed my eyes and tried to stay calm. "Get a bucket" was all I managed to say. Mom switched into emergency mode, disappearing and returning seconds later. She reached me just in time, capturing in the bucket—in five nasty installments—the entire contents of my stomach.

"I'm so sorry, honey," she said. I thought she was referring to what had just happened, but when I looked up I saw that she was putting on a new pair of gloves. She took the bucket from me and reached into it, pulling out one pill and then another, wiping each one off with a tissue and setting them next to me.

"You've got to be kidding, Mom," I said.

She shook her head. "Orange juice or water?"

•

My stomach ended up going through a week of hell. Even though Paul begged me to come, I told him there was no way I'd make it to the Bahama Lanes reunion.

The evening before the get-together, after a dinner with Mom and Dad when I was just poking at my food with a fork, Dad came downstairs with a pink bottle in his hand.

"Mother told me you had a bowel disturbance this afternoon." His words—"bowel disturbance"—made me cringe. The last thing I felt like doing was having a discussion about diarrhea.

"Uh-huh," I said.

"She mentioned this might be inhibiting you from attending the bowling event tomorrow with your friends."

"Yup."

"Well, I periodically have disruptions in my bowels." My toes starting curling. "I find this helpful," he said, handing me the bottle. I grabbed it to get him to stop talking but couldn't even look at it. I really needed the conversation to end.

"Gotcha." I faked a yawn. It looked like he might continue, so I stretched my arms. Still, I wasn't sure he was finished. And I needed him to be. "Boy am I wiped, Dad," I finally said. "Think I'd better hit the hay."

"All right, son. Good night." I wasn't the slightest bit tired, but I switched off the lights as he closed the door so he wouldn't feel insulted. A few minutes later, I switched them back on. I grabbed the bottle, poured myself a dose, and downed it. It was disgusting.

The next day, I woke up feeling great. My stomach, for the first time in a week, was calm. I looked over at the bottle and laughed to myself. Maybe Dad was on to something. I called Paul to let him know that maybe, just maybe, I'd be seeing him that evening.

●

Mom dropped me off at Bahama Lanes a few minutes past five. I saw my friends gathered near the building's glass double doors. Paul was chatting with Tony. Cara was in a conversation with Ryan and Dave. Nobody had noticed me. The last thing I'd done before stepping out of the car was pull down the vanity mirror and adjust my baseball cap, but as I walked over I found myself tugging down on the left side to make sure my scar was fully covered.

Paul saw me when I was about fifteen feet away. "Jeff!" he said with a big grin. He started walking toward me.

Tony spun around. He was smiling, too. He stepped off the curb and quickly passed Paul. I felt goose bumps popping up all over my forearms.

"Did Jeffy get a buzz cut?" Tony asked when he reached me. He leaned forward, staring at my head and shifting from one side to the other. I rubbed my nose, not because it itched, but just so

I'd have a hand ready. That was when Tony grabbed my hat. I clamped down hard on his wrist.

"Stop, Tony," I said firmly. My other hand swung around and I pressed down on top of my head.

His fingers were locked on the brim of my cap. "Lemme see your cut, Jeff," he said, tugging upward.

"Let go of my hat," I said, louder now. In the corner of my eye, I could see Cara, Ryan, and Dave walking over.

Tony didn't listen. He yanked on my hat. "Dammit!" I finally yelled. "Will you let go of my goddam hat? I had fucking brain cancer, okay?"

His jaw dropped. He let go and stepped backward. My other friends had heard everything and were staring now, along with a bunch of people I didn't know who were passing by.

"You're joking," Tony finally said. He turned to Paul. "Jeff's joking, right?"

"He's not, Tony," Paul said. "He had brain cancer."

It wasn't what Paul and I had discussed. I didn't get to calmly tell everyone what happened. I went through an inquisition in the Bahama Lanes parking lot, with friends and strangers alike staring at me. The interrogation didn't stop when we got inside, because other friends showed up. I wanted nothing more than to leave. But I knew if I did that, everyone in our group would spend the evening talking about me, their friend who looked different, who maybe *was* different, so my only option was to stay. Even the thought of stepping away to the bathroom scared me, because I would become a topic of discussion, and likely pity. It took a rumbling in my gut for me to finally excuse myself, and then it was only because my fear of the humiliation that would come if I crapped in my pants outweighed the fear I had of becoming the subject of a conversation I'd never hear. I went off to the bathroom, which prevented an accident, but I still came back feeling disgraced.

It felt like eons passed before our rides showed up. I was desperate to get out of there. I walked toward my mom's headlights, and she had figured out something awful had happened by the time I stepped into the car. "Oh, honey, what's wrong?" she asked as I got in.

"Drive, Mom," I told her as my eyes welled up. "Just drive."

CHAPTER SIX

Polytechnic School started its new year on a Thursday—this time without me. I could've made it, but my stomach was a little unsettled. Plus, I didn't want a repeat of the Bahama Lanes disaster, with somebody running up to me and yanking off my baseball cap. I mentioned to my mom that it sure would be nice if someone just let my classmates know what I'd gone through that summer and that I wasn't up for answering a bunch of questions. She passed that message to Mrs. Hager, our upper school director, and she, Paul later told me, shared it with the school.

I showed up on Monday. Mom drove me, and as she turned onto Cornell, the road that ends at our school, I practically had a panic attack. Paul had promised to meet me out front, but I didn't see him anywhere.

After Mom reassured me five times that my hat looked great (she'd insisted that morning that I wear the black velvet one she'd gotten me for my birthday instead of my beaten-up Dodgers cap) and that everything was going to be fine, I stepped out of the car with my fingers tingling. I took two steps forward and practically ran into Anjali Senanayake, a really cute girl from Ted's class.

"Hi, Jeff," she said. She had a beautiful smile on her face. "It's good to see you."

We'd never really had a serious conversation, considering she was two years older. I tried to think of something to say. "How was your summer?"

"Pretty good. We were here for part of it and also back in Sri Lanka." I felt awkward. I had no idea where Sri Lanka was, and I sure didn't want to talk about my summer. She seemed to pick up on my discomfort.

Her face got serious. "I know yours wasn't easy, Jeff," she said, gently touching my shoulder. "I'm honestly very pleased you're here."

It felt good to hear that, and I think it showed, because she smiled again.

Just then, I saw Paul. He was leaning under the eave of the Garland Theater roof, looking cool in his new Sideout Sports sweatshirt, his index fingers pointed at Anjali, which he quickly switched out for two thumbs-up as he winked at me. I wanted to kick him. "Excuse me, Anjali," I said, walking toward Paul and praying she hadn't seen my face turn red.

"Look at you, making your way with a senior," Paul said, laughing.

"Give me a break. Seniors don't go after sophomores. Or invalids, for that matter."

Paul's smile disappeared. He pointed at me forcefully. "Dude, you're not an invalid."

"Fine, I guess I'm just nervous."

"Don't sweat it, man. People are cool about your situation. Nice hat, by the way. Shall we?"

●

Even though I'd missed the first two days of school, I was ready for my classes. Paul had gotten me up to speed over the weekend on the ones we had in common, and I'd made sure to call Cara about Mrs. McKendrick's English class, since she could be such a headache. I'd already done all the reading, too, and not just a quick skim. I was ready to answer questions, even the obscure kind she liked to formulate.

I'd gotten myself in trouble with her the previous year, showing up late two days in a row, which she never seemed to forget. The concept of "late" for Mrs. McKendrick was anything other than early. Forget about "on time." Students either showed up five minutes early and sat there as she compulsively cleaned every square inch of the chalkboard, or else they were late, even if they made it while the bell was ringing. Today I arrived with plenty of time to spare.

I was chatting quietly with Cara when, at eight a.m., Mrs. McKendrick wrote MORALITY on the chalkboard in big block letters and spun around to face the class. "What," she said, followed by a dramatic pause as she adjusted the chopsticks holding her hair bun in place, "are the central elements that constitute *To Kill a Mockingbird*'s moral infrastructure?"

Not a single hand went up. Given how things had gone between us the previous year, it felt like an opportunity to get on her good side.

I raised my hand.

She noticed, but she didn't pick me. I looked around the room. Everyone else's hands were either frozen in their laps or glued to the table. I was the only one offering an answer, but still she just waited.

Finally, Allison Fowler raised a finger, and Mrs. McKendrick immediately called on her.

She ignored me two more times. I didn't get it. Was she holding a grudge?

By the time the bell rang, I wanted to fling my book into the trash can right next to her. I was imagining exactly that when I felt my stomach rumble slightly.

I zipped up my backpack along with everyone else and headed toward the door.

"Jeffrey," Mrs. McKendrick said in her serious voice just as I was leaving. My neck muscles tightened up as I turned around. "I'd like to have a word."

"The administration has brought to my attention that your medical condition may require certain accommodations."

I thought some clarity might help.

"I've got five more rounds of chemo," I said. "They're four days long, and I can't attend school during those periods. I'm starting radiation at the end of the month. My doctor said I might need to take a break then, but I'm not planning on it."

"You will of course need to do whatever your medical experts advise. With regard to my class, I will accommodate you to the extent necessary, but I will not treat you any differently from your classmates."

I couldn't believe what I was hearing. For the last hour she already had. Not only that, I really didn't like her tone. Neither did my intestinal tract, which reacted by rumbling again. I wanted to set her straight, but I needed to find a toilet.

"I don't want to be treated differently," I said, shifting on my feet. The pressure in my stomach was building. A disaster was imminent.

"That means reading all the same works, completing all homework assignments, and . . ."

I jumped to my feet.

Mrs. McKendrick's eyes quickly narrowed. "Jeffrey," she said in an even louder voice.

"I forgot something very important," I said, and started toward the door. I literally had seconds.

"Jeffrey!" was the last I heard from Mrs. McKendrick, with incredulity in her voice, as I raced toward the administrative building. It was an old house, and the previous year I'd discovered a lesser-known bathroom accessible through a small outside door. I prayed it was unlocked.

•

After school, I was waiting for Mom to pick me up by Garland Theater, reflecting on how the day had gone—not bad, actually, other than that situation with Mrs. McKendrick—when the theater doors swept open and Lucia appeared with two of her girlfriends. For the whole day I'd managed to hide from her, even during lunch, which I'd eaten with Paul in our math classroom.

But now she'd found me, and her eyes opened wide, and she shouted my name. That got half the people waiting for rides to turn toward me and stare. Boy, did I ever want to disappear.

She ran over to me. Her friends stayed behind. "Hi, Jeff," she said, this time breathless. I could smell her perfume, Poison, the same stuff she'd been wearing when we made out in her bedroom.

"Hi, Lucia," I said nervously.

"I've been trying to reach you forever," she said, tossing her head back and running her fingers through her hair. She'd called so many times in the past week that Mom no longer spelled out her name on messages. It was just *L called*, along with the time.

"Have you? I'm so sorry. Things have been really busy."

She nodded. "That's okay." Her eyebrows were furrowed. Her lips were pursed. She looked like . . . my mother. "Tell me, how *are* you?" Hearing that made my toes curl.

"I'm fine. Really. Everything's going great."

She wasn't listening. Her eyes had been focused on mine, but now they were moving, from my forehead to my cap, to the left side of my head. It was like she was searching for a deformity.

"You know, you can't even see anything," she finally said. I quickly adjusted my cap. "The scar, I mean."

My stomach tightened. Then—nausea. For a second, I really thought I might throw up.

She continued, saying how she wanted to help, but now I was the one who wasn't listening. My eyes were on the road in front of us.

Lucia was in the middle of a question when Mom showed up. I think I gasped. "Looks like I've gotta go," I said.

Lucia frowned. "But what about—"

I cut her off. "Sorry, can't keep my mom waiting."

I let out a huge breath as I hurried toward the car.

●

A month into my sophomore year, just as I'd finally settled into my classes, Dr. Gourevik told me it was time to start radiation. It wouldn't be at Huntington Hospital, where I'd had my surgery, but at City of Hope hospital in Duarte, half an hour away without traffic, and double that when the freeway was packed with cars. For six weeks, I'd have to go there every day to get zapped. Somehow, I'd keep up with my classes.

Mom could tell I was stressed as she drove me out for the first appointment. She reached over and clasped my hand, giving it a couple of squeezes. It took me right back to when I woke up from my brain surgery, when she was sending me her hand-pulsed Morse code messages. I decided not to mention that to her. On our way out to Duarte, we passed C&H Surplus, the store that carried the parts for my laser. I'd sort of put the project on hold. It was still sitting there in my bedroom, in the corner by the window, but I hadn't once asked Mom to drive me out to C&H. I guess it was because of the cancer diagnosis. If they couldn't cure me, there was no point in trying to get into one of the top science schools. So much for becoming an astronaut.

Mom and I sat down with the radiologist, a brawny man in his fifties with wiry red hair, who explained how everything would proceed. He'd first review the scans Mom had brought with us. Then his team would lay down a triad of barely visible tattoos on my head (one between my eyes, another in front of my left ear, and the third behind it) to help line up the radiation beams. Last, I'd be taken to the radiation chamber, where I'd get zapped for the first time. Only this first visit would take a few hours, because of all the preparation they had to do. After that, I'd be in and out in fifteen minutes.

He asked if I had any questions.

"Two, actually. Dr. Gourevik said I might have to leave school, but you're saying I won't feel anything, so who's right?"

"You won't experience any discomfort during the sessions. But you're likely to experience fatigue, which typically increases over the treatment period. In a few weeks, you may find it necessary to take a break from school."

I really didn't want to leave school. I sighed quietly.

"You said you had two questions."

"Oh, right. Well, there was this guy in the waiting room who had a huge bald spot in the back of his head. Is that gonna happen to me?"

"It might. Hair follicles are sometimes sensitive to radiation."

I hated hearing that. Mom could tell. She squeezed my arm.

I looked at the radiologist. "If my hair falls out, will it grow back?"

"Sometimes it does, sometimes it doesn't. It's not something we're able to predict." He could tell I didn't like that answer. "Look, I think it's important to focus on the priority."

"What's that?" I asked. I honestly didn't get what he was saying.

"Hair is cosmetic. Our priority here is to eliminate cancer cells."

Mom's jaw dropped, which she quickly corrected when

she saw me look at her. I couldn't believe what I'd just heard. I groaned, shook my head, and sank into my chair.

●

After just one week of radiation, I was exhausted. I'd fall asleep on the ride back from Duarte, napping as Mom drove me to school. By the end of the second week, I was misspelling words, or incorrectly substituting one for another, or leaving them out altogether. Sometimes, in class, I'd ask the same question twice. My Spanish teacher, Mrs. Pendorf, was understanding. So was Mr. Stelter, in chemistry, where I got just about every term wrong. But after I misused "their" for "there" in Mrs. McKendrick's class, she suggested I take a remedial spelling course. And then, when I got confused about which pages we had to read from *All the King's Men* and raised my hand to ask, she snapped at me. "Whining again, Jeff?" she asked. The whole class went silent. I felt like screaming at her, but I didn't have the energy.

●

The first couple of days of my radiation-imposed school break were absolutely necessary. I slept tons—ten hours each night, along with a few naps during the day. But soon, it was boring. I had to go to radiation each morning and study and do homework when I got back, but that went much faster when not having to listen to self-centered twats like Mrs. McKendrick drone on for an eternity. After accounting for the radiation trips, extra sleep, study time, and meals, I had five free hours a day with nothing to do, and Mom definitely didn't have five hours to hang out.

One Saturday, after my fourth round of radiation, Mom came home from running some errands. Ted and Dad were out independently. I was lying on the couch, in front of the TV.

"Guess who I ran into?" Mom asked.

"Darth Vader?"

Mom frowned.

"Okay, tell me."

"Joni Ashworth." Not only was Mrs. Ashworth my favorite teacher in elementary school, she was the mother of the first girl I'd ever kissed. I pressed mute on the remote and sat up. "She asked about you. I mentioned you were taking a break from school and had some free time, and she said she could really use your help."

"Me? What could I do for her?"

"She needs a teaching assistant. I told her you volunteered at Head Start last year."

"Was this her idea or yours?"

"I'm not sure who came up with it. Here's her number, though. She'd love to hear from you." Mom handed it over. "I've got to put the groceries away."

I ended up speaking with Mrs. Ashworth for nearly an hour that afternoon, talking about her daughter and her fifth graders and the ways I could be helpful. On Monday, after a morning dose of radiation and a nap, Mom dropped me off at my old elementary school.

"Pencils and paper down, everyone," Mrs. Ashworth said. Her students, ten and eleven years old, instantly complied. "Let's welcome my new teaching assistant. This is Jeff, who happens to have once been a student here, just like you. Shall we?"

The kids nodded, and Mrs. Ashworth cued them up. "Good morning, Jeff," they said in classic elementary school monotone.

The kids got back to their U.S. history projects, and I walked from table to table. They were putting together posters of famous historical figures, like George Washington and Eleanor Roosevelt.

"What's your name?" I said to one girl.

"Linda."

"Well, Linda, that's a lovely picture of Thomas Jefferson you've drawn."

She frowned. "That's not Thomas Jefferson. That's Zachary Taylor."

"Thank you for correcting me," I said, smiling. Linda smiled back.

With each new day of radiation, my fatigue increased, and each day away from Poly, my friends felt more distant. Paul called whenever he could, but he was super busy and could never talk long. Without being around those little kids, I would've felt isolated and alone.

One afternoon in Mrs. Ashworth's classroom, five weeks into my radiation, I was helping the kids with the questions they had to write for their U.S. history game show. It was just like *Jeopardy!*

"Jeff, what should my Eleanor Roosevelt question be?" a girl named Edna asked.

I knelt next to her. "Did you have anything in mind?"

There was a poke on my shoulder. I turned around to see Robert, who was sitting at the table behind Edna's. He had a quizzical look on his face. "Why do you have a blue dot on your head?" he asked.

It couldn't be tempera paint. We'd used that a few days before, but I'd definitely showered since then. Plus, none of the bottles was sitting out. I wiped my face and looked at my hand, just to make sure. "No, not there," Robert said loudly. The students around him looked up. He extended his index finger and pointed at the side of my head, touching a spot behind my left ear. "There!" he proclaimed.

The radiologist's team had tattooed a point behind my ear, but the dot was hidden by my hair. How could this kid see that? I ran my fingers through the area. Small patches of my own hair fell like snowflakes.

"That's your hair!" Edna said.

Robert followed. "Ooh, your hair is falling out!" The children quickly assembled around me as I stood there, dumbfounded. Some were pointing at me. Others were picking up strands of my hair that had fallen on the table and floor. They started laughing, and that got Mrs. Ashworth's attention on the other side of the room. She walked over quickly and found me frozen in place.

"Back to your work!" she barked at the kids. She tugged on my arm. "Come on, Jeff," she said, and led me out of the room.

We stood for several minutes in the afternoon sun. I wasn't really with her. I didn't know it at the time, but I was compulsively tugging at my head. She touched my shoulder and then my hand, slowly pulling it away. In it was a fistful of hair. "Can I take you home?" she asked.

"Your students need you," I said after a long pause.

In a daze, I walked home. I never, ever went back.

CHAPTER SEVEN

My favorite thing to do as a kid, other than launching rockets, was to see the Dodgers play. Their stadium was pretty close to Dad's office. The reason I liked it so much wasn't just because Dad, as a senior partner, had access to such excellent seats behind home plate. It was also because going to games was one of the few things we did together as a family. Nothing—not a toothache or homework or the worst cold imaginable—ever kept me from going.

We had tickets for an evening game just a week after the absolute humiliation I experienced in Mrs. Ashworth's class when my hair fell out. I now had a large bald spot on the side of my head, along with patches missing from the front and back. I'd been getting something called stereotactic radiation, where twin beams were sent in on the left side of my head at ninety-degree angles, meeting a few inches inside my head where the tumor had been growing, and exiting far apart, through my forehead and the base of my skull. In all those locations, I'd lost hair. The beams had also torched the skin on the tip of my left ear, leaving it covered with bloody scabs. I looked like a freak show.

Mom had been downstairs twice that day to see if I would join the rest of the family for the game. She was stunned to hear me say no. After the second time, she called in the cavalry: Dad.

I heard his plodding footsteps on the staircase. He knocked on the door and I told him to come in. He skipped saying hello. "Do I understand correctly from Mother that you're not joining us to see the Dodgers this evening?"

"I'll join you on television. I'm definitely not leaving this house."

"I thought Fernando Valenzuela was your favorite pitcher."

"That doesn't mean I have to see him in person."

"But we have tickets. You *can* see him in person."

"Fernando could personally invite me and I still wouldn't go."

Dad shook his head. "I don't see the point of your staying home."

"Well, you're not bald, Dad."

"Neither are you, Jeff."

I lifted my hat and rotated my head. "What do you call these three massive hairless patches?"

"Then wear the baseball cap you've just removed."

I jumped off the couch, fuming, and turned, pointing to the back of my head. "What, so the open space in the rear of my baseball cap can highlight my freakishness? I don't think so."

"You're missing out—and over something of no importance." He shook his head in disgust. I wanted to kick him. I mean, he was sixty-one, and he had more hair than I did. When he finally walked out, I grabbed a pillow, pressed it hard against my face, and screamed.

●

Skipping the Dodgers game made it clear to my mom that something serious needed to happen. She called around, ultimately finding a wigmaker in Hollywood, and in no time at all I ended up with three hairpieces I could clip over the exposed spots in just a couple of minutes. They made me look normal, and I felt like celebrating.

I wore my wigs to City of Hope during my last week of radiation. It made everything take longer, but man, was it satisfying when Friday rolled around. The technician locked me in place, gave me my last dose, and set me free with a high five. When I came out of the dressing room with my wigs back in place, Mom smiled and hugged me. "Congratulations, sweetie," she said. "I'm so proud of you." I was pretty proud of myself.

I wanted to leave right away, but Mom said we had to see the radiologist. We ended up waiting fifteen minutes, which felt more like three hours.

"Congratulations, Jeff," he said. "How are you feeling?"

I let out a long yawn. "Happy to be done with this place."

"Well, you're definitely finished with brain radiation."

That sounded great. It was like he was certain my cancer wasn't coming back. I just wondered why he wasn't smiling.

"Um, just to be clear, what do you mean, exactly?"

"Yes, well, you've had the maximum dose of radiation your brain can take."

"You mean for this six-week treatment protocol?"

"I mean permanently."

"So what if I get a recurrence?"

"Radiation, in that case, would no longer be an option." I sank into my chair. What felt at first like a triumph ended up being a major letdown.

Mom had a few questions for him and then we said our good-byes.

"Good luck," he said as we walked out. Those two words only made me feel more insecure.

I was exhausted—like I always was after getting my brain zapped. But this time, I was angry, too. I had no idea there was a lifetime maximum radiation dose for my brain, and I was pissed the doctors had never bothered to mention that. Mom went off to get the car, and I sat by the hospital entrance. I usually struggled to keep my eyes open as I waited, but that day my anger kept me fully awake. When Mom pulled up, it was pulsing through me.

Mom knew something was up. "Is everything okay?" she asked as I got in.

"Everything is fine," I said robotically. The anger wasn't going anywhere. I had to do something about it.

My eyes scanned the interior of the car, looking for something to crush or throw, but I didn't see anything. I did notice the button for the sunroof. As we approached the hospital parking lot exit, I turned to my mom and said, "Don't freak out now."

"What are you talking about?" she asked as I opened the sunroof. Her eyebrows were squished together.

I popped my seat belt. "Jeff, what are you doing?" Mom asked, sounding anxious.

I climbed onto my seat, stood through the sunroof, and turned my body toward the hospital entrance.

"What in God's name . . . ?" Mom said frantically. I ignored her.

I looked at the hospital, raised my middle finger, and shouted, "Fuck you!" at the top of my lungs. Some staff who were out smoking looked at me, startled. A doctor heading into the building spun around. Mom gasped.

I sank into my seat, put my belt on, and smiled to myself.

Mom's jaw was hanging open. The car in front of us had just left the lot. Mom didn't appear to be moving. I looked back and there was a car behind us, patiently waiting. "Um, Mom?"

"What?"

"We can leave anytime you're ready." My smile broadened.

Mom snapped to. She glanced in her rearview mirror. "Sorry," she said, lifting a hand and waving as she took her foot off the brake.

As we rolled onto the street, Mom looked over at me and shook her head. Then she laughed. "You really are a nut sometimes, you know?"

I nodded.

•

With radiation out of the way and my energy slowly returning, my plan was to head back to school. I was definitely ready for it. Home felt lonely.

One Sunday, with the house empty and me deep into a book on the space race with the Soviets, the doorbell rang. I figured it was someone for my parents, so I lingered on the couch downstairs. But Amiga was barking and the bell kept ringing, so I scrambled into the bathroom to snap my wigs into place, then raced up to the entrance.

On the other side of the glass door, standing next to his bike, was Paul.

"What are you doing here?" I asked. I was honestly dumbfounded to see him.

He snickered. "A hello would be nice."

"Oh, sorry. Hello. I just wasn't expecting you."

"I know. I've been a little distant. Which makes me a little bit of a shit." He scratched his head. "That's why I'm here, though. Do you wanna hang out?"

It was really good to see him. "Are you seriously asking?" I said. "Of course I want to hang out."

After he raided the fridge upstairs, we went down to my room. He got me caught up on everything going on at Poly, like classes and the dating scene and whatnot. When he finished, he stiffened, shoving his hands into his pockets and biting his lower lip. "How's the, uh . . ."

"Cancer?" I said.

Paul nodded. He was never into talking about heavy stuff.

"It's fine. I'm done with radiation, thank God. I've got four more rounds of chemotherapy, and then it'll just be keeping my fingers crossed."

"Gotcha," Paul said. He looked around the room, then down at the bag he'd brought with him. "Say, are your parents still heating the pool? I've got trunks with me."

It wasn't the slickest subject change, but I didn't want to linger on cancer talk. "My dad put in solar last year," I said. "The water's always heated."

Paul smiled.

A couple of minutes later, we were standing by the pool. We had a tradition of jumping in with a flip—something he usually screwed up. "Who's first?" he said.

"I'll do it." I looked at the water, focused, and jumped. My rotation was perfect. I didn't really have time to extend, so I entered more like a ball, with my head hitting first. The water was warm. It felt welcoming. I swam to the bottom, touched the floor, and came back up.

I looked up at Paul. "What did you think of that?" I said, wiping my eyes. He didn't respond. His eyes were fixed on the water behind me. He raised one hand to cover his mouth, then pointed with the other.

I spun around in the water. Floating there, a foot away, was one of my wigs. I'd forgotten about them—swimming was so normal for us—and I suddenly wished I could disappear. I snatched it up, swam to the shallow end of the pool, and stepped out. I hurried toward the house. I couldn't meet Paul's eyes.

When I returned with my baseball cap on a few minutes later, Paul was standing by the pool. He hadn't gone in.

"You can swim if you want," I said, scratching my arm. He was quiet, which I couldn't stand. I faked a yawn. "I'm just, you know, really tired."

"Maybe I'll just head back home, then," he said.

My chest suddenly tightened. "Um, Paul," I started, with my eyebrows scrunched together. I was staring at my toes.

"What's up?"

I looked at him. "Truth you won't tell anyone about this?"

He looked back at me. "Truth."

•

For hours after Paul went home, I replayed the pool scene in my head. It wasn't far off from what had happened at Monterey Hills School, though I didn't exactly feel humiliated, just embarrassed. The more difficult thing was that Paul was my best friend, and he just didn't get my situation. He couldn't.

That's when it hit me. It wasn't just Paul. It was all of my friends. My whole family. Not one of them really understood what I was going through. I could call every single person I knew and spill the gory details of surgery, chemo, and radiation, or describe how hard it was for my battered brain to stay focused for even a couple of minutes, let alone a whole day, or what it felt like to be bald at fifteen, and still, nobody would get me.

That realization was followed by something that was more like a revelation: there had to be people out there, guys and girls my age, who were going through the same nightmare.

If I was ever going to be understood, I had to find them.

•

The very first meeting of Teenline took place in the living room of our house in South Pasadena. When I shared my thinking with my mom, she found a social worker, Aura, who'd been helping teenagers with cancer at Children's Hospital Los Angeles. Aura and I had a long conversation, and what came out of it was a solid plan.

"Welcome, everybody," I said nervously. "Maybe we can go around the room and introduce ourselves. My name's Jeff. I had brain cancer. I guess I've been feeling kind of alone, so I'm really happy to be meeting all of you." People smiled at me and nodded. It felt good.

Chris went next. He was short and chubby and direct, with thinning brown hair and bright blue eyes. Mom was serving trays full of drinks and snacks, and he grabbed a plateful of cookies as she was passing. "Y'all think I'm bald from chemo or something, right? I'm actually an old guy who showed up for free food." People laughed a little uncertainly.

Sylvia followed. She was also heavyset, with long, thick black hair and a slight Spanish accent. After talking about her cancer, she said, "My stepfather told me I'm stealing his wife, since she's always with me in the hospital. My sister hates me, I think for the same reason." It was really hard to hear.

Mom, who'd toted the trays back to the kitchen, reappeared on the staircase, accompanied by two teenage girls. They looked like they'd been pulled off a Hollywood set.

"Sorry we're late," one of them said, a bunch of bracelets sliding down her arm as she tucked some strands of hair behind her ear. She was friendly enough. The other one seemed chilly.

"Welcome," I said. "Sit wherever you like. We've been introducing ourselves and talking about what we're dealing with. Go ahead and jump in."

"Oh, cool," the warmer girl said. "I'm Beverly. I'm seventeen and in remission from leukemia. I'm just glad to meet other people my age dealing with the same stuff. So hi."

Eyes turned to Beverly's friend, who looked like a prom queen—pretty, perfect hair, and smug—but without the smile. She didn't make eye contact with any of us. She didn't seem nervous. Just rigid and cold. She finally said, "I'm Monique, also seventeen. Same story as Bev's, basically." She looked down at her watch.

The five remaining people introduced themselves. By the time we got to Oscar, people seemed pretty comfortable. He talked for a while. When he finished, he flopped back on the couch. "I gotta say, it feels good to finally be around people who really get you." Everyone in the room was nodding.

Aura probed deeper into the challenges we were facing, and people were engaged. Everyone had something to add—except Monique. I wondered why she'd even bothered coming.

Overall, the meeting went well. "I hope this has been helpful for you," Aura said to us when it was over. "Do you want to meet again?"

"Yes," everyone said.

"We're totally open to suggestions," I added. "Like if there's something specific you're looking to do."

To my surprise, Monique raised her hand. "Go for it," I said. It wasn't like we were at school or anything.

"I think it's great to get together and talk about the tough things we're going through," she said. "But I also think we should have fun."

She won over the entire group with a sentence. Before that, the room felt settled, maybe even tuckered out. Now, everybody seemed energized.

"What about a party?" Chris said.

Oscar, smiling, gave him a thumbs-up.

Monique jumped at the opportunity. "Yes," she said, "a *dance* party! We can have it at my house."

•

A month later, I was out in the city of Tarzana, standing in Monique's dining room next to a table full of appetizers her mother, Hugette, had prepared. "Eat, *Jef-fer-rey*, eat," Hugette said, with a thick French accent.

"Did you make all this?" I asked. The food was delicious.

"Everything," she said.

"You're amazing," I said.

"Stop charming me. I'm married!" I think my face turned red, because standing right next to me was Norman, Monique's father.

He and I ended up talking a lot, and he was in the middle of a story about his childhood bout with polio when I felt a tug on my sleeve. I turned around to find Monique and Beverly. They looked alarmed.

"What's up?" I said.

"Nobody is dancing," Beverly said.

Monique jumped in. "You've got to help us."

"Your dad's in the middle of a story." I prayed he'd continue. I wasn't into dancing.

"Don't let me keep you from responding to an emergency of such proportion," he said.

Monique winked at her father and she dragged me out to the patio.

In spite of my initial reluctance, Beverly and Monique got me onto the dance floor. The three of us burned the place up. It was infectious. When "Like a Virgin" came on, most of the group and their dates were out there with us. One of the guys was spinning his wheelchair.

I danced with Monique. I didn't know the first thing about her, I realized. She'd been so cold the day we met, and that's how I'd seen her as a person ever since. But it was just self-defense, or shyness, or something like that. The girl twirling and swaying in front of me couldn't have been warmer or more vibrant—more *alive*.

My eyes went over every inch of her face, stopping on her lips, which were absolutely perfect. I must have smiled at her, because she looked at me and started grinning.

Back home that night, I couldn't sleep. I didn't even want to. Monique was occupying my head. Both versions of her were there—the anxious, pouting girl who begged me to dance and the liberated one who moved so freely, effortlessly, with that infectious smile and those beautiful lips. What blew me away was the transformation that had taken place, not just in how she looked from one moment to the next, but in how I saw her, and how much, how *very* much, I wanted to see her again.

PART 2

CHAPTER EIGHT

All sorts of cool conversations had taken place at Monique's dance party, but the most interesting was the one I stumbled upon between Oscar and Chris. They were in the kitchen, each holding a cup of Hugette's fruit punch, and talking about wishes. "What was yours, Jeff?" Oscar asked totally matter-of-factly as he took a sip.

I had no idea what he was talking about. "What, like if I die?" I said.

Oscar's eyebrows shot up toward the ceiling. He spit into his cup.

Chris stepped in. "No, dude. Wishes, like a day at Disneyland or meeting Tom Cruise—you know, the kind the Starlight Foundation or Make-A-Wish offer. What was your wish?"

"I never had one. I mean, I thought that was for kids. I'm almost sixteen."

"I'm fifteen," Oscar said, "and they just gave me one."

"Yeah, and I'm sixteen," Chris said. "I've had two."

"How'd you get two wishes?" I asked.

"My cancer came back. You see, recurrence ain't *all* bad."

The three of us cracked up when he said that.

That was what got me started on wishes. In the days after the party, I thought about them a lot, though not nearly as much as I thought about Monique.

Paul told me back in eighth grade that you're not supposed to call a girl immediately after meeting her or she'll think you're desperate. I don't know where he got that from—it wasn't like he had a girlfriend—but I always took it as fact. It seemed like a decent strategy to use with Monique, given that she was a whole year older than me, in her junior year, and I knew how clueless and desperate freshmen sounded to me. So after a lot of debate, I settled on two days—that was how long I'd hold off before giving her a call.

After a day and a half of thinking about her nonstop, I couldn't hold out any longer. Plus, with Ted at the gym, Mom out shopping, and Dad at work, I had the house to myself. I perched on the edge of my bed, drew in a deep breath, and made the call. I was so nervous dialing, I had to do it twice.

"Jeff—I was hoping you would call!" Monique said. "Did you like the party?"

"I loved it. Everybody did."

Monique let out a satisfied sigh. "I was so worried because hardly anyone was dancing. But you totally saved it."

I snorted out a laugh. The only saving I might've done was to demonstrate to everyone that at least one dancer there was worse than they all thought they were.

Our conversation turned out to be the easiest thing in the world. We had a million things in common, like school and parents and doctors. Just a few minutes into it, I couldn't believe how nervous I'd been calling her in the first place.

After talking about her life plans—she was thinking of becoming a nurse, just like her mom—I remembered the conversation with Chris and Oscar about wishes. I asked her if she'd ever had one.

"Yes, but it's embarrassing."

I laughed. "Even better."

"Mine was for a personal water polo lesson from the Olympian Terry Schroeder."

"What, like the two of you swimming in a pool together?"

"See, it's totally embarrassing."

"Not at all. It sounds like fun. I'd love to get a water polo lesson from Madonna."

"I totally didn't know she was into water polo."

"Heck, I don't even know if she can swim. But I'm sure I'd enjoy anything she'd be willing to teach me!"

Now Monique was the one snorting out a laugh. "All right, playboy, what was your wish?"

"Never had one. I thought you had to be a kid, like five years old or something."

"No way. Eighteen is the cutoff. You should definitely do it. What would you wish for?"

"Me? I have absolutely no idea."

"Just relax for a second. What's the first thing that pops into your head?" The image was of me on the beach in Marina del Rey when I was a kid, launching a rocket with my dad. I'd never forgotten the look on his face after seeing that thing take off.

"I wonder what my dad would think was cool," I murmured.

"Um, Jeff, this is *your* wish we're talking about."

I rubbed my nose. "Yeah, I know. I was just curious."

"Can you maybe stop thinking for a second and try again?"

"Funny, that's exactly what my brain tumor was trying to get me to do."

"*Jeff.*"

"Okay, okay—for you, anything."

"Finally," she said, exhaling sharply. "Now just close your eyes for a second. Relax. Take in a deep breath. Blow it out." I did exactly what she told me. "Now imagine you're offered an actual wish, something you can't do on your own. It's something you really, really want. Something that excites you."

"Okay." For several seconds, my mind was blank. "Nothing's coming."

"That's okay. Just keep breathing. Something—maybe someone—will pop up."

An image slowly formed, of myself as if viewed through a camera lens. I was strapped into a seat, wearing a helmet. The lens pulled back, revealing more of the scene. I was on the flight deck of the space shuttle *Columbia*, in the mission commander's seat, with the pilot next to me. The image broadened further, and now I could see the shuttle on the launch pad, strapped to a fuel tank, with booster rockets on either side and white vapor streaming from the bottom. I was about to go for a ride.

The thrill of it surged through me. It's what I'd spent my whole childhood dreaming about—becoming an astronaut. Could that somehow be my wish?

I must have sighed. "You've got something, don't you?" Monique said.

I told her I did.

"Ooh," she said, when I revealed what was going through my head. "That *definitely* sounds interesting."

I heard a voice in the background—Monique's mother calling her to dinner.

"Sounds like you've gotta go," I said.

"Yes, but I really love the idea of you somehow getting yourself to outer space."

"Seriously?"

"Of course. I mean, it's kind of crazy, but so are you." She giggled. "Seriously, keep thinking about it. I've got to run, but I really enjoyed our conversation. Keep me posted on your wish, 'kay?"

"I promise." We hung up and I lay back on my bed. At that moment, my wish had everything to do with Monique.

•

Astrocytomas, the kind of tumor Dr. Egan had removed from my brain, tend to grow back pretty fast. You always have to be on the watch for recurrence, and that doesn't just mean being on the lookout for symptoms, because you might not have any. It means brain scans, like those CT scans I started with, or the much more intrusive MRIs, which Dr. Gourevik ordered for me every three months. A nurse would pack me like a sardine into a tube, and then a technician would blast me with deafening pulsations. They gave me earplugs, but that hardly seemed helpful. After forty-five minutes in that tube, with every inch of my brain bombarded, I'd get up feeling half dead and completely woozy.

I went in for an MRI a few days after that conversation with Monique. When I finished and was escorted to the waiting room by a nurse, Mom took one look at me and wrapped me in a bear hug.

On our way home, Mom stopped in front of Fair Oaks Pharmacy.

"Do you have to pick something up?" I asked.

"Yes," she said, smiling. "Two ice cream cones."

"Seriously?"

"You need to have a little fun. And I need an excuse to have ice cream."

That cracked me up. I followed her in.

We ended up getting sundaes. Halfway through mine, my headache mostly gone, Mom asked me what I was thinking about.

"Monique's party. I talked to some guys there about wishes." I paused, then looked at Mom. "If you were offered a wish, what would it be?"

She gazed out the window for a second, then turned back. "I'd wish for you to be completely healthy."

I pinched her cheek. "That's really sweet, Mom. I was actually talking about those organizations that grant wishes to sick kids."

"Oh, I've heard of them. Are you interested in that? What would you wish for? Something space-related, I assume?"

I figured it was best not to specifically mention trying to get myself on a space shuttle flight. "Yeah, definitely something space-related."

"That's very exciting, Jeff. I'll bet your dad would be interested in hearing about that. I remember how much he enjoyed launching that rocket with you out at the beach."

"I never told you that."

"You didn't. He did."

That sent a tingle through my spine. "Do you think he, like, would be supportive of a wish?"

"If he thought it would make you happy." She thought about what she'd said, then nodded. "Yes, I'm sure he would."

That was all we said to each other until we left. The rest of the time we just sat there, the two of us smiling, scooping away at our cups.

•

Dad got home relatively early that night—a quarter to six—and I met him at the front door. Amiga beat me to it, her tail wagging. I slid open the door and she rushed to him, with his arms opening wide as he dropped to a knee.

"How'd your scan go?" Dad asked as he gave Amiga a belly rub. "It was one of those MRIs, correct?"

"Yup." I considered telling him how much the pounding bothered me, but he didn't like hearing complaints. "It went fine."

"Good, Jeff. That's good. Did they share the results?"

"I'll get them from Dr. Gourevik in a couple of days."

"I see," he said, standing up. He tugged back the left sleeve of his suit jacket to reveal his watch. I was sure he was thinking about his news program.

"You've still got thirteen minutes," I said. "By the way, I wanted to talk to you about something."

"May I say hello to your mother?" I turned to find her at the entrance to the kitchen, wearing a warm smile.

"Hello, Bob," Mom said. He walked over and they did their classic chicken-peck kiss. Seeing it always made me think I was the result of an immaculate conception. I followed Dad down the hallway to the old playroom after he hung up his jacket, and we sat on the couch in front of the television. I looked at the clock on the wall. Ten minutes. It was enough time to get a decent conversation started.

"Have you ever heard of Make-A-Wish or the Starlight Foundation?" I asked.

"I believe so."

"Well, some of my friends in the cancer support group have made wishes with them, and I've been thinking about making one myself."

I was expecting him to ask what I had in mind. Instead, he slowly rubbed his jaw. I hadn't given him anything to consider, but it was like he was deep in thought.

After several seconds, he spoke. "I was under the impression that these organizations only serve children."

The muscles in my neck started to tighten.

"Isn't a child defined as someone under the age of eighteen?"

"A *minor* is so defined, not a child."

He was being so difficult. "Okay, Dad, so they offer wishes to minors. I happen to be a minor, you know."

"Indeed," he said. "And minors have things other than wishes that require their focus and attention."

"Like what?"

"Like schoolwork."

He'd recently seen my quarterly grades. The one I got from Mrs. McKendrick wasn't stellar. I was also a little behind in biology homework, but he wasn't aware of that.

"I can participate in a wish and still complete my homework, Dad. Practically all the other kids in my cancer support group have managed to do it."

"Perhaps they have. But you've got a lot on your plate. Not just a demanding school environment, but three more rounds of chemotherapy, and they might have to be administered in the hospital."

I shook my head.

"Is that not correct?"

"Only if my white blood cell count stays low. But I don't see—"

He lifted a finger. "I'm afraid I need to use the bathroom."

He got up and I groaned. Mom had witnessed our exchange from the kitchen. She came over and put her hand on my shoulder. "I'll talk to him, Jeff," she said.

"You'd think he could be, like, supportive," I said.

She nodded.

Dad came back a minute before his show started. It was like

he timed it. "Shall we watch *NewsHour?*" he said, lifting the remote off the television projector.

I shook my head, exiting toward the stairs. "Apparently, I need to be focusing on my schoolwork."

•

For a dad who had denied his son a wish, you'd expect him not to follow up with a gift. But when my sixteenth birthday rolled around, Dad did exactly that—to the extreme.

It was a week before my actual birthday. The whole family was having brunch together, something that was increasingly rare, since Dad was always swamped with work and Ted had so many precollege events. These days, whenever we had a family gathering, Mom seemed to go into a wistful state, touching her face and saying something like "I wonder how many more of these we'll have together."

We'd finished our eggs and waffles and were flipping through sections of the *Los Angeles Times.* I had the front page but wasn't really reading it seriously. For days, two things had occupied my mind, competing for my attention. One was the wish, which got me into a funk. The other was Monique, who always made me smile.

"How would you like to celebrate your birthday, Jeff?" Mom asked.

"I don't know," I said. "Definitely not a big party like Ted had when he turned sixteen."

"Well, you'd need friends for that," Ted said, smirking.

"Wow, Ted. That was so funny I forgot to laugh." I handed the front page back to Dad. He didn't ask me what I wanted to read next. He just gave me a folded-up section. I opened it. *Automotive.* I looked at him and raised an eyebrow.

"You might find it helpful—in selecting a vehicle," he said.

My eyes widened. I glanced at Mom. She winked.

"Seriously?" I said.

Mom and Dad nodded.

"Wait a second," Ted said to Dad. "You don't mean *any* car, right? You guys totally didn't do that for me."

"Yes, that's a good point," Dad said. He turned to me. "Considering how your brother managed to carelessly slide his car across an entire lane and smash it into a curb, I would suggest you choose a four-wheel-drive vehicle."

Ted rubbed his face and moaned.

My eyes landed on an ad for a brand-new, turbocharged, all-wheel-drive Toyota Celica—with a huge price tag. I pointed at it, only half seriously. Dad nodded. I was speechless. Mom's jaw dropped, but then she broke into a broad smile. Only Ted was disappointed.

"Seriously?" he said to Dad, who ignored him. Ted pushed the newspaper away, crossing his arms and slowly shaking his head. "This family is insane."

•

After I passed my driving test and got my license, Mom and Dad drove me out to the car dealership. We were there for a couple of hours, which was how long it took Dad to negotiate the salesman way below his "absolute bottom line." Mom and I were sitting on a bench in the showroom when Dad appeared, lifting his hand and jingling the keys. "Why don't you take your new car for a drive?" he said to me, smiling. "Use it in good health."

I thanked them both, shaking Dad's hand and giving Mom a hug. It took her a while to let go. When she did, she had tears rolling down her face. The last time that had happened, I was in the hospital. I started to say something, but she stopped me. "I'm fine, sweetie. You're just all grown up." She pulled a tissue from her purse and dabbed her eyes. "Do what your father said—go for a ride."

The 210 Freeway, the one we had to get on to go home, just happened to connect with the one that went directly to Monique's house. It was the weekend, so she'd probably be home. She'd definitely be impressed with the car—and the fact that I was driving it. I decided to pay her a surprise visit.

On my way out to Tarzana, I thought about this car my parents had just given me. It was so powerful—pressing the pedal to the floor engaged a turbocharger, and the car took off like a rocket. Compared to the one they'd gotten Ted a few years before, it was crazily expensive. Our entire childhood before that, Dad insisted that everything be exactly equal between us. I wondered what was different this time around. The only explanation that made any sense—and when I came to it, a chill shot up my spine—was that he thought I was on my way out. This car was his way of telling me he cared.

My mind switched back to Monique. I reached the off-ramp

to her place a little past four. Her house was just off that main road, but I couldn't remember if it was north or south of the freeway. I drove up and down the boulevard for nearly half an hour before conceding I'd have to give her a call.

I pulled into a gas station, bought a pack of gum to get some change, and headed over to the pay phone. After a quick call home to let my parents know everything was okay, I dialed Monique.

Her father answered. He never picked up the phone, I think because his wife or his daughter would beat him to it—he moved around on crutches because of his childhood bout with polio. "Hello, sir. My name is Jeff. I'm in your daughter's cancer support group. I met you at the party you hosted."

"Of course, Jeff. You charmed my wife when you complimented her food. And I enjoyed our conversation. How are you?"

"I'm great, thanks. Is Monique around?"

"You just missed her. She's out with Edward."

He said the name like I already knew it. There was no one named Edward in our support group. I had to find out who this guy was.

"Is Edward her cousin?"

"No, Edward is . . . well, I guess he's her boyfriend." She definitely hadn't told me she had a boyfriend. I was speechless.

"Right," I finally said. "Look, my mom is waiting to use the phone, so I need to go." The second I said that, a lady in a VW blocked by a truck that had stopped in front of her honked her horn. I was sure Monique's dad could tell I wasn't exactly hanging out at home.

"No problem," he said. "I'll let Monique know you called."

I felt like telling him not to bother, but I held back. I thanked him and we hung up.

I walked back to my new car and sank into the driver's seat, rubbing my eyes and mulling over what I'd just learned. It felt like a really crappy birthday present. After a couple of minutes I sat up straight, turned the key, and drove off.

On my way home, where the highway turned toward the hills near a cemetery, an instrument light popped on. Dad had told me never to ignore those lights, so I put on the emergency blinkers and pulled over to the shoulder. I scanned the panel. The temperature gauge was a millimeter away from the red zone, which meant the engine was close to overheating. I'd already noticed it was a little high on the way out, but now I wasn't using the turbo-charger, and it definitely wasn't hot out. I sat there for nearly half an hour, practically steaming myself—about my new car failing and the relationship I'd been dreaming about coming to an end before it even got started.

CHAPTER NINE

One Sunday morning, after waking up late, I decided I was going to drive out to the beach. It wasn't warm out or anything. I just wanted to go to Marina del Rey, where our family spent a few summers when I was a kid. It was so beautiful there, the water and the waves, and I hadn't been back for ages. The idea of a quick visit felt really nice.

I'd tied my shoes, snapped in my wigs, put on my baseball cap, and was in the process of looking for my keys when I recalled that my car, the one I'd gotten as a birthday present, was in the shop. It had overheated again, and the radiator was apparently suspect. For a second I thought about firing up our old Jeep Cherokee, but Dad had told me not to use it, as it only had liability insurance. I was carless, it seemed. But maybe Mom would want to go.

I went upstairs and called out a hello. The only response came from Amiga, who raced to the playroom with her tail wagging. Dad must have been at the office; otherwise he would have taken her on one of his morning runs. Ted's car was gone, but Mom's was there. "Mom?" I said loudly. Nothing.

I found a note from her in the kitchen. *Morning, sweetie,* it said. *Ted and I are out college shopping. Dad's at the office. Enjoy your day.*

I sighed.

Over breakfast, I decided I'd watch a movie. We had a few tapes lying around, though Ted had probably grabbed the good ones. On the shelf was Dad's favorite, *Chariots of Fire*—about running, of course—and one Mom really liked, *On Golden Pond,* about a kid spending a summer on a lake with a guy who was actually a lot like Dad. The other tapes were *MacNeil/Lehrer NewsHour* recordings, which didn't fit at all with my kick-back-and-watch-a-flick plan.

I was considering biking down to VideoWorks, the rental shop not far from the pharmacy where Mom and I had had ice cream a few weeks earlier, when I stumbled upon a tape with Dad's scribbled handwriting on it. The title was *The Day After*—the movie he'd made the whole family watch, the one that had given me a week's worth of nightmares.

I popped it into the VCR.

It was a totally different experience from the first time I saw it. It wasn't that scary. The special effects were lame, especially an hour into the film, when the nuclear missiles detonated and people's bodies suddenly turned into orange skeletons. If nuclear missiles really hit, people's bodies would either splinter into a gazillion tiny pieces or burn up in a firestorm.

What got to me this time was the movie's ending. The main

character, the white-haired Dr. Russell Oakes, is wandering around the decimated remains of his hometown. His hair has dramatically thinned—radiation exposure caused it to fall out—and there's a patch of skin on his face that's badly burned. One look at him took me right back to my own experience in Mrs. Ashworth's class, when I was standing there in a daze, with my hair falling to the floor, and then to a week later, when my irradiated left ear started to scab up and bleed. The movie, fake in the earlier parts, suddenly felt real.

Dad got home from the office not long after the movie ended. I was sitting there in front of the television, the screen blue because the tape had stopped.

"Everything okay, Jeff?" Dad asked.

It wasn't, but I couldn't tell him exactly why. There was this tension in my gut, a kind of frustration, that felt like a smoldering fire. "I just rewatched *The Day After.*"

He came over and sat down on the couch next to me. Amiga tucked her head between us. "I certainly remember the film." He picked up the remote and switched off the TV.

"Yeah, well, it wasn't as scary this time, but something about it kind of—I don't know—pissed me off."

"What, exactly?"

"The radiation from all the nuclear warheads exploding. Remember the end, when the doctor is doddering through his decimated hometown and you see his hair all thinned out and his face kind of torched?"

"I believe so. What disturbs you? Your own experience with radiation?"

"I mean, yes, but it's more than that." I crossed my arms, tilted my head, and looked through the window at the top of the staircase. "It's like, people. Humanity, as you like to say."

"What about humanity?"

"Take radiation. We use it to destroy cancer cells. It's gross, I can promise you, but we're using it to save ourselves, in a way. But then we also use it to randomly kill—and threaten to kill—huge numbers of people. Innocent people. *Humanity*."

Dad tipped his head toward me. "You're growing up, Jeff."

"That's the weird thing, right? The only reason I'm still growing, and not, like, dead, is because of humanity and technology and all the things we've learned. And yet I'm threatened—so are you; everybody is, for that matter—by the fact that we're a bunch of idiots."

●

The second half of sophomore year was tough. The classes alone would've been hard enough, but add to that chemo, which absolutely blitzed my immune system, and Mrs. McKendrick being an unsympathetic pain in the butt, and I was really struggling to stay on top of things. Thank God I had Paul to help me with math, because I wouldn't have made it through that class without his regular consultation calls.

When the phone rang one evening close to eight o'clock, the time Paul and I usually reviewed our homework, I grabbed the receiver and said, "Welcome to Jumbo Jeff's homework completion service. May I take your order?" I expected Paul's extra-loud laugh, but instead got a giggle.

"Hi, Jumbo. It's Monique."

I could feel my face turning red. "Oh, hi. I was just . . ."

"I'd like one simplified explanation of differential equations, a short paper on the cause of the Vietnam War, and an essay on Dylan Thomas's poem 'Do Not Go Gentle into That Good Night.'"

I laughed.

"Oh, and I'll also say that Jumbo Jeff totally works as a name for you, despite the fact that it makes my name kind of boring."

"How about Majestic Monique?"

"That's a bit too aristocratic."

"Mesmerizing Monique?"

"Obviously accurate, but a touch long-winded."

"Magic Mo?"

"Perfect!"

My tension disappeared in an instant. We talked for ages, catching each other up on just about everything—except Edward. I loved her voice, how it would change in pitch and pace as she told a story, and her giggle, too, which was infectious. She had lots of questions for me; nothing invasive, but ones that made it clear she was really curious about what was going on inside my head. I found myself wanting to share everything with her.

"Say, what's up with your wish?" she asked. "Any progress on getting yourself to outer space?"

"Not really. My dad said wishes are for kids, and I have more important things to focus on."

"Like what?"

"School, for example."

"Seriously? I *loved* my wish."

"Slipping into a swimming pool with an Olympian hunk?"

"Ha. Yes. And maybe it *was* a distraction from school, but that was momentary. And it put a huge smile on my face."

"Which seems to return every time you think about Terry Schroeder."

"You remember his name!"

"I remember all the guys you're after." I bit my lip, worried that was a little too revealing.

"Yeah, well, it wasn't like the two of us ever dated. But let's get back to your wish. Did you talk to your dad about ideas?"

"No, we didn't get into it at all. He literally just tossed out the whole idea."

"Wow. He seems like a bit of a . . ." She paused.

"You can't possibly stop there."

"Okay, a hard-ass. Wait, was that too strong? I'm sorry."

"Are you kidding me? This is music to my ears."

"Oh, good. So look, here's how I see it. We're still officially kids, right? Wishes are for kids. Every kid I know who's dealing with cancer has done a wish. You're like, I don't know, the misfit."

I pretended to be offended. "Thanks a lot."

"Here's my million-dollar opinion, which I'm going to give you for free: I don't think you should turn down the possibility of a wish just because your dad doesn't get it."

"Why, exactly?" I really wanted to know Monique's thinking.

"Because I know for a fact you'd love it. That's what's important."

I smiled but didn't respond. I was considering what she said.

"Come on, Jeff. Even if you don't make it all the way to outer space, you could take some kind of step in that direction, right? And for you, that would be a blast."

"*Blast* isn't the best choice of words, Mo." Space shuttle *Challenger* had blown up just a year before.

"Oh, shoot, right, my bad. I'm sorry. Look, all I'm trying to say is that a wish could put a huge smile on your face. That's the only thing that matters. At least, that's the only thing that should."

•

I was pretty surprised one Monday to show up to school totally up-to-date on my homework. It was the first time that had happened in ages, and I noticed that my shoulders weren't in their typical position, bunched up around my ears, but actually hanging loose. I liked the feel of it.

Practically the moment I stepped onto campus, I noticed a weird vibe. It seemed as if there were a million hushed conversations going on. The patio where the seniors typically hung out, normally the source of loud morning laughs, was practically silent. Several people had their mouths hanging open or a hand pressed against their lips. Clearly, something major had gone down.

I saw my friend Cara and hurried in her direction. Just before I got to her an announcement was made over the PA, asking students and faculty to gather in the main courtyard. "What the heck is going on?" I whispered to Cara as we walked together.

"I think someone committed suicide."

"Who?" I said. Cara shrugged and motioned toward Mrs. Hager, the upper school director, who was tapping on the mic.

"There are rumors going around, and I think it's best for everyone to know the truth," Mrs. Hager said. "Julie Siegel, a member of our junior class, attempted suicide over the weekend." There was a sudden wave of moans and sighs. Mrs. Hager quickly reassured everyone. "Thankfully, she is alive. She's in the hospital in stable condition and is expected to fully recover." She let that sink in, then continued. "High school is challenging, and it's particularly so here at Poly. We put a lot on your shoulders. We expect a lot from you. But most important to us—more than anything else—is your safety. Your well-being." Her eyes traversed the student body, underscoring her point. She let out a long breath and looked over to our school counselor, who nodded at her and stepped up to the mic.

"Hi, everyone. Sean here, if we haven't met." He was tall and thin, with a gentle smile. I'd never actually spoken to him. "I know it's really hard to hear news like this, especially if Julie is a friend of yours. If you're hurting over what happened and need to talk, or if you're feeling down yourself or if you just need a sympathetic ear, please feel free to drop by my office anytime."

He lifted a stack of papers from the mic stand. "The faculty and I are going to pass around these information sheets on depression. Please make sure to take one before you go to your first class. It has questions that can help you determine whether you're experiencing depression."

A guy standing across from me rubbed his neck. Cara fiddled with her ring. Sean sensed the uncertainty. "People with depression aren't always aware of what they're experiencing. This sheet really can help. Anyway, I'm just asking—okay, I'm demanding—that you read this. And again, if you want to talk, my door's open."

Sean stepped back. Just as Mrs. Hager was returning to the mic, the stack of papers reached me. I grabbed one, took a quick look, and put it into my backpack.

"Okay, everyone," Mrs. Hager said. "I'm sorry to start your day like this. I'm also really sorry for Julie. There's a card for her in Mrs. Fox's office if you'd like to show Julie your support." She stepped back from the mic, thought for a second, and then returned. "Please," she said in a voice that was pleading, "be good to yourselves."

•

I got home from school that day and Mom waved at me from her office. She grabbed a portable phone and walked it over to me, saying, "He's right here." She had a smile on her face.

The lady on the other end was from the Starlight Children's Foundation. "This is just a preliminary call," she explained as I sat down in the old playroom. She told me about the organization, and when she finished she asked if I had any questions.

I only had one. "Who called you?" Because I hadn't.

"The notes here say your mom was in touch."

I turned around and saw Mom standing behind me, pretending to clean up the already perfectly clean kitchen. The smile on her face had gotten bigger.

"We'll be sending you an application," the lady from Starlight said. "If it's approved, some of our volunteers will interview you about your wish. Do you happen to have one in mind?"

"Not exactly," I said. "Maybe something related to NASA and outer space."

"That sounds very nice. No need to decide on anything until you've been approved and have the interview. If you don't have any questions, I'd like to speak to your mother."

I thanked her and walked the phone over to Mom, who eagerly took it, and then I headed downstairs.

For a few minutes, I thought about Julie trying to commit suicide. But it wasn't long before my mind shifted to something else: daydreaming about my wish. As soon as I realized that, I felt a little selfish.

My backpack was next to me. I figured I'd better get to my homework. I unclipped the top and pulled out my math textbook. Some papers fluttered to the floor. I bent over to pick them up, and a moment later I was reading about depression.

•

Almost to my surprise, I made it through sophomore year. My third round of chemo had really laid me out—to the point where my oncologist said I'd have to do my final three rounds in the hospital—but despite falling way behind at times, I somehow managed to get myself caught up. The fact that I didn't have a car—mine turned out to be a lemon and there was a waiting list for a replacement—ended up helping me, because I spent more time around the house. Even though homework was boring, it was better than watching a bunch of reruns or doing nothing at all.

The week classes finished, Dave, an old friend of mine, called out of the blue. He and his buddy Ryan were headed to a movie, and Dave was calling to see if I wanted to join them. I told him sure, but I needed a ride, and he said they were actually hoping to get one from me. "Let me call you back in a sec," I said.

Mom was in her office. "How are you doing, my dear?" she asked.

I told her I'd just been invited to a movie, but that none of us had a car.

"I'd give you a ride, honey, but I wouldn't be able to pick you up. I've got something this evening."

I sighed. "There is the Jeep, you know."

"Dad doesn't want anyone to use it. It only has that one kind of insurance on it."

"Liability. I know. But all we'd be doing is going to a movie. That's it."

"He's at the office. You can call him and ask."

There was no way I was going to do that. He'd get irritated. I decided to play the sympathy card.

"Mom, I've got another round of chemo in the hospital in just a couple of days."

"I know you do, honey."

"I'd really like to have a little fun. I promise I'll be super careful. Can I please use the Jeep this one time?"

She looked at me for several seconds, and when I put on my best puppy-dog eyes she finally gave in.

"Please don't get into an accident."

"I promise I won't," I said, planting a big kiss on her cheek after she handed me the key. I called Dave to let him know that I'd come up with a set of wheels.

We got to the theater, which was in the crappy part of Pasadena they were trying to revive as "Old Town," with just a few minutes to spare.

"If you give me some money, I can grab tickets while you guys park," Ryan offered.

We handed over six bucks and he hopped out. Dave and I drove around to the new lot.

"Holy crap," I said to Dave, pointing at a sign showing the parking fee. It cost as much as the matinee did.

"Let's park on the street," Dave said.

We found a spot and I swung open my door. Just as I was about to step out, a man wearing a ski mask shoved a machine gun into my stomach. The look of it jolted me. An actual machine gun. I was so stunned it took me a second to understand what the guy was saying. "I said put your keys back in the ignition! Put your wallets on the dashboard!"

With shaking hands, I followed his instructions. I looked over at Dave, who was pale and had a dark stain growing on his pants, and nudged him for his wallet. I slid out of the front seat with my hands up and yelled at Dave to get out of the car. The guy told us to run or he'd kill us, that if we were slow, he'd kill us, and it didn't take anything more. We were already twenty feet away when the doors slammed shut and the engine started, and it was only when we heard the screeching of tires that we looked back, catching a glimpse of the Jeep as it raced around the corner and disappeared.

Two hours later, we were at the Pasadena police station. We had all called our parents. Ryan had nothing to add to the police report, so he left the moment his mom showed up. Dave and I sat with an officer for a while, answering all the questions he asked in his monotone voice. Dave had his legs crossed tight, the dry one over the wet one. I was fidgeting away, my fingernails scratching at my thumbs, thinking how I wasn't supposed to have used that car. Dad was going to be upset.

Dave's dad showed up. He ran to his son, leaning over and wrapping his arms around him, holding him for several seconds the way my mom did when I came back from summer camp. He kissed him on his forehead. "Are you okay?" he asked.

Dave nodded a yes.

His dad pulled him against his chest and said, "Praise God, praise God."

The officer finished with his questions and pushed forward some paperwork to sign. Dave's dad asked me if I'd like them to wait for my parents to arrive, but I saw Dave look down at his pants, and I told his dad I'd be fine.

After they left, I found a seat near the entrance and focused my eyes on the door. My fingers kept fidgeting away, picking the dead skin from my cuticles. I kept shifting in my seat, my mind flipping between seeing the machine gun in my gut and visualizing Dad's arrival.

After another fifteen minutes went by, I saw my father on the building steps. He pushed the door open vigorously and walked directly to me.

I quickly stood.

"Are you injured?" he asked.

"No," I told him. I hoped he would hug me, like Dave's dad had hugged him.

Dad pressed his lips together. He drew in a deep breath, slowly, but then blew it out fast enough to make his nostrils flare. "Do you realize," he said, his voice deeper now, "the motor vehicle you *insisted* on borrowing was insured only for accident liability since, as Mother turns out to have *incorrectly* stated, it was never being used? That amounts to a loss of thirteen thousand dollars."

For several seconds, I felt like my legs were going to give out. I did everything I could not to collapse. My eyes welled up, like I was pleading with Dad for something, but he just stared at me with his jaw clenched, his own eyes flinty and cold.

He finally stepped away to talk with the officer. I told myself he'd be calmer when he came back, that he'd tell me he was grateful I survived, that either the look on his face or the words that came out of his mouth would steady me. The thought of it got my shaking to stop.

Dad signed some paperwork. He shook the officer's hand. Then he stood, turned, and walked past me toward the door. He didn't hold it open. He didn't look back to see if I was following.

CHAPTER TEN

It felt pretty ironic that the follow-up to nearly being killed by a machine gun was being admitted to Huntington Hospital so chemo could get injected into my veins. The idea of chemo was ironic enough on its own — toxic poisons kill off parts of you so the whole of you doesn't otherwise die. But add to it that the nurses were shooting me up just after a guy nearly shot me down. Life, at least mine, felt strange.

For four days, I was stuck in a room that was totally depressing. The brownish-yellow walls matched the smog outside. The only view was of a parking lot. There were no pictures or paintings or anything interesting to look at, just the tall metal pole next to me where nurses would step in periodically to hang a new bag full of poison. It was like the room was designed to reflect the dual dejection of chemo and carjacking.

Dad didn't visit the first day, and on the second morning Mom told me he'd called to say he was stuck in the office.

"It's because I got his Jeep stolen," I said to Mom.

She shook her head. "He's just on overload with his case, honey." She patted my arm but I looked away.

I slept most of the day, waking up that afternoon to find Loretta sitting in the recliner where Mom normally planted herself. She was flipping through a magazine—*Cosmopolitan*.

"I thought that was for teenage girls," I said.

"God knows I've got three of them," Loretta said. She set the magazine on the side table. "Your mom's out running some errands. How are you feeling?"

"A little nauseous. Not as bad as usual. I guess it's a little easier when they inject the poisons directly instead of my having to swallow all those disgusting pills."

"I'm just happy you're less likely to puke on me," Loretta said with a wink.

"Be careful there. I still managed to puke once. Keep talking and I might again."

We chatted about all the usual stuff, like her daughters, one of whom had a skinhead boyfriend, and how Ted had gotten a lot nicer, probably because he was getting ready to go off to college, just like Loretta's oldest daughter. Then I told her about Dad's car.

"Your mother shared that with me, honey," Loretta said. Her eyes turned toward the ceiling. "I'm just grateful to God that you're alive."

"I wish my father felt that way. Seriously, Loretta, from the look on his face when he came to the police station, I think he would've preferred his Jeep survive over me."

Loretta's face crumpled into a frown. "How can you say that, Jeff? Of course he wouldn't have."

"You weren't there, Loretta. He was furious. He hasn't visited me once. It's like he's moved into his office downtown."

"Maybe he's just overwhelmed with work."

"Maybe he just hates his son."

Loretta reached across the bed for my right hand. The one closer to her had a bunch of tubes going into it. I gave it to her and she kissed it.

"Okay, on to brighter things. What's up with the wish?"

"Well, I had a phone chat with someone from the Starlight Foundation, but they haven't accepted me yet."

"Have you come up with a wish?"

"Not exactly. I mean, I'd love to do something space-related, but I'm not sure what my options would be, given the state of my body. Plus, Dad thinks wishes are stupid."

"Did he actually say that?"

"Well, not exactly. He said they were for kids."

"Look, Jeff, if you're no longer a kid, then I'm an old hag! You're definitely a kid." Loretta started laughing. I rolled my eyes and sighed. Her laughing stopped. "Seriously, maybe this wish could be a way for you to connect with your father."

I sat up a bit. "How's that?"

"I'm just thinking of this world we're in, and everything that's happening. Your father actually fought in a war. He's concerned whenever there's conflict. And you, sweetie, you're *very* mature for your age. I remember how much you worried last year about that nuclear reactor that blew up in the Soviet Union—"

"Chernobyl."

"Yes, that one. And also how you wish the U.S. and the Soviets would collaborate more in outer space."

"We could do amazing things."

"I'm sure we could. My point is, as different as you are from your father, there are things in this world that are important to both of you. Maybe your wish could be about that."

I looked over to the window, thinking about what she'd said. It was so different from what normally came out of her mouth—jokes and laughter and much less serious stuff. But it felt like she'd landed on something.

"What are you thinking?" she asked.

I didn't say anything for a moment.

"Tell me."

I looked at her and chuckled. "I'm just surprised that you managed to say something that truly makes sense."

●

Not long after getting out of the hospital, as soon as my energy came back, I headed down to the South Pasadena Public Library to do a little research. Ever since that conversation with Loretta, I'd been thinking about something that did actually connect me with my father: nuclear weapons and the Cold War.

In no time at all, the librarian and I had pulled out a ton of books. I parked myself at one of the reading tables, neatly stacked everything in front of me, and dug in.

Almost every book had something that blew my mind. The first one talked about nuclear yields—the amount of energy that came out of nuclear weapons. I mean, I'd already heard they were insanely powerful. Dad had told me that the bomb we dropped on Hiroshima in 1945 was equivalent to fifteen thousand tons of TNT, and that it killed something like seventy-five thousand people in an instant. I knew the bombs we had now were even larger, but I couldn't have been further from grasping the extent of it.

What this first book said was that by the early 1960s we'd developed a nuclear bomb, the B-41, that was equivalent to at least fifteen hundred Hiroshima bombs. The Soviets responded by building—and actually blowing up over an island in the Arctic Ocean—one that was twice as powerful as ours, the Tsar Bomba. Everything within a radius of forty miles was completely destroyed.

I sat back for a second, scratching my head. What if the Soviets dropped just one of those bombs on downtown L.A.? The whole city would be flattened. That sent a shiver down my spine. And our house was just ten miles to the north. All the beaches we ever went to, like Santa Monica and Long Beach and Marina del Rey, where I'd launched my rocket, were within that forty-mile stretch. Heck, with the exception of some cousins in New York and San Francisco, my whole family, and certainly all my friends, were within that radius. That single bomb could kill everyone I knew.

And that was what just one Soviet bomb could do. I quickly learned that they had stockpiled something like thirty thousand nuclear weapons—of all different sizes—which could be delivered by bombers, by missiles, by submarines. And we had at least thirty thousand of our own. If we actually got into a nuclear war with the

Soviets, the outcome wouldn't look like *The Day After*. There would be no story to tell. Human beings would no longer exist.

I didn't stop reading. I was scared at first—to the point where I almost got up and walked out—but I kept at it. A boring book about the price tag of nuclear weapons helped, at least at first. It had all these statistics about what it cost to develop new weapons, maintain existing ones, come up with new ways to deliver them, and develop systems—like Reagan's Star Wars program—in the hope of preventing the Soviet missiles from blowing us up. The total cost could be as high as four trillion dollars.

That didn't mean much to me—the numbers were so huge—until an author said it was also hard for him to understand. We should think in terms of what that money could be spent on instead—the opportunities we lost, the things that were stolen from us. My mind went straight to cancer. What if some of that money was spent on research? There might be better ways to treat people. I felt my jaw tightening. Maybe Dr. Egan wouldn't have had to carve my head open. Maybe some of my friends in the cancer support group would be living normal lives.

I had just closed the book with all those numbers when the librarian stopped by my table. "Everything okay?" she asked.

My whole face was crumpled into a frown. I could feel it. "Oh, yeah, fine," I said, straightening in my chair.

"Well, this was just returned," she said, holding up a book with a smiling little girl on its cover. The title was *Journey to the Soviet Union*. I accepted it from the librarian and thanked her.

Samantha Smith wasn't the best writer—she was the kid on the cover and the author of the book—but her story was amazing.

It was also pretty heartwarming, especially considering the super-dark stuff I'd just been through. When Samantha was just ten, she wrote a letter to the head of the Soviet Union, Yuri Andropov, asking why they wanted to blow us up. He wrote her back, saying they desired peace, and he invited her to visit. She went the following year.

The librarian came by a while later to tell me that the library was closing. I pointed to Samantha's book. "I really loved this one," I said.

"It's delightful," she answered. "I wish that young girl was still with us."

I frowned. "What do you mean?"

"She died in a plane crash with her father."

My hand flew to my chest.

"In the Soviet Union?"

"No, back home. She was in one of those small planes."

I couldn't believe it. I must've just sat there blinking, because after a while the librarian gave me a sad smile. "I'm really sorry," she said. "But the library is closing."

●

The interview with the Starlight Children's Foundation took place just a few weeks after my visit to the library. It was a Sunday, and I'd slept in late, lying in bed after waking up with a smile on my face, finding it hard to believe things were actually moving forward. A week before, a Starlight representative had called to let me know that I'd qualified for a wish, and the next step was the interview. Only one parent technically needed to be present for it, but I wanted both of mine to be there.

Dad had calmed down a bit since the night when the Jeep got stolen, yet he seemed distant. I'd been wondering if he was still angry with me. Mom encouraged me to invite him to the interview, but I held off. At dinner on Saturday night, the day before the volunteer couple was coming over to our house, she brought it up.

"Jeff, tell your father about the interview."

"What interview would that be?" Dad asked.

I wiped my lips with my napkin and sat up straight. "Some volunteers from the Starlight Children's Foundation are coming over tomorrow afternoon to interview me about my wish."

"I didn't realize you'd made one."

"I haven't yet. That's what we're going to talk about."

"I see," Dad said.

Mom looked at me. "And?" she said.

"So maybe you could sit in on the interview, if you want. I mean, they'd like you to."

"I see," Dad said again. He stayed quiet.

Mom turned to him.

"Bob, did you hear your son?"

"I did, Phyllis. I'm afraid I have to head to the office this weekend."

I felt a lump in my stomach. I was a fool to even think he might no longer be upset with me.

Mom frowned. "Well, I'm sure I can have them come another

time, Bob. When would work for you?" I couldn't believe she said that. She hardly ever pushed Dad.

For several seconds, Dad rubbed his jaw, finally pinching the tip of his beard. "All right," he said. "Let's go ahead with the meeting tomorrow."

The morning of the interview, after showering and putting on some nice clothes, I headed upstairs. I was grabbing the milk out of the fridge when I practically bumped into Mom, turning the corner with a stack of fine china. She looked a little winded— she'd probably been scurrying all around the house, standard practice for her when people were coming over.

"Where's Dad?"

Mom set down the plates and put a hand on my shoulder. My eyes shot to the carport. Dad's slot was empty. "You've got to be kidding, Mom," I said, shaking my head. "Did he actually ditch me? Is he at his office?"

"I'm sorry, Jeff," she said.

I pushed her hand away. "Why are you sorry? Why bother? *You* can't do anything. It's me. *I'm* the problem, Mom. He doesn't want to spend time with me."

"That's not it, honey," she said.

"Then tell me what it is." I watched her. She searched for something to say, but found nothing. "See? I knew it."

Then I noticed the pools forming in Mom's eyes. In an instant, my rage drained out. It was replaced with guilt. How could I put all my problems with Dad on Mom's shoulders?

I gave her a long hug. "I'm sorry." With one arm still around her, I quickly wiped my own eyes. "Honestly, Mom, everything is cool. Let's do this meeting."

She dabbed her eyes with a tissue. "Okay," she said. "Have some breakfast. I've got to finish getting ready."

The folks from Starlight arrived exactly on time. When the doorbell rang, Mom emerged from her room beautifully dressed. I buzzed them in so they could open the gate from the street.

A couple walked down the stairs. They looked like total yuppies, neatly dressed and nicely tanned, with perfect hair. We greeted them at the front door, along with Amiga, who gave them a comprehensive sniffing. They introduced themselves as Matt and Teri Haymer.

"It's an honor to have you here," Mom said elegantly, and she escorted everyone to the living room.

My eyes almost popped out when we got there. It wasn't just the fine china that Mom had been carrying, which was beautifully set up on the coffee table. There were also crystal water glasses, bowls full of fresh fruit, and a serving tray loaded with cookies. We hardly ever have cookies in our house. She'd seriously prepared.

We chitchatted for a while, until Teri asked if I'd come up with my wish. "We understand from your mother that you've got a deep interest in the U.S. space program."

"That's definitely true," I said to Teri. I focused on her eyes. There was something I had to get out of the way. "You don't think there would be any way to get me on the next space shuttle flight, do you?"

Mom was sipping from her coffee cup; she actually spit some out.

Matt jumped in. "I can say with confidence that the organization would be unable to grant a wish like that."

Mom exhaled sharply, wiping her lips. I sighed. Teri gave me a sympathetic smile.

"I figured. I mean, I knew that. I just had to ask. Anyway, I've been trying to come up with something more meaningful."

"What do you find meaningful?" Teri asked.

"Like maybe doing something good for the world, not just for me."

"That's very kind of you, Jeff," Teri said.

Matt leaned in. "Do you have anything in mind?"

"Kind of. Do you know that girl who wrote a letter to the head of the Soviet Union a few years ago, Samantha Smith?" I'd been thinking about her off and on since my visit to the library.

"Yes," Matt said.

"I remember her," Mom said. "Didn't we see her on TV?"

I nodded.

"I think she wrote a book," Teri said.

"I just read it. And I found out she died in a plane crash a few years later." Mom winced, touching her lips. "Anyway, she didn't live very long, but she did something meaningful." I looked at Matt, then Teri, then my mom. "That's what I mean by something meaningful. Something that could build bridges, that could matter, you know, beyond me. I just can't quite figure out what."

I reached for my water glass and took a sip, my eyes shifting toward the wall of windows behind Teri and Matt. I could just make out the hills across from us. The smog made them seem so distant. Even the sun was obscured, the normally yellow daylight more orange. It reminded me of a picture I'd seen at the library, of a nuclear detonation in French Polynesia in the 1970s, with the orange gaseous plume of the explosion penetrating grayish-white clouds.

"Wait a second," I said. Something was coming to me.

"Tell us," Teri said.

"I want to follow in Samantha Smith's footsteps. Not just play with Soviet kids, though. My wish is to travel to the Soviet Union and meet with Mikhail Gorbachev so that we can discuss bringing an end to nuclear weapons and the Cold War."

Mom's jaw dropped. Teri and Matt looked at each other, smiling, eyebrows raised.

"That's quite a wish," Matt said.

Teri nodded. "Indeed it is. It's also a really big one. Just in case we can't make it happen, do you have another?"

"A backup?" I asked.

"Exactly," Teri said.

I thought about it for a second. What I'd come up with definitely wasn't something for kids. It was substantive, truly meaningful. It might even make my father proud.

I shook my head. "It's my only wish. If you can't grant it, I'd totally understand, but I don't want anything else."

●

"That was the most absolutely fantastic meeting in the history of the universe," I said to my mom after Matt and Teri left. I plopped myself on the couch in the living room, leaning back against the pillows with my fingers locked behind my head, feeling completely satisfied. Mom didn't say anything. She was loading a tray with coffee cups and dirty plates. "Mom, wasn't that just amazing? I mean, I didn't even know what I was going to wish for going in, but it all came together so perfectly."

"It was definitely interesting," she said. She kept stacking plates. I sat up, raising an eyebrow and wrinkling my nose.

"Interesting?" I said. "You don't think that was the world's most perfect wish?"

Mom's eyes were pointed at the floor. "I'm just not sure how safe it is to travel to the Soviet Union." She looked up at me. "The Communists happen to be our enemies, you know."

Oh. My mother was freaking out.

I hopped to my feet and pulled my mom over to the couch. She sat down with me. I cupped her hands in mine. "Mom, think about that little girl, Samantha. She went there when she was ten. She came back in one piece. Plus, I can absolutely guarantee you that Dad is going to be blown away by this wish. He soooo wants to end nukes."

Mom wasn't convinced. "You're sure it's safe to go there?"

I put on the most confident face I could and squeezed her hands. "Mom, I'm absolutely completely totally one hundred percent certain." I honestly was. If a preteen could go there all by her lonesome and come back without incident, an almost-adult wasn't going to have the slightest problem.

"Okay," she said, sighing. I let go of her hands. She stood to pick up the tray.

I leapt to my feet and snatched it. "Let the cancer-conquering purveyor of world peace get this," I said. That finally got her to laugh, and boy, was I grateful.

Even though I was furious with my dad for missing the meeting with the Starlight folks, I wanted to tell him about the wish. He made it home in time for dinner, which I wasn't expecting—Ted did, too—and I decided to share the news with everybody.

Dad interjected just as I began. "Excuse me," he said, "but I wanted to say that I regret missing today's meeting with the wish-granting organization."

"The Starlight Children's Foundation," I said.

"Yes, that one. I simply had too much work on my plate. But I am eager to hear how things transpired."

Ted and I looked at each other. We'd only heard an apology from our father once, when we were seven and nine and he came home angry one evening. He clomped down the outside stairs with his briefcase in a death grip, and then, at the dinner table, shared an animated story about how the judge that afternoon had ruled against his client. He was quiet for a few seconds when he finished, but then his jaw started flexing, and everyone's tension grew. Suddenly, he slammed his fist onto the dinner table, hitting it so hard that his wineglass launched into the air. It shattered when it came back down, leaving pieces of glass in the chicken and rice Mom had cooked for us. Dad stopped by our rooms that night to apologize, saying, "My behavior at the dinner table this evening was discourteous and undignified."

I didn't know what either of those words meant, and I'm not sure Ted did either, but we could tell he was saying he was sorry, and we never heard that from him again. Until now.

But I didn't focus on that. I went through the details of the afternoon meeting. When I got to the part about asking if I could get onto the next space shuttle flight, Ted shook his head in amazement, his jaw dropping. "You on the space shuttle? No way. Is that even possible?" I loved his reaction. I looked for one on Dad's face, but there was nothing there.

I told them I wanted my wish to be more meaningful.

"More meaningful than going to outer space?" Ted asked.

I nodded and smiled. "Yup, more meaningful." I told them how the conversation with the Starlight people switched to the Cold War and nuclear weapons, and then I revealed my wish. I was happy to get it out there. I even felt proud of myself. I leaned back in my chair, grinned, and looked around the table for reactions. Ted, for once, was stunned into silence. Mom was beaming. Dad's face hadn't changed at all.

I watched as Dad poured himself another glass of wine. He asked Mom if she wanted any. She said no. He took a long sip and let it swirl around in his mouth, like he did when we went to nice restaurants and the waiters gave him a taste from the bottle he'd ordered. Still he didn't say anything, or seem to notice that the whole table was waiting for him to speak.

"Was your wish accepted?" Dad finally asked.

"They're considering it," I said, straightening in my chair. "Why?"

"I'm simply curious," Dad said.

I waited for more. He just sat there, occasionally sipping from his glass. It really seemed like not only was he not proud, but he just didn't care. I was stunned. I couldn't believe that was all he had to say. Slowly, I squeezed my eyes shut, furious.

"I've got some calls to make," I heard Ted say as he pushed back from the table.

"Please clear your plate, honey," Mom told him.

I felt so small. So completely unimportant to my father. If that was all he had to say, it meant he didn't care about me. He didn't want me in his life. Hell, he couldn't even say "I love you." Maybe it was because he didn't.

After several seconds, I opened my eyes. I fixed them on my father's. "Is your *curiosity*"—I said that word slowly—"producing any other questions?"

Mom, picking up on my frustration, turned to me. "*Jeff*," she pleaded.

"What, Mom? I want to make sure I answer *all* of Dad's questions. Is there a problem with that?" She moaned and rubbed her forehead.

"I have none at the moment," he said. It felt like confirmation of everything I'd suspected, of my father not caring if I was in his life.

I started to cry.

"You know what I think, Dad?"

He was silent.

"I think life would be easier for you if the tumor had killed me."

"Jeff!" Mom said, gasping. Dad stiffened, but he didn't speak. I grabbed my napkin out of my lap and threw it on the table.

"Don't you worry, Dad. The doctors seem pretty sure it's going to come back."

He stayed quiet as I stormed off to my room.

●

An hour later, downstairs, after telling Mom I didn't want to hear any excuses for the jerk she'd married and sending her back upstairs, I decided I really needed to call someone. I'd been avoiding Monique, since she didn't seem too supportive of any wish that wasn't one hundred percent pure fun, but my only other option was Paul, and I knew he'd be busy doing something with his family. I figured I'd better call Monique.

She was happy to hear from me. "I was wondering when you'd call me back. Is everything okay?"

"Sure," I said. "Things are fine." They weren't, not at all, but I didn't want to waste a single word talking about my dad. "How are you?"

"I'm really good, thanks. But I want a wish update. Have you come up with anything?"

I felt my stomach tighten. "Yup," I said. I cleared my throat. "Actually, I met with the Starlight people."

"Oh my God, Jeff—how come you didn't tell me? I mean, that's fantastic! Did you give them your wish?"

"I did."

"Tell me!"

I drew in a breath and blew it out. "I asked to travel to the Soviet Union so that I could meet with Mikhail Gorbachev and make an appeal for an end to nuclear weapons and the Cold War."

"Oh," Monique said. For several seconds, she was silent, not that different from what had gone down upstairs. I kept quiet, just breathing into the phone. She finally added, "I mean, that sounds really good."

"You sound about as enthusiastic as my dad."

"I'm sorry, I didn't mean to. It's just—"

"What?" I said sharply. I felt a surge of anger go through me.

"Well, you seemed really excited when you were talking about catching a ride on the space shuttle."

"The Starlight people vetoed it. Even if they hadn't, the missions have been grounded ever since *Challenger* exploded last year. And if Starlight said yes and the space shuttle flights were running, do you really think NASA would let brain-tumor boy hop onto one of them? Not a damn chance."

Once again, Monique was quiet. "I just want to make sure you're doing something you love," she finally said softly.

"I wanted to do something meaningful, you know? What's wrong with that?" I tugged at my hair as my voice fell away. "Why is everyone against me on this?"

"I'm not against you, Jeff."

"Maybe. But you're definitely not with me." She was with Edward, and she probably always would be. It finally hit me that I was completely alone. "I need to go," I told her.

"Jeff, please," she said.

"No, Monique," I said firmly. "I really need to go."

With that, I hung up.

•

Ted left for college in Philadelphia that week. The day before he took off, he came downstairs to get an extra suitcase from the storage closet. We bumped into each other in the hallway.

"I've been thinking about that wish of yours to go to the Soviet Union," Ted said.

I braced myself. I was pretty sure an insult was coming.

"What about it?"

He looked off for a minute, then snickered and shook his head.

"The whole thing was kind of funny," he said.

"Thanks a lot, Ted. Just what I needed to hear."

"Not your wish, you dork—Dad's reaction." My brother instantly gained my complete attention. "Your wish is exactly the kind of thing you'd think Dad would be thrilled about—or at least as thrilled as that man is capable of getting."

I spread my fingers out against my chest, slowly shaking my head. Ted didn't notice I was in shock.

"You just never know with that father of ours."

I snorted. "That's for damn sure."

"But I'll tell you something, bro—and then I've got to finish packing. As wishes go, yours ain't bad."

My jaw dropped. It stayed that way for a couple of seconds before my face broke into a wide grin.

"Easy there, cowboy," Ted said. "Don't have a seizure on me."

That made me laugh out loud.

He headed upstairs. I couldn't get over the exchange. My brother was leaving for college on a high note.

CHAPTER ELEVEN

Junior year started with three major changes. First, no one, Lucia included, rushed up to me on day one like they had the previous year to ask me how I was doing. Second, I switched my foreign-language class from Spanish to Russian. (The signup sheet for fall classes came in the mail, and I'd filled it out before Dad had crapped all over my wish.) Third, I ended up with a new English teacher. Dr. Dillon's Russian class, which I soon discovered was insanely challenging, put me in a time conflict with Mrs. McKendrick's English class. I signed up for another one, taught by a Ms. Hamilton, who was the new kid on the block as far as teaching at Poly went. Nobody had ever seen her, but word on the street was that she was practically a kid herself.

That first day, I walked into her classroom a couple of minutes early. It was empty, save for a blond, blue-eyed woman in her late twenties or early thirties in a well-worn long-sleeve plaid shirt. She was sitting on the teacher's desk at the front of the room, the long hardwood table with a U-shaped seating arrangement in front of her for students. She was flipping through our textbook, the extra-thick *Norton Anthology of American Literature*.

I plopped my own copy down on the table, several seats away from her. She looked up and smiled warmly. "Are you here for English?" she asked. "I really hope so." I nodded. She hopped off the desk, dropping her anthology in the process, and walked over to shake my hand. "I'm Ms. Hamilton. I'm your English teacher." She picked up the book on her way back and tossed it onto the desk. She turned toward me and laughed. "I guess you probably knew I was your teacher."

"Oh yes, I was able to determine that with the powerful deductive reasoning skills I've developed at this fine academic institution," I said with a smirk.

Her eyes shot wide open; then she gave her thigh a hard slap and boomed out a laugh. It was enough to get Mrs. McKendrick, who was passing by outside, to pause and look in. She seemed puzzled, her tongue poking into the side of her cheek. Ms. Hamilton turned back and saw her.

"Sorry, Matilda," she said. "We're just having a little fun here."

I was tempted to wave at her, but I didn't. Inside, I was thrilled.

Ms. Hamilton started her class with a round of introductions. She seemed really interested in her students, most of whom were pretty cool, except for an obnoxious guy named Tim who had teased me endlessly in eighth grade. With all the questions Ms. Hamilton asked, the introductions took a third of the period.

When the last student finished, she picked up the anthology but changed her mind after checking her watch. She set the book down and turned to us. "Let's do a neat exercise," she said.

She started by telling us what constituted a good story. "As we read through the remarkable stories in this book, you'll see they have something in common. They're fundamentally about challenges. Someone *wants* something, but they can't get it. There are barriers to achieving it—sometimes another person, sometimes an actual physical obstacle, sometimes a belief. The stories finish with some kind of resolution, which is often a transformation. Maybe the person gets what she wants, maybe she doesn't, but she changes so much in the process of pursuing her goal that in the end it no longer has the same significance. That concept— transformation—is often what's behind a good story."

She motioned toward a wooden bowl filled with pens and index cards at the center of the table where we were seated. "Grab one of those pens and a card," she said. "Now write down, in a sentence, two things: a challenge you're facing, or one you've faced, and the resolution you hope for, or have attained, which might be your personal transformation. Be bold—but not crude. Don't put your name on it. Take no more than five minutes. When you're done, we'll read a few, and then I'll tell you your homework."

Cancer jumped to mind, of course. It was my most obvious challenge. Still, I didn't feel like writing about it, and I wasn't sure what the resolution was, other than my not dying. I looked over at my friend Cara. She'd already started scribbling something down. I tried to focus. Monique came to mind next, but whatever story I could tell about her wouldn't lead to a transformation. I got nervous looking around the room, because it seemed like everyone was throwing their completed cards into the bowl. In the last half minute, I finally came up with something.

Ms. Hamilton motioned toward the bowl. A student slid it down the table to her. People sat up in their seats, their eyes focused on her, and she closed hers and mixed the cards. At last, she pulled one out. Watching her was amusing.

"Okay, here's our first grand challenge. It says, 'Getting a certain boy to notice me.'" Everyone looked around the room, trying to figure out who wrote it. Ms. Hamilton continued. "'Resolution/transformation: making his girlfriend disappear.' Aha, we have unrequited love here, followed by machination and possible subterfuge. Love, in all its forms, is a very powerful basis for a number of the stories we'll read."

Ms. Hamilton closed her eyes again, steadying the bowl with one hand while swirling the cards around with the other. She withdrew one and read it once to herself. "Okay, this one says, 'My father doesn't care about things that are really important to me.'" She looked up. "I'll bet that feels familiar to a lot of you." Several people in the room were nodding. "Lots of us feel like our parents simply don't get us. What's this person's resolution? 'Achieve something that truly blows my dad away.'"

Eyes darted around the room, with everyone trying to play detective. Ms. Hamilton was on to the next card before an identity could be determined.

The bell rang and everybody hopped to their feet and started gathering their stuff. "I hope you're not that eager to get out of my class," Ms. Hamilton said, smiling. "Grab a homework sheet—there." She pointed to the end of the table. "You've got plenty of reading for tomorrow—stories strong on struggle and transformation. And know this: I accept praise, ideas, and complaints—but not homework excuses."

Ms. Hamilton stood near the door as we walked out. I ended up being the last to leave. Just as I walked past her she said, "I have a book you might like to read." I turned around and she handed me *East of Eden* by John Steinbeck.

"Is this, like, homework?" I asked, flipping through it. It looked pretty long.

"No. It just happens to be one of my favorite books. And it's about father-son relationships, among other things."

I put two and two together, impressed. I looked at her and smiled. "How did you know the card you read was mine?"

Ms. Hamilton laughed. "Everyone else followed my instructions."

"How's that?"

"They wrote their challenges with a black ballpoint they took from the bowl. You used the blue pen you're holding."

●

During my first week of school, I came down with a killer cold. Chemo always leaves patients vulnerable to every bug floating around, and this one was bad. Dr. Farbstein, my oncologist, said I was at risk for pneumonia and gave my mom orders to keep me home for a few days.

I didn't complain. Something had sucked me into *East of Eden*. Halfway through, this nice old man, Samuel Hamilton, visits a farm owned by Adam Trask, and the two of them get into a discussion about conflicting translations of the Bible with Lee, a very philosophical guy. Lee, the philosopher, explains that the King James Bible has the Hebrew God saying that Cain, the guy who kills his brother Abel, in Genesis, *shall* conquer sin. The word "shall" is pretty much a ruling—straight from God. There's no room for choice. That's simply the way it's going to be.

But Lee says another translation of the Bible, the American Standard, suggests something completely different: that Cain *may* conquer sin. The word "may," it seems to Lee, means that Cain has some say in his own fate—actual choice, free will. One word, translated differently, turns the meaning of the whole passage upside down.

I found myself thinking about my father. In our house, he might as well have been God. One word coming out of his mouth became a command for the rest of us. It made me think about my wish. I was seriously considering abandoning it, just because sharing it with him had produced nothing but a wintry detachment—or maybe just prolonged the one that had started when I got his car stolen. I was letting Dad determine my fate, the same way one father in *East of Eden* tried to lay out his son's.

I was thinking about that when the phone rang one afternoon. No one picked it up, so I did. It was Aura, the social worker I'd set up the cancer support group with, whom I'd kind of been avoiding. After having that blowout with Monique, the last thing I wanted to do was schedule another group meeting.

"So look, Aura," I said, once we got past the pleasantries, "as much as I'd love to plan a get-together, I'm swamped with school. I really don't think I can do it this time."

"That's okay, Jeff. I understand." I thought she'd be upset, but she sounded fine. "Actually, I was also calling to let you know some news. Sylvia had a relapse."

The news hit me hard. I felt it like a punch in my stomach. Sylvia was the girl who'd told us how her stepdad and sister blamed her for hogging her mom.

"Oh, jeez, that's the last thing any of us needs. And she's got the worst family on the planet."

"It's difficult. She's definitely lacking support. I'm sure she'd appreciate a visit—she's at Torrance Memorial—or even a call."

At that moment, it felt like a wave hit me—starting in my gut, building, and crashing into my brain. I was suddenly light-headed. I lost focus. I could make out sounds—Mom calling down from the top of the staircase, Aura's voice over the phone—but I couldn't respond.

Seconds passed, and I finally mumbled to Aura that I had to go.

Mom knocked on my door at the same moment, swinging it open. At first, she looked relieved, as if she was satisfied to find me home and awake, but her expression quickly turned into one of concern. "Are you okay, honey?"

I wanted to calm her, but I couldn't formulate a response. She hurried to the couch, her eyes scanning my body, briefly pausing on the book resting on my lap, quickly glancing at the phone beside me, then landing on my face, my eyes. Slowly, my mind cleared. I drew in a long breath, then blew it out.

"Too much reading," I said, my fingers tapping on the book cover. "But I'm fine." An expression of protest, maybe disbelief, blanketed her face. I wasn't sure what had just happened, but I was lucid enough now to make sure I appeared calm to her. "Really, Mom," I said, totally faking confidence, "everything is fine."

●

The day after I finished *East of Eden*, which had gotten me thinking so much about Dad and my wish, the head of the Starlight Children's Foundation called me. Carol Brown introduced herself with her voice full of enthusiasm. "I've been so looking forward to speaking with you," she said. "I can honestly say your wish is the most extraordinary one we've ever received." I really liked the sound of that.

Carol told me that her team had made progress. "We've found an organization, Youth Ambassadors of America, that coordinates international youth summits. They've got a trip to the Soviet Union next year, and they'd *love* for you to join them. We're separately working on the meeting with Mr. Gorbachev, and we might have found an angle on that."

I was speechless. I couldn't believe what I was hearing.

"Jeff?"

"I'm here," I said, jumping to my feet. "It's all just kind of amazing. I thought you might be calling to let me know it wasn't going to happen."

"Not at all. We really, really want to make this happen." She sighed. "Now, a couple things. First, your parents will have to sign off on this wish. Can I assume they're supportive?" Mom was scared about me going overseas. Dad considered the wish a distraction from school.

"Oh, absolutely. They love it. No problem at all."

"Great. The other thing is making sure you're healthy enough for the trip."

"I'm in great shape. Almost done with chemotherapy, in fact."

"That's good to hear. Who is coordinating your cancer treatment?"

"I've got *tons* of doctors. I guess the main one is my neurologist, Dr. Gourevik."

"We'll need him to certify your health." The second she said that, I felt like kicking myself for offering his name. The chances of him doing anything that would help me were slim to none.

Carol went on. "We'll send you the release forms and information about Youth Ambassadors of America. I've got to run now, but we're really excited. It's a beautiful wish."

I thanked Carol and we hung up. It was great to hear her enthusiasm. But I really screwed up in mentioning Dr. Gourevik. Getting my parents' support would be hard enough. Hooking his would require a miracle.

Before talking to Dr. Gourevik about clearing me for the trip, I had to get an MRI scan, which always stressed me out. But this time it wasn't just the prospect of my tumor coming back; it was also the fact that any evidence of recurrence would ensure I'd never be allowed to go on the trip.

The absolute worst day to get an MRI, I'd learned from experience, is a Friday, because you end up waiting the whole weekend and then some to get the results. Of course, the only appointment they had available that week was on Friday. What made it worse was that Monique was the only person who'd ever succeeded in chilling me out while I was waiting for the verdict, and now we weren't speaking. The only good thing was that I got to transport myself in my own set of wheels. The dealer had called the day before to say the new car was ready, and Mom kindly chauffeured me out to pick it up. Needless to say, it took tons of reassuring to convince her to let me drive up for the MRI on my own.

The whole time I was in the tube, as my head was getting pounded, I wondered if there was some way I could get an early copy of the radiologist's report. By the time the machine stopped scanning my brain, I'd come up with an idea.

I heard the muffled sounds of the technician, who looked like a younger version of my mother, as she entered the room. She slid me out, removing the cage over my face and the band across my forehead. I yanked out the earplugs.

"How are you feeling?" she asked.

"Really good," I said, which couldn't have been further from the truth.

"Sit up when you like," she told me. "There's no rush."

Instantly, I swung myself up. I put a particularly warm smile on my face. She smiled back. "You look great," she said. "Let me get you a step stool."

As she was positioning it on the floor in front of me, I noted the location of the door that accessed the control room, where the radiologist and his crew were sitting.

"Are you ready to stand?" the technician said.

My head was still tingling, but I said yes and hopped to my feet. I was lucky I didn't fall over. She motioned toward the door, but I shook my head. She pursed her lips and raised an eyebrow. I extended my arm toward the exit, winking at her, and said, "Ladies first." She cracked up and nodded.

The second she started walking toward the exit, I took off in the opposite direction, swinging open the door to the control room. The radiologist, an athletic older guy with an oversized mug in his hand, nearly choked on his coffee. "Sorry to trouble you," I said, "but considering it's Friday, I'll go through a hellish weekend of worry waiting to hear the results of the scan you just completed. Of course, a man with your expertise could tell me right this moment."

"The exit is this way," I heard someone say behind me. It was the technician. I ignored her, but she tugged on my sleeve.

"Ouch," I said to her, flinching from faked pain. She instantly let go. I turned back to the radiologist. "Please. I'm begging you. And I promise this will be completely off the record."

"Not just off the record, but never again, agreed?" he said.

"Absolutely."

"No recurrence. No changes. Things are looking good."

I thanked him and followed the technician out. She shook her head and laughed.

When I got home, Mom rushed to the front door faster than Amiga. "How was it? Are you okay?" There was tension in every inch of her face, from her furrowed brow down to her pressed lips. I quickly relayed the news, including the trick I'd pulled to get the results, and she laughed out loud. The tension drained from her face.

Smiling, she looked at me and slowly shook her head. "How did my son become such a talented trickster?"

I smiled back at her. "Genetics."

•

I returned to school on Monday and blew Ms. Hamilton away with the news that I'd finished *East of Eden* in addition to all the other homework she'd assigned. On Tuesday, Mom took me to the appointment with Dr. Gourevik. "Is something wrong?" she asked as we drove up to his office.

I was agonizing over getting his approval for the trip, but I thought it best not to mention my concern to Mom. "Are you actually worried I'm not full of excitement to see Dr. G? Come on. If I was excited, that's when you should worry." Mom thought that was pretty funny.

We waited twenty-five minutes for His Highness to call us in, and he sat down behind his desk and picked up the MRI results. I had already told Mom to pretend she didn't know, and when I saw her scoot to the edge of her seat, I nearly cracked up laughing.

"The most recent MRI shows no sign of recurrence," Dr. Gourevik said.

"Thank God," I said, wiping my forehead. "That's such a re-lief." Mom gave my hand a squeeze and smiled.

"Yes, I'd say it's something to be happy about." He pointed toward his exam room. "Let's proceed with a quick physical." I walked straight to it, trying to look as confident as possible. Mom waited back in his office.

He went through all the standard checks, like thumping on my chest and listening to my heart and lungs. Then he proceeded with the neurological stuff. I walked across the room with one foot directly in front of the other. I sat down and he had me touch his finger and then my nose a few times as he moved his hand around. I touched my nose with my eyes shut. All good. Then I followed a light with my eyes, trying to keep my head straight, but when he got far over to the left, my head started shaking. "Interesting," he said. That got me a little concerned.

"It's been that way since I was a kid," I said. It was a total lie, though I'd never consciously tried to keep my head straight and swing my eyeballs all the way to one side.

"I understand," he said. "All right, let's return to the office." He didn't seem terribly worried. My stress level dropped by half.

I sat back down next to Mom as Dr. Gourevik plopped down on his throne. "I see no changes," he said.

Mom sighed. She never seemed to know that people could hear her when she did that. "Jeff is demonstrating certain effects from the trauma to his brain, and as I've said previously, I think it would be a good idea for him to undergo a neuropsychological evaluation."

"What is that, exactly?" Mom asked.

Dr. Gourevik described it. It sounded like the IQ test I'd taken to get into private school, along with some exams to figure out if everything in my head was working properly. What if the test revealed something was wrong? He wouldn't let me go on the trip.

I either had to avoid it altogether or make sure I only did it after coming back from the Soviet Union.

"Sounds good," I said. "Is that it?"

Dr. Gourevik nodded.

This was my moment. "Say, I wanted to get a quick signature from you on something." I reached into my backpack and pulled out the medical release form that the Starlight people had sent us. "If you could just sign right here," I said.

"What is this?" Dr. Gourevik said. He reached for his pen, which was good.

"Well, I'm going on an overseas trip next year and the people coordinating it just wanted to make sure I'm medically cleared, so if you could just sign on the bottom left there, we're all good."

"Where is the trip to?" Dr. Gourevik asked.

"Well, the Soviet Union. But I'll be accompanied by a whole bunch of adults and other people my age. So no risk. I certainly don't want to bother you, so if you could just sign, that would be great."

Dr. Gourevik looked up at me. "If you want me to sign something, I have to review it."

I slumped into my seat. "Fine," I said.

He took forever to read the thing. It was short, too. I'd already read it. It had three yes or no questions, a line for his signature, another for his printed name, and a space for today's date. I'd even filled out the last two for him, just to make it convenient. He scanned each sentence with his finger, and, now, for the third time, he went back to the top and started over. I was getting worried.

"Jeff," Mom said to me quietly.

"What?"

"Did you want to ask Dr. Gourevik about the problem you had while reading the other day?" I couldn't believe what I was hearing. Was she selling me down the river? I frowned at her, praying that Dr. Gourevik missed what she'd said, but he looked up.

"What problem would that be?"

"Nothing," I said. "Just spent eight hours on my couch glued to a book."

Mom couldn't keep her mouth shut. "You had difficulty speaking to me. And I spoke with Aura, who said you had trouble during your phone call."

I couldn't believe she'd had a secret conversation with Aura about me. I rubbed my arms as my lip started to curl. My own mother was betraying me.

"Mom, I was just exhausted from tons of homework and all that reading. There was no problem."

"Fatigue certainly increases seizure vulnerability, Jeff," Dr. Gourevik said. "And that does sound like a possible seizure." I was stunned by where this was going. "Have you had any other episodes where your ability to communicate was adversely affected?"

"No, Dr. Gourevik. I'm fine. My scan is clear. Everything is perfect. Honestly, I just need you to sign the paper."

He set down his pen, rubbed his nose, and then cupped his hands together. "I'm not going to sign this now," he said.

"But, Dr. Gourevik—"

"I need to think it over. My initial sense is that I'm not in a position to certify you're okay to go on this trip."

"The Starlight Foundation thinks you are," I said.

"I'm lacking information."

"What kind of information? You've got the scan results in front of you. You just did an exam. What more could you possibly need?"

"A full evaluation from a qualified neuropsychologist."

"Are you serious?" I said, crossing my arms. "What has that got to do with my head buzzing a tiny bit after reading for twelve hours straight?"

"You said you'd been reading for eight hours."

I rolled my eyes. "Whatever. Eight hours, then."

"A neuropsychological evaluation has the potential to identify specific areas of cognitive impairment, which is important in determining your well-being."

"Impairment? You've gotta be kidding. I'm perfectly fine."

"If that's the case, the examination will confirm it. In any event, I will consider your request and give you a response when I'm ready. In the meantime, please consider undergoing this important evaluation."

"You're such—" I started to say, but Mom pinched my arm—hard.

"Thank you, Dr. Gourevik," she said. "Please hold on to the form."

I walked out of his office completely silent, continuing to the elevators. I didn't bother waiting for Mom. I stood by her car outside, steaming for what seemed like ages, until she finally showed up.

"What the hell, Mom?"

"Honey . . ."

"Don't 'honey' me! Do you realize you destroyed my wish?"

"I didn't mean to, Jeff."

"You didn't mean to? You gave Dr. Gourevik the reason he needed not to sign the damn release. I thought you were on my side. But you're just like Dad."

"I only wanted—"

"You got what you want. I don't need to hear anything else about it. Just take me home."

We didn't exchange a word on the way back. It was *exactly* like me and Dad.

I hurried from the car to the house to use the bathroom just off the kitchen. Mom went to check the answering machine, and the messages started to play back.

As I stepped out of the bathroom, I heard Aura's voice drifting off the tape. "I'm afraid I've got some bad news, but I wanted to make sure you got it. Sylvia passed away last night. Her funeral will probably be this weekend. I'll let you know the details when I find out. I'm really sorry, Jeff. Bye."

CHAPTER TWELVE

I woke from a bad dream about Sylvia with my hands clasped together and my shirt damp with sweat. For several seconds, before I was fully awake, I thought maybe her death was just part of that nightmare. But then my consciousness kicked in, and along with it the awareness that Sylvia was indeed gone and my mom had ruined my wish. In an instant, the morning felt gloomy and bleak.

It took ages to pull myself out of bed, and the only thing that got me to do it was knowing that if I didn't, my mom would come downstairs to get me. I really didn't care to see her.

In the shower, I lathered up with soap, rinsed, and did it again. I was so fixated on Sylvia that I didn't even realize I was doing it until I was halfway through—my showers were typically quick, and I never went for two rounds unless I was filthy. But I *felt* dirty, knowing that Sylvia died without hearing from me. It's like I was trying to rinse away the guilt I felt for not being there for Sylvia when she needed me. The least I could do was show up at her funeral. From what she'd told us about her family, I worried they wouldn't bother to attend.

I stepped out of the shower and reached for a towel. My focus was shifting from Sylvia to my mom. I still couldn't believe what had happened in Dr. Gourevik's office. She had to know that saying what she said would freak him out. Now, thanks to her, I had to go through a neuropsychological evaluation, whatever the hell that was. Just another obstacle to a wish—one that I really, deeply wanted, but one that was starting to feel impossible.

Mom was in the kitchen when I appeared at the top of the staircase. "Good morning, honey," she said as Amiga ran over to me. "I made you some breakfast."

I'd had to make breakfast for myself since I was twelve, with the exception of weekend brunches, so I knew she was trying to get rid of her guilt. I wanted her to feel it, like I did. "I'm not hungry," I said.

Mom frowned. "Please, Jeff," she said. "I didn't mean to create problems for you with Dr. Gourevik."

"'Didn't mean to'? Seriously, Mom? He was about to sign that form until you opened your mouth. If you didn't want me to go to the Soviet Union, you should've just told me outright instead of stabbing me in the back in front of that jerk."

"I wasn't trying to ruin your wish. You'd just had that episode in your bedroom when you couldn't speak—and it *worried* me. I wanted him to know."

"Well, he knows. And now I've got to do this damn evaluation and I wouldn't be surprised if he discovers something that gives him an excuse not to let me go overseas. So congratulations, Mom. I think there's a reasonably good chance you've killed my wish."

She sighed and looked at her feet. "I didn't want that, Jeff."

I knew what she was looking for now: a hug, my understanding, for me to eat the breakfast she'd made and head off to school with a smile on my face. But I was pissed, and I couldn't just wipe all that anger away.

"Want it or not, Mom, that's what you got." I looked at the clock. "Anyway, I don't want to get in trouble now for showing up late to school."

●

The whole morning at school, I didn't listen to a word coming out of my teachers' mouths. All I could think about was the neuropsychological test Dr. Gourevik was so hell-bent on me taking—not only whether I could pass the damn thing, but what it was in the first place. I had to figure it out.

Halfway through my Russian class, while I pretended to be reading a sentence in Cyrillic along with everyone else (it took me twice as long as my classmates to make out the letters, even when I was paying attention), it struck me that Sean, our school counselor, might know what the test involved. He had to, actually—he was a psychologist, after all. I decided I'd stop by his office during lunch, which was what he was always asking people to do anyway.

After grabbing a sandwich from the food truck, I hurried over to the administrative building. I'd never visited Sean's office, and it took me a few minutes to find it. The door was halfway open. I knocked.

"Come in," Sean said.

"Hi, I'm Jeff—in my junior year. I was wondering if you had a moment."

"Sure, Jeff," Sean said with a smile. "Have a seat—the couch or one of those chairs, whatever you prefer."

"Thanks. So, like, I was wondering if you could explain to me what a neuropsychological evaluation is."

One of his eyebrows rose, which made me nervous. "Is your doctor making you do one following your surgery last year?"

"Oh, no, it's someone in my cancer support group. She's kind of nervous about it. So I thought I'd ask you—you know, so I could reassure her."

"I see. Well, I'd be happy to talk with her directly if that would be helpful."

"She's at a different school, actually. You can just tell me. I'm pretty good at communicating details."

Sean smiled. "All right. Well, neuropsychological evaluations— or comprehensive neuropsychological testing, which is what it was called when I was in school—are a series of tests to measure how a person's brain is functioning compared to the norm. They're usually given to people who are experiencing a brain illness, like Parkinson's disease, or to someone who has had a brain injury, say, from a car crash."

"What kind of tests, exactly?"

"It's all paper-and-pencil-type stuff, often timed. They don't use any diagnostic equipment, like scanners or that kind of thing."

"Gotcha." Sean's explanation had made things clearer—mostly. A piece was still missing, and Sean could tell.

"Is there some other aspect of it you'd like to hear about?"

"Well, I guess most of what you said sounds like neurological testing. I've done stuff like that. You heard I had brain cancer, right?"

"I have."

"My neurologist had me do tests like these in his office. But this is neuro*psychological* testing we're talking about, right? What's the psychological part?"

"Sure, I get what you're asking. Yes, most of the tests, as I recall, are neurological. But in addition to an interview, there's typically at least one psychological test—a long series of questions—that looks at personality type, quality of life, and things like depression. Remember that sheet I passed around about depression after Julie's suicide attempt?"

I nodded.

"That had similar questions on it. Anyway, the psychological questions are included in this type of testing because brain injuries or diseases can impact a person psychologically."

I wondered where I'd stashed that information sheet.

"Jeff?" Sean said. I looked up at him. "It would be *totally* legit if you had been asked to take this test and were coming to me out of fear or concern. That's why I'm here—to help students who are facing challenges. If that's what's going on, there's no need to feel embarrassed, and I'm happy to help."

For a second, I thought about telling him the truth. But what if it went into my record that I was seeing the school shrink? Or he had to tell my parents I stopped by?

"Thank you very much for your answers," I said as I stood. "I'm sure this will help my friend."

●

After school, I came home to a tail-wagging dog and a note from Mom taped to the sliding glass door: *I'm checking out retirement homes for your grandfather. I'll be back around 5:30. I hope you had a good day.* I crumpled it up and threw it into the trash, gave Amiga a quick tummy rub, and headed downstairs.

I probably should have just asked Sean for another one of his information sheets on depression, but I didn't want to tip him off on anything. Plus, I knew I had the original copy—I'd tucked it away. Where, exactly, I couldn't remember.

With my irritation building as I foraged through notebooks and textbooks and backpack compartments, all the while thinking that I wouldn't have to do any of this if Mom hadn't opened her mouth, a picture popped into my head. It was a young African boy, dressed in rags, covering his head with his hands as a tear rolled down his bony cheek. I snapped my fingers and spun around, pulling the August 1987 edition of *National Geographic* from my bookshelf. The day I came across the article, I'd been feeling sorry for myself, just having finished a round of chemo, but that poor kid and the hell he must have gone through put things into perspective for me. Earlier that same day, I'd pulled

Sean's information sheet on depression out of my notebook and was thinking about taking his little five-question test. But when I saw this kid—and how badly he was suffering—I decided I had nothing to complain about.

I held the magazine up and shuffled through the pages. The sheet I was looking for fell onto my bed.

It was divided into two parts. The first was a short description of teen depression. *Being a teenager isn't easy,* it said, *and it's natural to feel down sometimes. But depression is overwhelming sadness that sticks around for weeks or months or even longer. People experiencing depression can't just "snap out of it"—they often need professional help or adult support. And there's nothing wrong with that. If you think you might be experiencing depression, please stop by the student counselor's office or ask a trusted adult for help.*

The second part was the quiz. There were five personal statements, and you had to answer with a number indicating how much each statement applied to you in the past month: one meaning hardly ever; two, some of the time; three, most of the time; four, all the time.

I'm finding it hard to concentrate. Definitely a four, but it wasn't like it was from depression. After all, a chunk of my brain had been removed and the rest of it had been irradiated. Whatever.

I have difficulty sleeping or I sleep too much. I wasn't having the slightest bit of trouble sleeping, at least in the past month. It was the other extreme. Sometimes I didn't even want to get out of bed. Four.

I feel like my friends and family don't understand me. That question kind of freaked me out. I mean, no one in my family understood me, that was for sure. As for my friends, Paul did, a little, but not the cancer stuff, and while Monique originally had that part covered, we'd had our blowout fight and she was out of the picture. I chose three.

I feel hopeless about my future. That was tough. Part of me definitely worried that I was going to die from cancer, even more now that Sylvia had, but I was pretty good at burying that fear. I had been *hopeful* about my wish—up until the point when Mom might have destroyed it. I guess I wasn't looking forward to what was ahead for me, but that wasn't, like, constant. Three.

I'm experiencing chronic pain, or problems from a physical disability or a serious illness. That statement seemed stupidly phrased—at least for me. What the heck were problems *from* a serious illness? I was pretty sure—based on personal experience—that serious illness was the problem itself.

Still, I had to give it a number, and considering I was not only going through chemo, but due for my next round, I put down a four.

At the end of the statements, it said to add the numbers.

> *If your total is between . . .*
> *1 and 5—Depression is unlikely.*
> *6 and 10—Depression is possible. Speak with the counselor or talk with an adult if these symptoms persist.*
> *11 and 15—Depression is likely. Definitely speak with the counselor or talk with an adult.*

*16 and 20—Depression is highly likely. Immedi-
ately speak with the counselor or talk with an adult.
Do not put it off.
No matter your score, if you have thoughts or plans
of suicide, immediately tell an adult.*

I seriously couldn't believe I scored 18. I mean, I didn't *feel*
depressed, and it wasn't like I was even close to thinking of killing
myself. But if this quiz put me in the "highly likely" range for depression, what would the neuropsychological evaluation reveal?

●

As I sat in the hospital for my last round of chemo, in the same
room as before—the one with a crappy view of the parking
lot—my gut was churning. It wasn't the chemo, either. I was on a
new drug that kept my nausea mostly under control. Instead, I was
filled with anger—the smoldering, persistent ire toward my mom
for crushing my wish, and a newfound outrage at my chemo doc.
I'd begged him to hold off for a few days, because I had a truly
important event to attend, but he absolutely insisted we "stick to
protocol." The result: I was going to miss Sylvia's funeral.

Mom kept trying to get a conversation going between us, but I
shut every attempt down. I'd tell her I needed to rest, or that I had
to "focus internally" so I wouldn't get sick to my stomach. When
she tried to put a positive spin on everything by asking if I was
happy this was my last round of chemo, I snorted and said, "Yeah,
Mom. I'm just *really* enjoying myself." She winced, but I wanted

her to suffer. Okay, maybe not *suffer*, exactly. But I wanted her to know what my pain felt like.

On the third day, she finally managed to give me some space. I'd told her flat out that it would be easier for me to rest if I had the room to myself, and after letting out a long sigh, she said she had some errands to run. I frankly didn't care what she was up to. I just wanted her to leave.

In her absence, the anger inside me faded. You'd think that would be good, but nothing came in its place. Without the anger to focus on her, I felt alone.

That's when I thought of my wish—what it meant to me. I'd turned to it so much, I realized. When I felt isolated, like today, I imagined it ahead of me. It had the power to connect me. When I longed for my dad's warmth, something I'd wanted my whole life, I saw a chance in my wish to earn some of it.

Without the wish, there was emptiness. The vacuum inside me was so deep, so profound, I felt like I was saying goodbye to my own existence.

•

After they released me from the hospital, as soon as I was no longer feeling miserable, I decided to say goodbye to Sylvia. Mom stared at me with a dazed look when she saw me appear upstairs in slacks and a button-down shirt. "You look so nice," she said. Then her eyebrows squished together. "You know it's Sunday, right?"

I tried to speak but started coughing.

"Are you okay?" Mom asked.

I nodded, grabbing a cup from the cabinet and pouring myself some water from the dispenser. I took a sip. My lungs seemed to calm.

"I'm going to visit Sylvia's grave."

Mom pressed her fingers to her lips. She set down the towel she was holding and stepped toward me, her arms opening.

I lifted my wrist to look at my watch. "I'll be back this afternoon," I said, slipping past her.

"Aren't you hungry?" Mom said. "I could make you something."

There was a large ceramic bowl on the kitchen counter filled with fruit. I pulled out an apple and held it up at eye level. Mom frowned, but I didn't acknowledge her.

"Breakfast to go," I said, and walked to the front door.

•

It took a while to get to the cemetery, and ages to find Sylvia's grave. I passed one headstone after another, gripping the flower arrangement I'd picked out at a market on the drive down, calculating how old each person had been when they died. Even though several had been born more than a hundred years before, very few were dead at seventeen. It wasn't fair. Seventeen was more like when your life was supposed to take off.

I was close to heading back to the entrance to ask the attendant for better directions when I found Sylvia's tombstone. It was the newness of it that drew me, in contrast to the decaying tablets all around it. When my eyes landed on her name, I gasped, feeling my body stiffen.

I stood there for several minutes, unsure what to do. I didn't know any prayers for this kind of thing. The ones they'd said at my grandma's funeral, when I was nine, were in Hebrew, and I couldn't remember a single word. Sylvia was Catholic, anyway, so I figured it wouldn't be appropriate. I didn't know how to proceed, and suddenly I didn't know why I'd come.

I looked across the road, where there was a small group gathered for a burial. I watched them for a moment. Everyone was gathered around a casket, focused on a minister standing out in front, with some of the folks weeping. The exception was a little girl, maybe five, who was shifting on her feet and looking around, like she was disconnected from the group. Disconnected was exactly how I felt.

Why had I come? I didn't really know. I mean, people went to funerals to say goodbye—that was how I always understood it. But I wasn't exactly feeling that. Or at least, not just that.

Sylvia and I had seen each other only a few times—at the first meeting of our support group, at another held in a hospital basement, and at Monique's party. We'd spoken on the phone just twice before Aura told me that her cancer had come back. After that, I'd sort of disappeared. So it wasn't really about saying goodbye.

I could feel a pit in my stomach. Sylvia had told us her family didn't give her any support. Aura had let me know, after Sylvia's recurrence, how much she would appreciate a call. So what did I do? I ditched her. Exactly at the moment when she needed me.

I was overcome. My breathing quickened, like Amiga panting

when it was hot out, but I couldn't get enough air. I became light-headed. I felt a sudden onset of nausea, which forced me to drop to one knee. I placed a hand on my stomach, trying to understand what was happening inside me.

The nausea wasn't the same as what I used to go through during chemo. It didn't have that chemical feel to it. It was like *I* was the source. Disgust—with myself.

That was when it hit me—why I'd come. Not to say goodbye, but to be forgiven. And how do you get forgiveness when the person you're asking it from is dead?

There was no way around it: I'd failed Sylvia. And with her gone, I couldn't give her anything.

Maybe I can give to others.

My wish came to mind then. It was about reaching out to the world, trying to make it better. It was so much larger than me. If I got to do it and my cancer came back, and, like Sylvia, I died young, my life at least would have mattered. And if I managed to pull through, maybe the realization of my wish would make it okay that I got to survive.

I couldn't give up. There were huge obstacles, but I had to overcome them. I owed it to Sylvia.

My nausea faded and my breathing calmed. I picked up the flowers I'd set aside and knelt next to Sylvia's grave. I imagined her body in the ground below. I placed the arrangement over her chest, where I thought her heart would be, and bowed my head. I said I was sorry, even though I knew she couldn't hear me. But then I made a promise: I would try, with all my heart, to do some good for the world.

CHAPTER THIRTEEN

I woke up in a daze, to Mom telling me I'd missed my alarm, and once again started coughing, which I'd been doing most of the night. Mom was opening the blinds but hurried over when she heard my lungs go into spasm. "That doesn't sound good," she said.

"I'm fine," I said. "Just overslept." I started to sit up, but she put her hand on my forehead.

"You're blazingly hot, honey. You need to see a doctor."

"Mom, I've got school." If I went to a doctor now, it would give Dad a reason to can my trip. The coughing got more intense. I grabbed a tissue. When I pulled it away from my mouth, I saw it was covered with speckles of blood.

It turned out I had pneumonia, which I'd thought was exclusively for old people, in my left lung. I guess I would've said the same about cancer before getting it, but still, I'd never heard of a teenager coming down with pneumonia. Anyway, Dr. Farbstein put me on strong antibiotics and banned me from school for an entire week. I was so wiped out by the time he delivered his diagnosis—he made me go through a ton of tests, including a chest X-ray—that I didn't even bother protesting.

I slept the whole afternoon, waking up to the rumble of Dad's car pulling into the driveway. A few minutes later, I heard his feet on the staircase, along with Amiga's. I quickly gathered all my used tissues and stuffed them under my pillow, then grabbed a math book and flipped it open just as he walked in.

"How are you feeling, son?" he said.

Amiga came over to the bed and sniffed me. I reached down and scratched her head.

"Me? I'm perfectly fine. Just been hunkering down on school stuff." I tilted the book toward him.

"What sort of math are you working on?" I had no idea what I was looking at. The page might as well have been written in Russian, another subject I'd fallen behind in.

"You know, the usual." I snapped the book shut and changed the subject. "Anyway, what's up? Did you need something?"

"I simply wanted to see how you were feeling. Mother informed me of Dr. Farbstein's pneumonia diagnosis."

Dad was building a case against me.

"Oh, that? Did she mention it's only one lung?"

"Yes, she did. Also that Dr. Farbstein said it was potentially dangerous."

"Well, I thought the same thing about brain cancer, but you told me from the beginning everything would be fine, right?" That got him to stop talking. "Anyway, I just need to take it easy for a bit, and of course I'll dedicate myself to my schoolwork in the meantime. I should probably get back to it."

"What about dinner?"

The last thing I felt like doing was eating.

"I had some chicken soup earlier. I'm still full. I think I'll just get to work here, if that's okay."

Dad looked at me for what felt like ages. I knew he was thinking about the trip. His mouth was slightly open, like he was going to say something, but then he bit his lower lip and finally nodded. He walked out. Amiga followed.

For several seconds after he left, I felt energized—and relieved. I noticed my heart beating quickly. I thought maybe I would try to get some studying done—God knew I needed to. But as my heart slowed, the fatigue returned. It wasn't long before I'd fallen back asleep.

●

Antibiotics never cease to amaze me. After just three days on them, my coughing had stopped. My energy was still a little low, but my body was on the right track.

Mom could tell. We weren't talking that much, but she had a habit of sticking around the house when I was sick, and that morning, after checking in on me, she decided to run some errands.

Over breakfast, I thought about whether I was being selfish, feeling all this anger toward her. After all, she was obviously concerned about me. But then I thought back to the appointment with Dr. Gourevik and how she had opened her big mouth. He was hesitant to sign the medical release, but he'd gotten so close to doing it. Mom *had* to know that saying what she said would fill him with doubt. I decided my anger was justified.

I took a nap after breakfast, waking to the phone ringing a few times but falling back asleep. When I went upstairs in the early afternoon for lunch, I checked the answering machine. One call was from our gardener, saying he couldn't come that week. The second, which got me fully awake, was from the Starlight Children's Foundation. They hadn't received the medical clearance form. Without it, I couldn't go on the trip.

I absolutely had to do something. What, exactly, I didn't know. That was when Dad popped into my head. I wondered what he'd do in a situation like this. He always said that to solve a problem, you first needed to identify it. That was clear enough. The problem was Dr. Gourevik. Once you understood the problem, Dad would say, you had to tackle it head-on. In this case, that could only mean one thing: I had to call Dr. Gourevik.

One of his secretaries answered. "I need to talk to Dr. Gourevik," I told her. "I'm one of his main patients."

"Are you experiencing a medical emergency?" she asked.

I thought about it.

"Not really."

"Then I'm happy to take a message for him." Clearly, I should've said it was an emergency.

I decided to reason with her.

"As I'm sure someone in your position knows well, privacy is of utmost importance to the doctor-patient relationship. I really need to speak with him directly."

"I'm afraid I can only pass along messages. Who can I say is calling?"

"Forget it," I said, and hung up. Sulking, I went back downstairs.

One of the things I'd always been good at was impersonations. I had President Reagan nailed, along with some famous actors, and I could rap like the Beastie Boys. Juniors and seniors at my school were all assigned to advisory groups—they were supposed to help us steer through things together—and I ended up in Mrs. Cocumelli's. She was our drama teacher. She once told me that my impersonations were "utterly convincing."

Twenty minutes later, after warming up with my Jimmy Stewart voice practicing lines from *It's a Wonderful Life*, I called Dr. Gourevik's office again. The same secretary I'd spoken to before answered. I put my thespian skills to work.

"Well, hello there," I said. "Would Hermann happen to be in the office?"

"Who may I ask is calling?"

"Dr. Huntington," I said. I did a very guttural throat clearing. "I'd greatly appreciate a quick chat about one of our patients in common whom Hermann is treating for glioblastoma multiforme."

"Just a moment," she said. It worked.

"Hermann Gourevik," my doctor said a moment later. His sinuses sounded even more impacted than usual.

"Hi, Dr. Gourevik. It's Jeff Henigson calling."

"Excuse me?" He did not sound like a happy camper.

"I'm sorry, your secretary refused to let me talk to you, but it's hugely important."

"I do not appreciate deceit," he said in an ice-cold voice

"Of course you don't. And I apologize for being anything
than honest and transparent. Here's the thing: You remembe
wish? Well, the Starlight Children's Foundation has once ag
asked for a copy of the medical release signed by you, and sii
I'm totally healthy and have no brain tumor recurrence, as t
latest scan has shown, well, all you need to do is to sign that doc
ment we left in your expert hands and send it on its way. I believ
we included a prepaid addressed envelope." There was a lon
silence. "Um, Dr. Gourevik?"

"I told you some time ago that a neuropsychological evaluation would be beneficial for you."

"You did, sir, and it's an excellent recommendation, which I
have every intention of following through with—as soon as I get
back from the Soviet Union."

"I'm not convinced. And that's not until May."

"April, actually. Mid-April."

"Fine, April. Months away, in any case. You could do a neuropsychological evaluation this week and have the results a few days
later."

"But—"

"No buts. You've been dishonest and manipulative, and I have
no reason to believe that you're not being the same about a promise to do the evaluation later. You will do the evaluation now. If
the results are good, as you seem certain they will be, then I'm
happy to sign the medical release for your trip."

"Dr. Gourevik . . ." I probably came across as a sniveling child
at that moment, but I couldn't help it. I *needed* his signature.

"Jeff, the evaluation is your only option. Also, don't ever trick my secretary again." With that, he hung up.

For several minutes after getting off the phone with Dr. Gourevik, I held my head in my hands. I'd confronted the problem directly, just like my father would have told me to do, but I'd also lost. If a neuropsychologist got to look inside my messed-up mind, I'd almost certainly lose again. And that would be the end of my chance to do some serious good for the world.

There was another possibility, I realized. Mom had a copy of the medical release form—we brought it to the appointment with Dr. Gourevik. What if I faked his signature and sent the completed form to Starlight? Dad would kill me if he ever found out, but it wasn't like I'd be hurting anybody. It was more like a white lie.

I thought then about the promise I'd made at Sylvia's grave— that I would try with all my heart to make my wish come true. Going in for the neuropsychological evaluation would be the same as giving up. Faking Dr. Gourevik's signature would give me a chance to go on my trip. The result would be contributing to world peace, and that would definitely outweigh one little lie.

I went back upstairs. Amiga ran over to get some attention, but I pushed her away. I walked down the hallway and looked out the windows. The carport was empty.

I stopped by the answering machine, replaying the message from the lady at the Starlight Foundation. After drawing in a deep breath, I pressed the delete button.

Next, I walked down to Mom's office. There were four stacks

of papers and letters on her hardwood desk, neatly organized into piles. To their right was her compact calendar, displaying that day. *Regency Park retirement community* was written next to the 1 p.m. slot. I glanced at the clock. It was 1:30.

I quickly slid open the top drawer of her file cabinet, flipping through folders until I came across one labeled STARLIGHT/ WISH. Inside was the information package we'd received about Youth Ambassadors of America. The release form wasn't there.

I went through the remaining drawers. The form was nowhere to be found. I turned to her desk. Just as I was digging through drawer number three, I heard the rumbling of a car engine.

In a panic, I slammed the drawers shut. I put the Starlight folder back in place in Mom's file cabinet. Then I took off.

She'd see me if I passed by the front door, so I raced down the three steps to my parents' bedroom. I crossed from there to the back deck, where I opened the sliding glass door. Amiga raced after me, barking, and I nearly slammed the door shut on her nose. I had to make it to my bedroom before Mom checked up on me, and the only way to do that undetected was to take a very long path around the back of the house. She had a much shorter path—a few steps from the car to the house, and then the staircase down to my room.

I bolted down the stairs off the deck and sprinted around the house. Amiga was far away, but I could still hear her barking. I wished she'd shut up. I came to the first door. It was locked. The only other possibility was the external door to my room. I raced down another set of stairs, up along the side of the house, and around to that door. My heart was pounding when I got there. Thank God it was open.

As I positioned myself on the couch, I heard Mom's steps on the staircase. Just then I realized I was dripping in sweat. I hopped to my feet, yanked open a drawer, grabbed a shirt, wiped myself off, and stuffed the shirt behind the couch just as Mom knocked on my door. "Come in," I said as calmly as possible.

She had a curious look on her face, almost suspicious, definitely not with her normal how-are-you-feeling nurselike demeanor. Her eyes scanned the room. They came back and fixed on me. "You're sweating," she said.

"Oh, yeah? I, um, was doing some pushups."

"So you're feeling better?"

"Much better." I smiled.

She didn't.

"And were you in my office while I was out?"

"Your office? No." I swallowed.

"Are you sure about that?"

I must have left something out of place.

"Oh, yes, you're right. I was looking for information from the group that coordinates the trips to the Soviet Union. I completely forgot. Sorry."

For several seconds, she didn't say anything. She drew in a long breath, just like Dad did when one of his judgments was pending, but then she calmly let it out.

"Okay," she said.

•

I returned to school on Monday, way behind in almost every class. Ms. Hamilton asked me for my opinion on a Robert Frost poem she'd apparently assigned for discussion that day, "Stopping by Woods on a Snowy Evening." When I told her I hadn't read it, she frowned. Tim, who was sitting across from me, smirked. For the remainder of the class, Ms. Hamilton, at least to me, felt cold.

The rest of that school day had a robotic vibe to it. People, both teachers and students, asked me how I was doing, which would always happen after I was out of school for treatment, but no one seemed interested in the answer. It didn't matter, because I didn't care to give one. I wanted to be anonymous.

I got home around four. Mom's car was there, and as I walked down the stairs to the house, I saw her on the phone, in her office. I slid open the front door. "Thank you, Carol," I heard her say. "Let me look into this. I'll be in touch." I froze in place. Just from the tone of her voice, I could tell I'd gotten caught.

The door to Mom's office swung open in a flash. She stormed into the entryway, stopping inches in front of me. She glared at me, her eyes tight and cold. She slowly shook her head. It made me feel small.

The question came out of her mouth in three parts: "What," she said, pausing, "in the world" — another pause — "do you think you're doing?" Her voice was icy.

If she'd revealed my manipulations to Carol, the wish would certainly be finished. If she'd said anything to Dad, he wouldn't want me in his house.

"Did you tell her?"

"Did I tell her that you lied to her by saying the medical release was on its way? Is that your concern?"

"I'm sorry, Mom."

"Don't 'I'm sorry' me. You're not. You're only worried because you've been caught, not about the immorality of lying in the first place. What else are you hiding?"

"Nothing."

She crossed her arms and waited.

"Well, I guess I did call Dr. Gourevik on Friday and kind of tricked his secretary to get him on the phone, but I told him I did that."

Mom threw her hands up. "I thought you were honest, Jeff. I really did. Now I feel like I need to check up on everything you've told me. Everything you've done."

"You don't, Mom."

"How do I know you're telling the truth?"

"I just told you—I lied to Dr. Gourevik's secretary!"

"And what else? What else have you been lying about?"

I shifted on my feet. "I also kind of went through your office the other day for a copy of the medical release."

Mom moaned. "I knew it. I knew you'd been in there. And when I asked, you lied to me about it." She blew out a mouthful of air. "Why exactly did you want the medical release?"

"I was sort of thinking of forging Dr. Gourevik's signature."

She grasped her head. "I can't believe it. I simply can't believe what I'm hearing. My own son, manipulative and dishonest . . ."

I hated hearing her say that. "What about *you*, Mom?" I said sharply.

She was caught off guard. "This isn't about me."

"Really? Dr. Gourevik was just about to sign the release—until you opened your mouth. Now just why did you do that? You were worried about me going to the Soviet Union. Did you figure you could just end everything right there?"

Mom gasped. "No, Jeff. I was worried about your health. That's why I asked Dr. Gourevik about that incident. I wasn't trying to scuttle your wish."

"Maybe not, Mom. But I think you basically did." I slumped against the wall as my eyes welled up.

The stiffness suddenly left my mom's body. She touched my cheek. "I'm sorry. Really—I am. But I don't think this is the end of your wish. You just have this extra step now, the evaluation, and I'm sure things will come out fine."

I looked at the floor. Tears dripped from my chin.

"Oh, honey, please tell me what's wrong," Mom said.

"The evaluation is going to reveal that I'm depressed. Maybe even seriously." I wiped my face and looked back at Mom. Her eyes were fixed on mine. "Ever since I got the cancer diagnosis, I've been trying to keep things positive in front of you. Dad told me in the hospital you needed that. I knew your mom had died—not months later, when you finally got around to telling me, but while I was in the hospital, just after my surgery. So I kind of got into the habit of putting on a happy face whenever I'm around you—even when things are pretty bleak."

Mom bit her lip, then pressed her hand against her face. "Jeff, I want you to always feel like you can tell me anything."

"I didn't think you could handle it." I rubbed my nose.

"School hasn't been easy. Nobody really gets me or what I'm going through. The only person who did was Monique, and we had a huge fight."

"I . . . I didn't know."

"Yeah, and then Sylvia died." Mom squeezed my hand. I took a deep breath and let it out. "Anyway, that's why I think I might be in trouble with this evaluation."

"Oh, that's all just awful. But your trip—if it doesn't work out this time, I'm sure there will be others."

I sighed.

"What, sweetie? You can tell me."

"I hate to say this, and it scares the crap out of me just thinking about it, but my chances of being around for some trip down the line aren't very good."

She swallowed, then closed her eyes. She stayed that way for several seconds, and I wondered if I'd completely freaked her out. I was pretty sure I had.

Her eyes opened. She touched my cheek, nodding at me. "I understand now, sweetie. I get it. I really do." She opened her arms. I walked into them and she wrapped them tightly around me. "I love you, honey," she said.

"I love you, too."

She hadn't let go. "I need you to be honest with me, Jeff. Will you do that?"

"I will, Mom." She took a step back and exhaled deeply. I couldn't completely relax, because I still had stuff on my mind. I figured I'd better just ask her directly. "Did you tell Carol I lied?"

Mom scratched her nose. "I told her there had been a mix-up."

That was a huge relief.

"And Dad, has he talked about canceling my trip?"

"He has expressed concern—especially when you came down with pneumonia. He's also worried about school."

"Will you, you know, talk to him?"

"I have, sweetie, but I really think *you* should. Tell him what you just told me. I think he'll understand."

I wasn't sure if he could. The doubt must have shown on my face.

"Hey," Mom said, poking me. My eyebrows shot up. I looked at her and she winked. "Just trust me."

•

When I went upstairs for dinner that night, Mom, who was serving salad in the kitchen, stopped me and whispered in my ear. "Tell your father what your wish means to you," she said. He was in the dining room, pouring two glasses of wine. The thought of opening up to him made me instantly nervous. Mom could tell. "Don't worry," she said, squeezing my shoulders. "I've got your back."

At dinner, I avoided bringing it up. Dad and I went through our typical conversation topics, me asking him about work and him asking me about school. Halfway through the meal, he finished his first glass of wine. Almost instantly, Mom refilled it. Dad's eyes went to his glass, and under the table, Mom nudged me with her foot.

I understood. "Dad, um, I'd like to talk to you about something." He looked at Mom to see if his beard was clean, and she gave him her approval.

"What would that be?" he said.

"The wish. *My* wish, that is. I know you're not all that big on it . . ."

"I do not recall ever having said that."

"Well, you definitely don't seem very *enthusiastic* about it."

"It's not a matter of enthusiasm, Jeff. It's about the consequences of your electing to pursue it. It has already been a source of interruption—this when your energy has been reduced by your medical treatment. Continuing to pursue that path is likely to conflict with your school responsibilities. That is one of my concerns. Another is your health. I'm not sure a trip overseas at this time is a prudent move."

"I'm doing fine, Dad."

"That sentiment is not reflected either by your quarterly grades or by the fact that you recently came down with pneumonia."

"Why are you obsessed with school?"

"'Obsessed' is a gross exaggeration. 'Concerned' is a more accurate sentiment."

"Then what makes you so concerned?"

"Education is the most significant determinant of your future, an evidence-based fact well supported by statistics."

"Dad, if you want to talk statistics, the chances are I don't have much of a future left. Do you not get that?" Mom and I watched him, waiting for the answer he was obviously working on.

"Well, I don't base my life on statistics," he finally said. "And I do not believe you should, either."

I didn't let up. "Really, Dad? You invest your money based on statistics. You constantly compare your running performance to stats you've found on people your age. You're always talking about statistics."

"I simply want you to have a successful future."

"That would be nice, Dad. I'd like to have one, too. But if I'm on my way out, I'd much rather go having done something meaningful with my life, like advocate for world peace."

He didn't say anything. He pushed back from the table, his usual way of ending a conversation. Mom quickly intervened. "Bob, would you please respond to what Jeff just said to you?"

Dad pressed his lips together and blew out a lungful of air. Then he scooted back in, looking at me.

"You complained recently about your neurologist not having cleared you medically for international travel." His comment immediately put me on the defensive.

"So what?"

"The argument you're now advancing is that you're not well, that you might be medically unfit for such a trip." I felt like I'd been dragged into a courtroom.

"You're twisting my words around!"

"I'm doing no such thing."

I nearly exploded, but Mom once again jumped in. "Let's get the facts straight, Bob. Jeff did not say he's too sick to travel. He said he wants to travel while he still can."

I couldn't believe what had come out of my mother's mouth. I was also amazed that it shut my dad up.

"Exactly," I said. "I'm feeling pretty good now. All I was saying is that if my cancer comes back, I won't get to go. Anyway, nobody's expecting you to give me a medical evaluation. That's Dr. Gourevik's job—and this neuropsychologist he wants me to see. I'm just asking you not to cancel my trip."

Dad stayed quiet.

"Bob, did you hear your son?" Mom asked.

"I did," he said sharply. I think he expected Mom to wither away in self-preservation, like she normally did when he snapped at her. This time she didn't move, sitting upright with her shoulders relaxed, one hand resting on the table.

I took my mom's lead, uncrossing my arms and allowing myself to breathe. I looked directly at my father. "Will you promise not to withdraw your permission?"

He lifted his glasses and rubbed his nose. Reluctantly, he said, "I shall abide by your doctor's decision." It felt like the world had just turned right-side up.

CHAPTER FOURTEEN

The morning of my last chemo shot—the final wallop in my cancer treatment protocol—I found myself pacing around my bedroom. I was thinking about what people in my support group had said about the end of therapy. At the time, I couldn't even contemplate it—I had so much ahead of me—but it really surprised me how intense people's feelings were. Sylvia had said that as much as she hated chemo, the idea of finishing it freaked her out, because then she'd just be sitting around and maybe waiting for her cancer to come back. Chris thought that was ridiculous. "Every excuse you have to party," he'd said, "you absolutely gotta use." Monique had been somewhere in between. She believed in having a good time, but she thought you could jinx things if you celebrated before you were totally finished.

I came upstairs to find my parents sitting in the kitchen, sipping away at their coffee, with the corners of their mouths turned up. I'd already told them twice not to mess things up for me by celebrating an achievement that hadn't yet happened, so they were trying to control themselves, but it wasn't convincing.

"How would you like to commemorate this achievement, Jeff?" Dad asked.

"Jeez, Dad, I already told you guys not to jinx things." I frowned at both of them and served myself some pancakes.

"Indeed you did," Dad said.

"We're sorry," Mom said. "No jinxing." Of course, they were still smiling.

The three of us went to Dr. Farbstein's office in two cars. I couldn't believe Dad was actually coming. I told him he didn't have to, but he insisted. I figured since he was going to all the trouble, I could at least ride with him.

His jaw was kind of protruding as he drove, the way it always did when he was thinking about the past, or proud of something, or both. I asked him what was on his mind. "Abraham Lincoln, actually," he said.

That came as a surprise. "What brought *him* to mind?"

"Well, I've been reading a book about him of late. He was a brilliant politician, as I'm sure you know. Also a master of the English language. But at the moment of your inquiry, I was thinking how he was a lifelong student. He didn't know anything about military affairs when he became president. What did he do? He launched a study of military strategy, and during the Civil War he provided solutions that were as effective as some of those of his top generals, better than most."

It seemed like a strange thing to be focused on at that moment.

"So what got you thinking of him as a student—of, like, military strategy?"

"You, quite honestly."

My eyes instantly widened. He had my full attention.

"Many months ago, you were presented with disastrous news. You could have collapsed, or given up. You did neither. You rose to the occasion. Not only that, you carried your mother through a storm I'm uncertain she could have navigated without your confidence. That is what had me thinking about President Lincoln. He had some wonderful qualities. He was resolute. Determined. Tenacious." We came to a stop sign then, and Dad looked over at me. "You have these things in common."

We got to Dr. Farbstein's office a few minutes later, and I went into my appointment with my head held high. I didn't feel like I was jinxing anything because I wasn't celebrating yet, but boy, did I feel proud.

I thought the neuropsychological evaluation would take place in some kind of medical facility, so when Mom pulled up in front of a house on Fair Oaks, a couple of blocks away from my parents' favorite restaurant, I was convinced she'd gotten the address wrong. "You sure?" I asked with my eyebrows raised.

She pulled out the letter she'd been sent, then looked at the number on the curb. She shrugged. "It seems to be correct."

A guy in his fifties, rugged and tall, with pale blue eyes and a thick white beard, answered the door. "I'm Dr. Kennedy," he said to my mom. "You must be Mrs. Henigson." She smiled and shook his hand.

"And you're Jeff," he said with a smile and a firm handshake. I was expecting a guy in a lab coat. Dr. Kennedy was wearing a green flannel shirt with red suspenders holding up his worn brown corduroy pants. With a little more hair, he could've passed for Santa Claus. He extended his arm toward the entry. "Come on in and we can get started."

Dr. Kennedy explained what the evaluation would involve, most of which I already knew from my conversation with Sean at school. No brain scans. No injections. Nothing electronic. Just an interview, which Mom would be present for, and then a bunch of games and quizzes. It would go on for a while, he said—roughly four and a half hours—but I could take a break if I wanted.

"Tell me about your family," Dr. Kennedy said. I gave him the basics—it was just the four of us, more like three now, with Ted in college. Dad was super smart and he worked endlessly. Mom was a sweetheart and sometimes hard to get rid of—that made her chuckle. I noticed he didn't ask Mom any questions. He'd just glance at her while I was answering, like he was fact-checking or something.

He asked about school—how I liked it, and how things were going. Mom had already told me that she'd mailed him a bunch of paperwork; I noticed he had a copy of my grades from sophomore year in his lap.

"School's fine," I said. Mom shifted in her chair. I rubbed my nose. "I mean, all things considered."

Dr. Kennedy didn't seem satisfied with my answer. He turned to Mom.

"Well, Jeff's behind in his classes at the moment—because of all the time he's had to take off for treatment," she said. I kind of rolled my eyes. "But he's working very hard to catch up."

Dr. Kennedy nodded. He focused back on me. "Tell me about your friends."

"Like, what exactly?"

"Just a general picture. Do you have some good friends? Do you get along? Do you feel understood?"

Now I was the one shifting in my chair. "Well, Paul's my best friend."

"They've been in school together since sixth grade," Mom threw in.

"Yeah. But he's really busy—you know, sports and AP classes and that kind of thing. Plus, he's never had cancer." Dr. Kennedy jotted something down on his notepad. "I helped set up this support group a while back—for kids like me who are dealing with cancer—but we haven't hung out for ages." I rubbed my face in front of my left ear. "One of them actually just died." I slowly exhaled.

"I'm very sorry to hear that," Dr. Kennedy said.

He asked a few more questions, including what I was hopeful about in life. I told him about the wish. He took tons of notes. When I finished, he said we were done.

"With everything?" I asked. I was hopeful.

He smiled gently. "With the interview." He looked at the clock, then at Mom, as I slumped in the chair. "Thank you, Mrs. Henigson," he said. "Jeff and I should be done by a quarter to five."

She blew me a kiss as he walked her out. I felt a surge of

anxiety. I swallowed when Dr. Kennedy returned. I think he could tell, because he smiled once again. "Let's continue," he said.

He pulled a small box from his desk. There were cards inside, each with a drawing of an object, and all I had to do, he explained, was name it. It seemed easy enough.

I got through maybe fifty of them—correctly, I was sure—until I came to one of a tool we'd used in math class a few years back. It was one of those curved rulers with a flat base that are used to measure angles. Two words popped into my head, but I knew only one could be right. I blew out a lungful of air and squeezed my eyes tight. "Compass," I said. "That's what I'm going with."

"No need to get stressed," Dr. Kennedy said. That was hardly helpful.

We went through eight more. I found it hard to concentrate; my mind was fixed on that damn tool. Still, I managed to get all the other pictures right except for one I absolutely didn't know.

The moment he said we were finished with that test, I slapped my cheeks with both hands and shouted out, "Protractor!" His eyebrows popped up, then quickly went neutral.

I pleaded with him. "The math picture—it's a protractor, not a compass. Can you change my answer?"

Dr. Kennedy chuckled. He flipped his pencil and corrected the entry. I felt my shoulders drop.

We did tons more tests, some of them just a few minutes long. As we went through them, I could feel my confidence building.

I only blew one of them—the two-minute test where I had to come up with as many examples as I could of four-legged hoofed animals. I just got three. But on everything else, from defining words to solving puzzles to memorizing long series of numbers and reciting them backward, I did really, really well.

Dr. Kennedy announced that there was just one more test. He'd give me a long list of statements, and all I had to do was say if they were true or false for me.

"How much time do I have?" I asked.

"As long as you need."

Up until that point, the tests felt neurological, like they were measuring how my brain was working. As soon as I read a few of the statements on this one, such as "No one seems to understand me," I realized the test was evaluating my feelings. I got nervous. Before, I could pretty much tell if I was coming up with the right answers; now I wasn't sure which answer—true or false—was right.

I have nightmares every few nights. I definitely did. But I was pretty sure nightmares were associated with people who had psychological problems. I circled false.

Much of the time my head seems to hurt all over. That was pretty much true, but it wasn't my whole head, more just the area where Dr. Egan had cut into the left side of my skull. Plus, I didn't want anybody thinking I had *another* brain problem. False.

I wish I could be as happy as others seem to be. That was often on my mind at school, like when I'd see jocks laughing as they walked out of the locker room, or a guy and a girl kiss. But I didn't want Dr. Kennedy to think I wasn't happy. False.

The questions went on and on. Not only was the content of them stressing me out, but I started getting uncomfortable with my own dishonesty. Some of the later questions seemed similar to ones I'd answered earlier, and I felt like I needed to go back and check, but Dr. Kennedy had his eyes on me. I started sweating. I hoped he didn't notice.

An hour into the test, after carefully answering several hundred questions with the goal of making myself seem happy, I realized that might make me come across as a psychopath. I let out a sigh. Then I remembered the promise I'd made to Mom—that I'd be honest—and I felt like a complete jerk.

Dr. Kennedy could tell something was up. "Is everything okay?" he asked.

I pulled at my shirt. "I, um, might have answered some questions incorrectly."

"Incorrectly?"

"So, maybe like, inaccurately."

"I see," he said.

I looked up at him sheepishly. "Do you want me to, like, correct them?"

He smiled gently. "Just go ahead and finish the test, Jeff."

Thirty minutes later, which felt more like three hours, I was done. The confidence I'd felt halfway into the evaluation was completely gone. I wanted nothing more than to leave.

I didn't bother making small talk. I just sat there, glancing at the clock, hoping Mom would show up soon.

•

A week after that miserable test, Dr. Kennedy called to say the results were ready. The *family* needed to be present at the appointment. It was the last thing I needed: three witnesses to failure.

The three of us drove independently to the appointment. Dad had to get straight back to the office, Mom had to take care of something for Ted, and I was going to meet up with friends. It did seem a little ironic that the three of us were going by ourselves to this thing that Dr. Kennedy pointedly stressed was for the entire family.

At the outset of our meeting, Dad asked how long it would take. Mom rolled her eyes, though I had the same question.

"Approximately an hour," Dr. Kennedy said. "Is that acceptable?"

Dad looked at his watch and nodded.

Dr. Kennedy started by saying what he planned to do in our time together. He'd quickly summarize the meeting I'd had with him, then present his evaluation, and would finish by offering some recommendations.

For the whole week since I'd seen Dr. Kennedy, I was fixated on the last test in the evaluation and its potential impact on my wish. I kept arriving at the conclusion there was hardly any chance he'd sign off on my trip.

Dad looked half asleep while Dr. Kennedy listed the tests. Mom was scribbling everything down. It was only when Dr. Kennedy said he'd now present his findings that Dad leaned forward.

"Jeff is highly intelligent," Dr. Kennedy said.

I liked hearing that.

"He is also high-functioning. Nevertheless, he is suffering from certain cognitive impairments—attention deficit and issues with language processing and memory."

"Are these because of the tumor?" Dad asked. "Will they improve?"

"They're likely related, and we now have a baseline test, so we'll be able to assess changes over time."

There was no way I was going to go through this again.

Dr. Kennedy continued. "A larger concern is where Jeff is emotionally."

I interrupted. "Could you please not talk about me in the third person?" It was irritating.

"I'm sorry, Jeff, of course," Dr. Kennedy said. "The psychological testing revealed a moderate to high level of depression." He looked at each of us, letting that sink in. I felt like I'd gotten caught—especially when he focused on me. "Part of this is related to the trauma you went through with the diagnosis and treatment—all perfectly normal, given what you've experienced. Another part is stress from your school environment. The last part is tension in your family dynamic, particularly in how you're communicating."

"How *I'm* communicating?" I asked. I felt my toes curling.

"How all of you are communicating—with each other," Dr. Kennedy said.

I glanced at Dad. He hadn't moved an inch.

"What can we do?" Mom asked.

"Let's discuss some recommendations," Dr. Kennedy said. Mom opened her notebook to an empty page. "Over the next six months, possibly a whole year, Jeff's academic course load should either be significantly reduced, perhaps to a single class, or he should take a break from school entirely. It is clearly a substantial source of stress, and this is something that would almost instantly reduce it. He can make up for it later."

Mom, as she took notes, was nodding. Dad frowned and leaned back.

"Are you aware of Jeff's wish to travel to the Soviet Union?" Dad asked.

"I am," Dr. Kennedy said. "Both Dr. Gourevik and Jeff discussed it with me in detail."

"Do you think the trip itself might be an unnecessary source of stress for Jeff?"

"*Dad*," I said, my mouth hanging open. I seriously couldn't believe what I was hearing. My heart started racing.

Dad ignored me and continued. "Specifically, would removing the trip from his agenda allow him to strengthen his academic commitments, as opposed to withdrawing from them, as you've suggested?"

"I'm glad you brought that up, Mr. Henigson," Dr. Kennedy said. "I'm firmly of the opinion that the trip gives Jeff something positive to look forward to. It's clearly a source of inspiration and drive for him. Removing it, I believe, would have a substantial negative effect. It is thus my recommendation that Jeff pursue the trip, and I'll convey this in writing to Dr. Gourevik."

The whole room went silent. The only thing I could hear was my own heartbeat, still racing, but now in a totally different way. It was like I'd just crossed the finish line of a very long race.

"That's good," Mom said to Dr. Kennedy. "The trip means a lot to him." She turned to me. "I just wish it wasn't to the opposite side of the planet." I squeezed her hand and smiled.

Dr. Kennedy cleared his throat. "I do have one other recommendation, and that is family therapy. This has been a collective trauma, and I believe this kind of therapy would benefit all of you."

Mom nodded slowly. Dad stiffened in his chair.

"If you believe therapy to be beneficial for Jeff, I will certainly support that," Dad said. "But I see no benefit in the three of us collectively undergoing therapy."

"*Bob*," Mom said in her protest voice.

"No, Phyllis," he said firmly.

His response was so frustrating. He couldn't possibly see himself as part of a problem — and a *family* problem, at that. Just sitting next to him at that moment made me feel nauseous. I looked at him with disgust. "Of course not, Dad. You might have to admit you're something other than perfect."

I watched the anger build in my father's face. I knew he was too disciplined to explode in front of a stranger, especially a fellow professional, which made me feel empowered. My eyes bored into his.

Dad swallowed in a roomful of air. When he exhaled, he lifted his wrist and checked his watch. "Thank you for your assessment, Dr. Kennedy," he said. "I believe our hour together is up."

•

At lunch with my friends, I didn't mention the wish. I didn't say a thing about the possibility of traveling "to the opposite side of the planet," as Mom put it, to save the world. I listened as Dave talked about a date, and Paul told us about a new band, and everyone shared what they were up to for Christmas and Hanukkah. The wish was still just my own, but with one huge difference: now it was actually going to happen.

PART 3

CHAPTER FIFTEEN

The twelve-hour flight from Los Angeles to Helsinki, on a plane packed with teenage ambassadors from the western half of the United States (we'd meet the Youth Ambassadors of America kids flying from the East Coast once we'd touched down), felt like a dream. The views—of an Earth so reduced that a hundred miles could fit inside a window inches across, of the shadowy layers of clouds, both snowlike and ashen, and the snapshot of the Milky Way that came when the sun had set and the sky was clear above us—were breathtaking. Teenagers talk—and the flight started that way—but the views brought long moments of silence.

For me, what made it even more dreamlike was that I hadn't been sure, not until that final meeting with Dr. Kennedy, that I'd be cleared to participate. When he delivered the news, it was like he'd restarted the countdown on a launch that had been paused— and one I'd been pretty sure would get canceled. For so long, my wish had been grounded, just like the space shuttle program after *Challenger* exploded. First it was because of my cancer treatment, which went on forever, and then it was because of Dr. Gourevik and my father, both of whom seemed to be making a case against me ever taking off. In an instant, Dr. Kennedy had jettisoned it, and I felt myself surging through the stratosphere.

The run-up to my departure wasn't tension free. If anyone needed a therapist, it was my mother. She started to seriously worry about my trip, in part because I was traveling so far away, but more because it was to the Soviet Union. When the information package from Youth Ambassadors of America arrived in the mail, Mom and I sat down at the kitchen counter and went through it, reading information about the organization, the trip, and all the participants, including pictures and bios, along with roommate assignments. I'd be sharing a room with Mike, a guy from Ohio who looked nice enough.

"I like the organization," Mom said after going over everything. But then she pushed the packet away. "I just hope those Communists don't try to brainwash you."

As the trip grew near, Mom's tensions mushroomed. She decided it was absolutely necessary that I call her after we got to the Soviet Union—not Finland, where we'd first spend three days in an orientation before moving on to Leningrad. She said it was to confirm my safe arrival. If I couldn't guarantee that I could call her from the Soviet Union, she wouldn't let me go on the trip. I finally had to get one of the heads of Youth Ambassadors of America on the phone to chill her out. "I can guarantee you'll be able to call home," Ed Johnson, the cofounder of the organization, said to me.

"Hang on a sec," I told him, pressing the speakerphone button. Mom was next to me. "Mr. Johnson, could you kindly repeat that?"

The situation with Dad was different. In the weeks before the trip, he'd become more distant than ever, besting his record for time spent at the office, skipping dinners at home with Mom and me, and working through the weekends. When he was around, he didn't hang out, and he never once mentioned the trip. I wondered if he was acting distant because he felt he'd lost a battle.

At dinner one evening—just Mom and me—I stayed quiet, mostly picking at my food. Dad was on my mind.

"Is everything okay?" Mom asked.

"Have you noticed how Dad is never around?"

She straightened in her seat. "He's been very busy with work."

"But even when he's here, it's like he's not."

"You know how focused he can get on a case, Jeff."

I rolled my eyes. "Mom, he hasn't asked a single question about my trip. He thinks it's all just a big waste of time."

She shook her head. "I'm not sure, honey. Maybe he's not asking questions because the trip hasn't happened yet." Mom took a sip of wine, then looked out the window toward the hills. "You know, years ago, before you and your brother were born, your father and I used to go on long hikes."

"I know. You told me."

"I remember once we were climbing Mount Whitney. It's the highest mountain in California, something like fourteen thousand feet. We started in the early morning. Halfway up, we broke for lunch. I'd barely finished when your father stood and strapped on his pack. 'We're halfway there,' I said. 'Can't we rest for a moment?'

" 'Which means we have halfway to go,' he responded. 'The hike will become more challenging at altitude. We can rest when we've reached the peak.' "

"What's your point, Mom?"

"My point is that your father celebrates when a goal is met, not before."

It was a decent argument. I actually finished my dinner.

I was thinking about that conversation when the captain announced we'd be landing at the Helsinki airport in thirty minutes. I had a surge of energy—clarity, too—and the dreamlike feel of the flight quickly dissipated. My wish, at least the beginning of it, was happening. In a matter of days, I might be sitting down with one of the most powerful leaders in the world to discuss how our countries could bring an end to the nuclear arms race. I still hadn't gotten any confirmation that the meeting would happen, but it wasn't just a fantasy anymore.

As we stepped off the plane in Helsinki, onto a tarmac darkened by a slate-gray sky, the cold instantly hit me. Unlike most of the other kids, I wasn't wearing a hat or gloves—back in sunny Southern California I'd stupidly packed them in my suitcase—and I definitely needed both. In tennis shoes that felt as thick as a sheet of paper, my feet were freezing, too. The biting, frigid air stung my face, which made me want to cover every bit that was exposed with my hands, but I didn't dare take them out of my pockets. I just wished everyone in front of me would get into the bus faster, and I prayed that it was already warm inside.

Two hours later, after going through passport control and customs and hopping onto another bus that took us from the airport to the center of Helsinki, we arrived at our hotel. We got into another line there—Chace, a nice guy I'd sat next to on the flight from L.A., who'd already been to the Soviet Union twice, told me I'd better get used to "processing." A lady with a clipboard checked us in one by one, handing each person a room assignment. When I gave her my name, she pulled me aside. "Ed and Linda would like to have a word with you," she said. Ed and his wife, Linda, were the directors of Youth Ambassadors of America.

My heart picked up. Had they gotten in touch with Mr. Gorbachev's office? Were Ed and Linda about to give me the verdict?

The kids behind me in line who were yet to be registered were trying to figure out what was going on. I hadn't told anyone so far about my wish. As far as I knew, only Ed and Linda and some other administrative people were aware of it.

"It's great to finally meet you in person," Ed said as he guided me down a hallway.

I found myself nervous, as if I'd swapped positions with my mother. When she and I were on the phone with Ed, she was the one who was worried.

We stepped into a conference room where a woman was sitting with papers laid out in a semicircle in front of her. "Linda, meet Jeff," Ed said.

Her face lit up with a smile and she jumped to her feet. "I've so been looking forward to meeting you," she said, grasping my hands. "How are you feeling? We have a nurse with us if you need anything."

The last thing I needed was medical care. God knows I'd had enough of it. But I didn't want her worrying about me. "I'm great. Never felt better." I wished one of them would get to the point.

"So about your wish, Jeff," Ed said. It wasn't the kind of intro you make to good news. My whole body tensed. It felt just like it had in Dr. Gourevik's office the day he gave me his diagnosis. "Our contact in Moscow has been in touch with Mr. Gorbachev's office. They are fully aware of your story and your interest in meeting the premier." I was tense, ready for the rejection. "As of yet, we do not have confirmation from their side."

"Oh!" It wasn't what I expected him to say. I felt like I needed some clarity. "Wait a sec, are you telling me they haven't rejected a meeting?"

"Oh, absolutely not!" Ed said.

I bowed my head.

Linda clasped my shoulder. "Nobody has rejected anything," she said.

"I didn't mean to worry you, son," Ed said, chuckling. I looked up at him and he gave me a pat on the back. "We think it's all good news. Not only were we able to reach his office, the person we spoke with was familiar with your story. That means the Starlight Children's Foundation got through to them as well."

"Yes, it's definitely good news," Linda said. "Now we just have to wait. I know that can be taxing. It's probably not helpful to hear, but please try to be patient."

I nodded, but I knew there was no way I was going to be patient.

Ed and Linda walked me back to the check-in line, mentioning along the way that there was nothing on the kids' schedule for the rest of the afternoon. We just had the evening welcome dinner.

"Glad you're with us," Ed said. "We're off to a counselors' meeting."

Linda looked me over. "You might want to rest now. We'll see you this evening."

I could still feel my heart pounding in my chest. As much as I probably needed a nap, I was way too excited to sleep.

●

I was inserting the key into the door of the room they'd assigned me when it suddenly swung inward. The guy holding it open was spewing energy, from the way he shifted weight from one foot to the other to the huge smile on his face to his athletic build—a football player's. "Jeff?" he asked, and I nodded. "I'm Mike," he said, and his smile got even wider. "We're gonna be roommates!"

I wished I had Mike around all the times I'd been accused of talking too much, which used to be a fair amount, because he would make me seem like the world's most patient listener. Over the next two hours, as I unpacked and lay on my bed, trying unsuccessfully to take a nap, he told me about his family, his hometown, his favorite sports teams, the most effective method for getting rid of athlete's foot, how in three easy steps any guy could get a girl to like him, and last, how he'd stumbled upon Youth Ambassadors of America. "How did you find them?" he asked. After his long monologue, I was amazed to be hearing a question.

"This organization called the Starlight Children's Foundation offered me a wish. I asked to come to the Soviet Union . . ." I nearly revealed the full wish, but decided to leave it at that, just in case the meeting with Mr. Gorbachev fell through. "The folks at Starlight connected me with YAA."

Mike, for the first time since we met, was silent. I knew the question that was formulating in his head, so I answered it pre-emptively. "And in case you were wondering, the reason I got a wish is because I had brain cancer."

For several seconds, Mike's silence continued. He plunked himself down on his bed—he'd been standing the whole time he spoke—and rubbed his jaw.

"Yes, it could come back, but I hope it doesn't."

"It's like you're reading my mind," he said.

The secret to my trick was that everybody I'd ever spoken with about my wish and my health asked the same questions.

"I'm a genius," I said, and then cracked up. "With half a brain."

"Wow. I just don't know what to say." He scratched his head. "I'll pray for you, man. For your health and happiness, every-thing."

The welcome dinner took place in the hotel's gala dining room. There were eighty of us, fifty kids and thirty adults, so even though the room was pretty big, we were elbow to elbow. The space was full of energy, enough to melt the snow outside. People were genuinely excited. When one of the coordinators wasn't talking to all of us, we were chatting with each other.

There was a girl at my table, my age or a little older, with tousled, shoulder-length blond hair, whose laugh caught my attention. It was just like Monique's—loud, warm, and infectious. She had pale skin and blue eyes, kind of like the attendants on our Finnair flight, but she spoke like a blue-collar American, saying the meat in the Finnish soup we'd just eaten didn't taste like any "sassage" she'd ever had. I didn't realize I was staring until our eyes locked and she smiled warmly.

A tapping sound came through the large speakers on the stage. Linda and Ed were standing there, checking to see if the microphone was switched on, and a counselor gave them a thumbs-up. Linda lifted the mic. With a big smile on her face, she shouted, "Hello, youth ambassadors!" She instantly had our attention.

She introduced herself and Ed and then welcomed us to Helsinki. "This is the official beginning of what we're certain will be a positively transformative trip for every one of you. Not only that, but for the world. You are here to make a difference, and the world needs it. More specifically, the world needs *you*."

I glanced around my table. Mike had straightened up. He held his chin high, as if he'd just been told he aced a test. The girl whose laugh reminded me of Monique's had a gleam in her eyes. Other people were nodding.

Linda talked about the purpose of the trip, to promote

universal peace and understanding, and to produce, along with our Soviet counterparts, a "declaration for the future" that would be sent to global leaders. Ed followed with the logistics. We'd spend three days in Helsinki, getting to know each other and learning communication strategies, after which we'd depart for the Soviet Union. We'd spend a day and a half in Leningrad and then take a night train to Moscow, the nation's capital. There, over the course of several days, we'd have our summit with young people from all over the Soviet Union. He added, a bit wryly, that we'd never be alone—Russian intelligence would be monitoring us—but that it was nothing to worry about.

Everyone in the room was excited about what was ahead. I shared their energy, but not the certainty—at least that I was going to make a difference. It depended on things I couldn't control—specifically, the meeting with Mr. Gorbachev going through. I had the same sense of purpose as the other people sitting at my table—to make the world a better place—but the measure of my success seemed different from the measure of theirs.

When Ed finished, a musician, Karl, took the stage. He had a guitar strapped to his chest and he sang a bunch of folk songs, getting the kids and the counselors all involved in the last one. Everyone clapped loudly when the song ended. Linda then told us we were done for the evening, and that while we were welcome to hang out and chat, we should try to get plenty of sleep.

I was the first to leave the room. I told the people at my table that I was exhausted, which was true, but I was leaving because I needed to think. I got back to our room, brushed my teeth, turned off the overhead light, and switched on the lamp next to Mike's bed. I was still awake when he came back an hour later, but I pretended to be asleep until I heard him start to snore.

For hours, I thought about the meeting: whether it would happen, what I would say to Mr. Gorbachev if it did, what I would say to my father if it didn't. The thoughts were consuming me—not allowing me to totally hear the music, to participate in conversations, to sleep—but also there was nothing I could do. Exhaustion always prevails, and it ultimately did. All those heavy thoughts turned into turbulent dreams.

I still woke early, at 6:22, minutes from when my dad typically headed out on his run. I'd asked him once why he ran so often, more in protest of his not being around than because I really wanted to know, but he gave me reasons I'd long remembered. He enjoyed the challenge of it. More importantly, though, it settled his mind.

I slipped out of bed and into a pair of sweatpants. I took some socks and pulled them over the ones I was already wearing, then stepped into my tennis shoes. I'd gone to bed in my sweatshirt, but I added a windbreaker, in addition to the ski hat I'd been missing while waiting for the bus outside our plane. Mike was snoring loudly. Quietly, I left the room.

The morning cold hit me the moment I stepped through the hotel doors. I began to run. The sky was a patchy gray, sometimes open enough for a beam of morning sunlight to come through the clouds and reflect off a building. I turned down one road, then onto another. I soon found myself on a street scattered with people. One woman was wrapped in a long fur coat, a man was wearing a wool jacket, and the rest mostly had parkas. Seeing their protection from the cold and noting the absence of my own, I ran faster.

There was a young woman walking with a little boy. I didn't notice him pointing at me, and my thigh crashed into his finger. Instantly, he started bawling, and I stopped in my tracks.

I turned and walked back to him, worried that I'd hurt him. He was clutching his mother's legs, and she was bending down to comfort him. When I reached them, she looked up, and I jerked back when I saw her. She had pretty, perfect hair, large brown eyes, and perfectly formed lips. With the sole exception of age, she looked exactly like Monique.

My heart had been beating so fast from the run I couldn't tell if the peculiarity of seeing Monique's doppelgänger on the opposite side of the planet had accelerated it—especially after hearing Monique's laugh replicated by someone in our group. The woman could tell I was worried I'd hurt her kid, and she smiled warmly, motioning with her hand to continue my run.

"I'm sorry," I said.

"All is good," she answered, gesturing again with her hand. I smiled at her and her son, whose bawling had softened to a whimper, and I took off again.

I was stunned to see Monique's twin, but the cold quickly forced me to refocus. It had gotten into my lungs, which were tightening. I didn't have my asthma medication with me, something Dr. Farbstein had prescribed after I came down with pneumonia, so I decided to turn back to the hotel. By the time

I stepped back through the large front doors, a deep freeze had gone through my whole body.

In our hotel room, with Mike still asleep, I slipped into the shower. The water was blazingly hot, though even cold water probably would have felt that way, too, at the moment. But soon it had soothed me, and my mind went back to the woman on the street, and then to Monique, and finally to a conversation we once had.

I'd called her on a Friday, and she'd asked me what I was up to over the weekend. I said I was thinking about seeing a movie with some friends, but I'd gotten a CT scan that morning and I wouldn't have the results until the following week.

"So lemme get this straight. You're actually skipping a movie—you know, having fun—because you're worried about possible bad news?"

I could picture Monique rolling her eyes when she said that.

"What, you don't get stressed about the idea of cancer coming back?"

"Duh, of course I do. I'm, you know, human. I just try not to let cancer take over my life, especially in *the moment.*"

"What does 'the moment' mean, exactly?"

"That's where we are, like, right now. That's where we live. Sure, my cancer might come back in a month or a year or never, and I definitely worry about it, but I'm not going to let my worry stop me from doing the things I want to do now. It's like that Buddhist thing—you know, living in the moment."

It struck me then that I could spend the whole trip worrying about whether I'd meet Mr. Gorbachev, or I could enjoy it along with everyone else, and be exceptionally happy if the meeting went through. I drew in a deep breath, then slowly let it out. For the first time in a while, I felt completely calm.

Just then, I heard a knock on the bathroom door. Mike was awake. "What's up?" I said.

"I just wanted to make sure you haven't drowned."

"I'm all good."

"One other thing, then, considering you've got this door locked," Mike said. "I seriously have to take a piss."

CHAPTER SIXTEEN

"Welcome to Leningrad!" Vitaly said, his voice—and thick Russian accent—booming through the speaker on our bus. Our tour guide was stocky, with a stomach that bulged beneath his buttoned blue wool sweater-vest and a smile so broad it nearly touched his closely cut salt-and-pepper hair. "Some of you look sad, but you should all be happy—you've been released from our notorious airport gulag!"

We'd touched down at Pulkovo Airport in the early morning. Compared to all the energy and activity in Helsinki, everything had slowed down. When we arrived, we were escorted through the cold to a door that opened into a long hallway. Soldiers wearing stern faces guarded every exit. We were told to form a line. With our passports and visas in hand, at a snail's pace, we appeared before uniformed, stone-faced men and women who sat behind walls of glass. Their eyes traveled back and forth repeatedly between our faces and our papers, until they finally stamped our passports and stiffly handed them back. Once we retrieved our luggage, we went through a similar process, with several of our bags subjected to searches. When we finally left the airport in the late morning, after hours trapped inside, the bar for our expectations had been set so low we could have tripped over it.

After Vitaly told us we should be happy, I looked at the other kids on the bus. A few were smiling. Most were looking at each other with their eyebrows raised. "Who knows what a gulag is?" Vitaly asked.

"A prison," Chace said. Maybe he'd learned that on one of his other trips.

"Exactly!" Vitaly said. "A shot of vodka for you. Joking! We have many gulags in the Soviet Union, not for you, but for us. If we show up to work five minutes late, they throw us in the gulag for sabotage. If we come five minutes early, we're thrown in for spying. Do you know what happens when we show up on time? They charge us for having a western watch!" Vitaly slapped his thigh so loudly that the mic he was holding picked up the sound. That made everyone crack up. Vitaly followed by laughing so heartily I thought a button might pop off his sweater.

On our way to the hotel, Vitaly asked us if we knew about the Siege of Leningrad. Some people nodded. My dad had told me a little about it, but I didn't really know the details. "I'm afraid there is no humor in this story," Vitaly said. "Beginning in September of 1941, the German army cut off our beautiful city from the outside world for 872 days. Our army had a small success on the eighteenth of January, 1943, when we opened a channel to the city, but it wasn't until the following year, on the twenty-seventh of January, 1944, that the siege was finally lifted. More than a million of our citizens were killed."

Everyone on the bus was silent as Vitaly told that story. For me, when he threw out those dates, a chill went through my spine. January 18 was my mother's birthday. January 27 was my own. I'd never been into astrology or numerology or any of that stuff, but those numbers made me feel a connection with Leningrad.

We checked in at the hotel, had lunch (thick brown bread and a big bowl of bright red soup—borscht, they called it—with beets and potatoes and little pieces of meat all stirred in), and then we returned to the bus. Vitaly was waiting for us. His smile and his belly were back in place. "A fantastic surprise is ahead," he said. "It is better than even your Disneyland. There are no rides—except for the thousands you will take inside your head!"

The bus plodded slowly through traffic, but no one really cared, because everything our eyes landed upon looked magical. The city seemed like it was floating, not just because of the massive river, the Neva, that meandered its way through, but because of the sequence of crisscrossing canals that cut through the land. We were pressed up against the glass, each of us carving out a spot so we could see, but doing it repeatedly as Vitaly pointed out sites on opposite sides of the bus. His laugh was nearly constant, which was warming, though the dates he'd mentioned before lunch, associated not only with the siege but with my mother's and my births, were very much on my mind. I kept trying to find meaning in them but never came to a conclusion.

"We Russians do not believe in religion," Vitaly said as the bus approached a large church. We'd seen half a dozen already, but none matched the scale of this one. "But each time I pass by the beautiful St. Isaac's Cathedral—that is the extraordinary structure you see off to your left—I wonder if I should reconsider."

The cathedral was like a multicolored version of the Capitol building in Washington, D.C., with a pale gray front, reddish-brown pillars, and a golden dome.

"If you're not religious, what do you use it for?" a girl named Mary asked. There was sarcasm in her voice. Some of the adults—two ladies—smiled. I'd already noticed the crosses on their necklaces.

Vitaly thought for a second. "For inspiration," he said. He was satisfied with his answer. "Yes, we use it for inspiration."

The bus continued along for a few more blocks before coming to a stop. There was a massive complex in front of us, a series of interconnected buildings with green and yellow facades, white pillars, and gold highlights. They surrounded an enormous open plaza with a red granite column rising from the center. There were people everywhere, pointing cameras in every direction or posing for pictures. Vitaly didn't have to tell us that we'd arrived at his Disneyland. The smile on his face revealed everything.

The Hermitage was the most spectacular place I'd ever seen. It wasn't just the five interconnected buildings, imposing on the outside, or their ornate interiors, with light pouring in through extravagant stained-glass windows, shining walls covered in sheets of gold, and parquet floors inlaid with complex designs. It was also the art inside. In Paris five years before, on our one family trip overseas, Dad had been excited—as excited as he ever got—to see the works of Matisse, Renoir, Manet, and others in the Musée du Jeu de Paume. All those masters, not to mention a bunch of others, were on display in the Hermitage. Dad would've been blown away.

After our group tour, the organizers said we could look around on our own, as long as we got back to the entrance by four-thirty. I'd hung out a lot with Karen in Helsinki during our orientation—she was the one who had a laugh just like Monique's—and during the museum tour we'd both been really impressed with the French masters. When she said she was heading back there, I asked if I could join her. "Of course," she said with a warm smile.

We walked through room after room. My eyes were on the art, but also on Karen. When she was struck by a piece, her eyes would widen, or she'd press her hand against her chest or slowly shake her head. She'd see me looking at her and smile, and I'd smile back, and we'd talk about the art. On a deeper level, I was feeling something, a draw to her, and I was wondering if she felt it, too.

In Room 319, we stopped in front of a work by Claude Monet, who the tour guide earlier had called the king of the Impressionists. I wasn't really into that kind of art, Impressionism, but Karen loved it. The first time we saw *Pond at Montgeron*, I even missed the people standing around the water, who blended into the background. Karen didn't. She saw everything. As she'd been doing throughout the tour, she examined the painting's surface, pausing here and there as she drew in a breath then let it out slowly. We were standing right next to each other, and when she shifted weight from one leg to the other, her hip touched my thigh. I turned toward her then, and she toward me, and I looked into her eyes. They seemed to be welcoming me. I leaned down to kiss her.

She dropped her head down, lifting her arm at the same time to look at her watch. I stepped back. "It's almost four-thirty, Jeff," she said. "We'd better head to the entrance."

I swallowed, then nodded. "Of course," I said, wanting to disappear. I started toward the stairs. She followed. It felt like an eternity passed before we finally arrived at the exit.

●

Back at the hotel, I passed by the phone booths. Mom was probably hysterical by then, not having heard from me. Even though I felt like hiding in my room after the embarrassing episode with Karen, this seemed like the best time to call.

Making a phone call to America turned out to be an extraordinarily bureaucratic process. I was told to wait in line, which was ridiculous, considering I was the only person there. They already had my passport, but I still had to fill out a form with my name and address and a bunch of other information. Then I waited in line again.

The lady processing my papers behind the front desk signaled to me that she was ready. She walked me to a booth and told me to sit. At six in the evening Leningrad time—eight in the morning for my parents—she dialed my number and handed me the phone. With all the hoops I'd had to jump through to make the call—and considering what Ed had said about us always being monitored—I wouldn't have been surprised to learn the call was being recorded.

After two rings, Dad answered.

"Hi," I said.

"Jeff," he answered, sounding surprised. "It's good to hear from you." I wasn't exactly expecting that. "Your mother has been anxious to speak with you. Just a second." Even with his hand covering the receiver, I could hear him bellowing her name.

"Jeff!" she said, breathing heavily. She'd probably raced to the phone. "How are you? Are you okay?"

"Hi, Mom. I'm great. They let us out of our cages today."

"Very funny. Where are you?"

"In Leningrad, at the hotel. It's a beautiful city, a lot like Paris, if you can believe it. We're only here until tomorrow evening. Then we'll take an overnight train to Moscow."

"Are the trains safe?"

"Mom, are you serious? We're fine. Everybody here is really nice."

"No one is trying to convince you to stay there, are they?" She was impossible sometimes.

"Mom, I'm with a group of Americans, remember? Several have been here before and they somehow managed to return to the good ol' US of A completely intact. I promise, I'll be home in less than a week." I thought about appealing to Dad to calm her down, but he was rarely good at that. Anyway, he threw in a question of his own, which got her to switch to listening mode.

"Have you heard anything from Mr. Gorbachev's office?"

"I haven't personally. The directors of Youth Ambassadors of

America told me that their Moscow contact has been in touch with Mr. Gorbachev's office, but there hasn't been any scheduling of a meeting yet."

"So it remains uncertain." In an instant, all the tension I'd left behind in the shower after my run in Helsinki came back. I wanted to get off the phone.

"Yes, Dad, it remains uncertain. Listen, on top of the connection fee I have to pay, it's four dollars a minute for this call. I need to go."

"We're covering it," Mom jumped in.

"I have to pay the hotel in cash. That's the only way. So I really do have to leave you now." I heard her sigh. "I'll see you in just a week."

"Okay, Jeff, but please, please be careful."

"I will, Mom. I promise."

"Take care of yourself, Jeff," Dad said.

Taking care of myself was precisely why I was trying to get off the phone. I honestly felt like telling him that, but I was glad I didn't. It would've spoiled Mom's "I love yous," and she needed to get in four of them. I probably needed to hear them. "I love you, too, Mom," I said, and hung up.

I stayed in the booth for a few minutes. The day had started so nicely, with Vitaly's energized city tour and our visit to the Hermitage. But things went south with Karen, which was awkward enough, and then Dad, in seconds, managed to reduce me to a bundle of anxiety.

The lady who'd dropped me off in the booth tapped on the window. Apparently, it wasn't okay for me to sit there. I wiped my face with my shirt and stepped out. She motioned toward the front desk, where she handed me a bill for eighty-five dollars.

●

The next day, after a hearty hotel breakfast—I deliberately sat as far away from Karen as possible—everyone boarded the bus to continue the city tour. We hadn't seen much the day before, only places on the way to the Hermitage, so the plan was to take in as much of Leningrad as we could before dinner at the hotel and our night train to Moscow.

Sitting next to one of our assistant coordinators, Bruce, was a new face. The stranger hid his eyes behind thick black-framed sunglasses. His hair was dense and puffy, kind of like Bob Dylan's in the 1960s. He was wearing a dark brown suit that looked like it came from the same period, over a blue shirt with a striped tie, and a silk scarf with so many shapes woven into it that it reminded me of the Hermitage's parquet floors. If Lucia had seen him, she would've immediately called the fashion police. I was more wondering if he was an agent for the KGB.

We spent the day exploring the city. Highlights included St. Isaac's Cathedral; a massive waterfront fortress established by Peter the Great that was now a museum; a monument to Peter the Great where he's sitting on a horse (it looked like the horse was trying to buck him off); and a walk down Nevsky Prospect, the main road, which apparently shows up in tons of Russian literature. I didn't realize what a big deal a street could be until Vitaly shared a few stories.

The fashion offender on our bus walked around with us, mostly talking to Bruce, the coordinators, and the adult volunteers. I noticed him looking at me a lot. Bruce knew my story—about the wish and everything—and the coordinators and volunteers had definitely talked about it. Several of them had told me what a beautiful wish they thought it was. "If it comes true," I had to remind them, though they said it didn't matter. Anyway, I figured the Soviet guy had been told my story. After I saw him glance back at me three times during our bus ride to St. Isaac's Cathedral, I decided I was going to do something about it. He and Bruce stayed on the bus as the rest of us got off. Just as I passed him, I suddenly turned and said, *"Dobri dyen,"* which means "Good afternoon." His eyebrows shot up and his mouth dropped open. I thought I'd freaked him out, but then his face calmed. He smiled, dipped his head, and said *"Dobri dyen"* in reply.

When we got back to the hotel, as I was stepping into the elevator to go up to my room, Bruce tapped my shoulder. I turned around. "What's up?" I said. He motioned for me to come out of the elevator.

"The man I was sitting with on the bus today—" Bruce started to say.

"The one who was staring at me?" I interrupted, with a smirk on my face.

Bruce laughed.

"Yes, that man. He's a journalist for a popular Leningrad youth newspaper. He came to do a story on Youth Ambassadors of America."

"Why were you guys all secret about it?"

"He didn't want to influence anyone's behavior—you know, just wanted to quietly observe. But he's very interested in your personal story, and he'd like to interview you."

"When would that happen?"

"Well, before we leave this evening for Moscow." I looked at my watch, then lifted my wrist so Bruce could see the time.

"After I pack. I'll meet you back here in half an hour."

•

Stepping out of the elevator, walking down the hallway toward my room, I saw Karen. She was knocking on the door to my room. My instinct was to retreat, but she saw me.

"Hey, Jeff," she said. "Do you have a second?"

I swallowed. "I'm kind of in a rush. I have to pack. Then I have to meet with a guy downstairs."

"I'll be quick."

I shuffled my feet. "Okay."

"Look, things got a little awkward yesterday."

I scratched my head. "Did they? When?"

"At the museum. When you tried to kiss me."

"I didn't try to kiss you."

"Oh, okay. Well, I just wanted to say, even if that's not what you were after, that I really, really wanted to kiss you. You're an amazing guy, Jeff. You really are. I love talking with you. The thing is, I've got a boyfriend back home. We've been going through a rough patch, but we're trying to make it work. That's why I need to keep us just friends."

"I get it."

"Do you?"

"I do. I really do." I glanced behind me to see if we were alone. The hallway was clear. "Okay, maybe I did try to kiss you. I didn't know you had a boyfriend."

"Of course."

"And I like you, too. Especially your crazy laugh. It kind of reminds me of this girl back home."

"What, your girlfriend?" A smirk appeared on her face.

It wasn't funny to me. "No. We're just friends."

Karen's smirk disappeared. Her eyes focused on mine. She was listening.

"She's also got someone."

Karen gave me a sad smile. I didn't want to get all emotional in front of her.

"It's no big deal," I said unconvincingly.

"Well, I'll let you get to packing. Just know for sure that I want to spend time with you, and talk about things, and be real friends. I think you're a cool guy, Jeff."

"Thanks, Karen. I think you're pretty cool yourself."

She walked off and I entered the room. When the door closed behind me, I leaned against it. My shoulders dropped. My breathing slowed. The stress, at least with her, had dissipated. Dad was still on my mind, but he was back home. Here, in the moment, I felt at peace.

●

"I am Nikolai Sivach," the reporter said in heavily accented English, jumping to his feet as I entered the sitting room. Bruce had dropped me off there, and we were steps away from the dining room, where everyone would soon be having supper. Mr. Sivach grabbed my hand and shook it vigorously. "It is great pleasure to meet you."

"Nice to meet you, Mr. Sivach."

"Please call me Nikolai. This is Ivan. He will translate."

I smiled at Ivan, a young man with short black hair standing next to him.

"Great. Shall we sit down?"

The room was like a cheap copy of the Hermitage, with wall sections covered in sapphire blue curtains and separated by shiny brass plates and marble tiles. There were three chairs in a corner, next to a table with a large recorder on it. Nikolai motioned in that direction.

"What made you interested in all the world's problems?" Nikolai asked through Ivan. I'd been asked the same question by a reporter who'd written a story about me and my wish in our local newspaper.

"Before I got sick, I didn't care too much about them. I knew what was going on from watching the news, but I was more interested in my own life. Everything changed when I got the diagnosis. I started seeing all the problems we have in our country, the homelessness and poverty, and how we weren't addressing them. Instead, we were investing in weapons of mass murder. And I noticed that you—the Soviet Union, that is—were doing the same. Frankly, it really angered me."

"What do you expect from your meeting with Mikhail Sergeyevich Gorbachev, if it takes place?"

"I have a lot of questions for him, but I also have a lot to tell him. I think he's receptive to other opinions, even those of young people. Our countries are no longer enemies, but we're certainly not friends. We're still pointing nuclear missiles at each other. We need to abandon this suicidal mission of mutually assured destruction and help our people let go of their fear, and even develop a friendship."

"So you believe one person can change the world?"

I thought about that for a minute. "I believe that in certain circumstances an individual can influence the course of events. What I think is unfortunate is when we don't try. Why can't we realize that the only way to bring about change is to make an attempt in the first place?"

"And you are one of these people?"

"I doubt I can bring happiness to the whole of humanity, if that's what you're asking, but if I'm able to do even a tiny bit, I believe I must try."

"Sorry, Jeff, but isn't that a bit naive? Young people don't have any political power."

All the coordinators in Youth Ambassadors of America had told us this wasn't true—and not to believe anyone who said otherwise.

"We do have power, Nikolai. It may not be immediate political power. But adults would be naive not to realize that we, in fact, are the future."

Nikolai seemed struck by that, because when Ivan translated it for him, his head cocked, his lips parted, and he slowly nodded.

He went on to a bunch more topics, from the cancer diagnosis to how I found out about the Starlight Foundation to—and this was truly odd—who my favorite general was.

"From everything we've just talked about, do you really think I have a favorite general?" I asked. I didn't want him to feel like a complete idiot, so I gave him a little smile, but it was a pretty stupid question.

"I think you probably don't."

"Let's get back to that question about whether one person can change the course of history. I think one can. Think of presidents, think of politicians. But I don't think it's necessary to be at the height of power to bring about change. Regular people, like me, can find friends in this world, people who are willing to work together right now to prevent the extinction of humanity. Youth Ambassadors of America came here for that reason, and I am here with them." I edged forward, my eyes focused on Nikolai's. "You chose to interview me because I have cancer and I made my wish and I might be on my way out, but there are all these people here who want to make the world a better place, and tons of Americans back home. All of us have a common goal. We want peace." I thought about that for a few seconds, then added, "If I really am going to die, I strongly hope we'll take solid steps in that direction before I do."

We heard sounds coming through the wall behind us—the clinking of silverware and glasses, along with laughter—and it seemed like a good place to end our conversation. I patted my stomach, and Nikolai picked up the cue.

"You have to eat dinner," he said, switching off his recorder. The three of us stood. I smiled and put out my hand to Nikolai. He grabbed it and pulled me toward him. He held me close for several seconds, then patted my back. Finally, he let me go. It was awkward, until I saw him pull a scarf from his pocket and wipe his eyes. "I hope to see you again, Jeff," he said.

"Yes, Mr. Sivach. I mean, Nikolai. I hope to see you again, too."

I thanked him and Ivan and left, hurrying next door to see if there was still any food. I was definitely hungry. Bruce, I quickly discovered, had been kind enough to save me a plate.

•

On the train to Moscow that night, I couldn't sleep. My mind revisited everything we'd seen in Leningrad, which I'd concluded was the most beautiful city in the world. I thought about Karen, who was probably asleep now. She'd sat next to me as I ate dinner, asking about the interview. I told her everything. She kept shaking her head, and finally she said, "You see, Jeff, I *knew* you were amazing." Even if she was never going to be my girlfriend, it definitely felt good.

Monique entered my mind, which wasn't a surprise, given that Karen and I had talked about her. I felt bad that we'd stopped talking. But I also wondered what she'd say about my wish. She'd tell me it wasn't the thing that truly made me happy or something like that, and I didn't want to hear it. But I did miss her.

As Mike snored in the cot across from me, I switched on the nightlight and pulled out my diary. I read through my notes on what Vitaly had said about the Siege of Leningrad, all 872 days of it. The dates—January 18 and 27, my mother's birthday and mine—really did make me feel connected to the city we were leaving behind.

A thought popped into my head. It probably came from a curiosity I had with numbers, like the way I'd calculated everyone's lifespan after reading their tombstones in the cemetery where my friend Sylvia was buried. I wondered about my own siege, starting with brain surgery on August 8, 1986. If I added 872 days to it, what date would I end up on? Maybe that day would be my liberation.

It took me several minutes to do the math. I ended up with December 27, 1988. Goose bumps appeared all over my forearms, and a chill shot up my spine. December 27 was my father's birthday.

It felt so strange, to have these dates and numbers so significant to Leningrad and its remarkable history connected in their own way to me and my family. I knew my mother, if I showed her what I discovered, would be filled with wonder. It would only be momentary. Dad would intervene, saying it was mere happenstance.

But there I was on a train, crossing the Soviet countryside, the world around me lit by stars and a waning moon. I was *actually* moving in the direction of my wish—toward Moscow, where it had the potential to be fulfilled. It didn't matter that the dates wouldn't mean much to Dad. What mattered was the wish. How would he react if I came home with the news that I'd met with Premier Gorbachev, that the two of us had sat down together and discussed how to bring an end to nuclear weapons and the Cold War? Dad would nod at first, only acknowledging what I said, but internally, he'd be analyzing it carefully. Slowly and steadily, a smile would form on his face, like the sun rising, and soon, even if he said nothing at all, he'd be beaming with pride. That prospect thoroughly warmed me, as if the whole windy moonlit sky overhead had been replaced by the sun at high noon, guiding me to a brilliant, beautiful new world. In that state, I quickly fell asleep.

CHAPTER SEVENTEEN

I was asleep, deep in a dream that had me trudging through endless fields of snow, toward a figure that kept moving farther away, when our train came to a halt. It had a few times already, stopping at dimly lit stations before lurching forward once again into the darkness, but this stop was different. It was a long one. Movement was the thing that kept me asleep, like it used to in my mom's car when she drove me back from radiation treatments, and I'd wake up automatically when the motion ceased. So it was in that particular station, where we were held in place, that I came back to consciousness.

Mike, in the bunk across from me, was still snoring. My attention turned to the hallway, where I could hear steps coming through the thin sliding door of our dark cabin. I'd heard some before, probably from one of the red-jacketed attendants passing through, since we'd been told to stay in our cabins, but these were different. The pace was accelerated and there was force behind each step, the sound of boots instead of shoes, coming from more than one person.

I tugged back the curtain covering our window, and after my eyes adjusted to the flood of light coming from the station lamps, I saw soldiers, dozens of them, with heavy jackets on over their uniforms. Some were walking toward the train cars. A chill went through my spine. "Mike," I said tersely, but he didn't respond. I switched the table light on, grabbed my pillow, and threw it at his head. He groaned.

"What's your problem?" he said.

Just then, the door to our cabin slid open. It was Bruce. He had his hat and coat on, but he was shivering. Behind him was a soldier.

"What's going on?" I asked.

"I'm not sure. We're being told to get off the train. Just get dressed and pack fast. Don't forget your jackets—it's damn cold out there. I'll tell you when to leave. Understood?" I nodded.

Bruce walked to the next cabin, but the soldier stayed in place. I tried to close the door, but he blocked it with his foot. "*Nyet*," he said coldly. When Mike and I stepped into the hallway, we could see a soldier standing in front of each cabin.

Minutes later, all of us were outside shivering. Some of the kids were whimpering. The adults on our team were trying to reassure them, but they kept looking nervously at each other, which hardly helped. We watched as the soldiers searched the train, for what, we couldn't figure out. Ed and Linda, with the help of one of our interpreters, were pleading with an official, and they followed him into the station after a uniformed woman unlocked a side door. I wanted to go to Karen, who looked shaken, but there were other soldiers who were watching us closely, so I stayed in place. The cold seemed to reach all of us, the soldiers excepted, and in a way it numbed our fear, forcing us to focus on our bodies as we moved about trying to keep warm. It seemed like a century had passed before Ed and Linda finally returned, and when they did, they found our whole team huddled closely together.

We returned to the train then, with no explanation of what had happened, other than a "misunderstanding" had taken place. Our only needs were warmth and sleep. The attendants, in their red uniforms, made us tea. I clutched my glass in both hands, holding it close to my chest. My earlier shock was reduced to unease, and the train resumed its journey to Moscow.

●

We pulled into the Leningradsky station in Moscow just before eight in the morning, and after a quiet, sleepy bus ride, we checked in at Hotel Cosmos, a twenty-five-story brownish-orange building curved like a rainbow that had been tipped onto its side. In the lobby, Ed waved me over. He was talking with a man in a striped black suit. "This is Gennady Vasilyev," Ed said. "He's our Moscow contact who's been working on your big meeting."

I quickly extended my hand, and Gennady shook it. He was thin and tall, in a suit that fit him well but clashed with his brown shoes. "It's a pleasure to meet you," I said. I was praying he was going to tell me that the meeting had been set.

"I am not yet have confirmation, Jeff," he said. I noticed my palms were almost instantly damp; I slipped my hands into my pockets. Gennady wasn't finished. His eyes were scanning my clothes. "You have suit, yes? Also tie, business shoes?" I definitely liked the sound of that.

"Yes, Gennady, though my suit's in this," I said, pointing to my suitcase.

"Put it out in your room. You might go to meeting with only, how you say, moment's notice."

"Definitely, Gennady. I'll be ready."

After breakfast, some of the group took a nap, but I spent the time getting out my suit and hiding it from Mike's view in the closet. I still hadn't told my roommate about the meeting with Gorbachev, and planned not to until the last possible minute, in part so I wouldn't be made a fool of if it fell through, but also because I wasn't up for all the dumb cracks that would inevitably come out of his mouth about a meeting with one of the most important people in the world.

Once we got all settled into our rooms and rested for a bit, we reassembled downstairs for our city tour. Something was going on—you could tell—because there was tons of whispering and eyebrows were shooting up all over the place. That's when I saw Mike, who'd skipped out on a nap. I walked over to him. "What's up?" I asked.

"You didn't hear the news?"

I shook my head.

"One of the girls in our group who hadn't gone upstairs for a nap went to grab her camera later, and there were a couple of guys going through her luggage."

I frowned. "What, like in her room?"

"Yeah, just a few minutes ago. Rumor is it's the KGB."

It was a little eerie, but Ed had warned us back in Helsinki that the Russians had been watching us. I wasn't worried. If they looked through my stuff, they wouldn't find anything interesting. I just hoped the same was true for Mike.

It took so long for us to get loaded onto the tour bus that all that excitement was mostly replaced with boredom by the time we pulled out of the hotel lot. The weather didn't help. It seemed overcast. But the sky was filled not with clouds, it turned out, but a curtain of thick gray smog. It came from the tailpipe of almost every car on the road, mostly boxy sedans that looked as if they'd been teleported from the 1960s, spewing black soot into the air. The sidewalks were packed with people trudging through the smog, which, along with buildings splattered across the landscape, some of them beautiful but most industrial and bland, reminded me of L.A.

Our first stop, our tour guide Igor told us, was Red Square. He explained that we'd be walking for a bit, so we hopped off the bus and followed. We were awaiting a story, but none came, so the conversations picked up between us, mostly about how much we missed our Leningrad tour guide, Vitaly.

I was walking with Mike and Chace. Another kid, Jeremy, hurried up alongside us. "Guys, I think we're being followed," he said.

"By who?" Mike asked.

By whom? I thought, though I kept my mouth shut. If there was anything Mike was good at—other than sleeping—it was mutilating the English language.

"He's fifty feet back or so. Wearing a trench coat."

It sounded ludicrous. All of us looked back. Sure enough, we saw a guy wearing a trench coat. He turned and looked into a store window, as if he was shopping.

"Give me a break," Mike said.

"I'm serious," Jeremy said. "I saw him right when we got out of the bus. He stops whenever we do. He's totally checking us out." Ed and Linda had told us back in Helsinki that the Soviet government would keep an eye on us but it was nothing to worry about. One of the coordinators said it could even get a little entertaining, because they act the same way they do in the movies.

"Then let's surprise him," Mike said, with a huge grin on his face, going on to describe his plan.

Chace liked it. "I'm in," he said. Jeremy nodded. For a second, I wondered if this might get me in trouble as far as my meeting was concerned. I reasoned this guy was watching our whole group, though, not just me, so I decided it would be fine.

"Me too," I said.

There was a slight hill with a road going up it that extended into Red Square. Mike took a casual look back. "Is he there?" Jeremy asked.

"Yup, still about fifty feet back," Mike said.

We passed a bland, redbrick building on our left, with nothing in particular to look at, and continued along. When we figured our target was near the building, Mike started his countdown. "In three . . . two . . . ONE!" The four of us spun around, hollered out *"Privyet"*—"hello" in Russian—and waved. Our man whirled 90 degrees to his left to do his pretend window shopping, but the only thing in front of him was a brick wall. We laughed so hard and for so long that I was wheezing when we reached Red Square.

The rest of the day wasn't quite as eventful, though we saw some spectacular stuff. Not far from where we pulled our prank on that blundering snooper was the most beautiful building in all of Moscow: St. Basil's Cathedral, a stunning domed church in Red Square. Honestly, though, even if I didn't feel that connection with Leningrad, I would've taken that city *any* day over Moscow. It wasn't just the capital's awful air quality, which we could all feel deep in our lungs by the end of the day, but the people. They weren't mean or anything like that, just distant and impersonal, focused on themselves, like New Yorkers seemed when I went to visit my cousin in Manhattan. Plus, while Moscow had some great sites, it was lacking the Hermitage, which Karen and I agreed was the most amazing museum either of us had ever been to. If I were charged with putting together the sightseeing aspect of the trip, I'd start in Moscow, since that would get people excited, but I'd finish in Leningrad, a place that would blow everyone away.

It was so hard not to say anything to Mike about my wish. With my suit hidden, and the almost unfathomable possibility of meeting the leader of one the most powerful countries in the world, I felt a bit like the spy who'd been following us. I thought about it in the shower, how I was hiding the truth, and it struck me that I'd been doing the same thing at home. When I was in pain, I never really let my mom know the extent of it. It was no different with Dad. I never told him how much it hurt sometimes to be his son. I didn't come to any grand conclusion there, as I let the hot water trickle down my back. I just realized it wasn't the best way to live.

We went downstairs together for breakfast. I saw Gennady in the main lobby, and he waved at me. I told Mike to start, that I'd catch up with him in a minute. He was voraciously hungry every morning, so he didn't require much persuading.

"Your suit, Jeff," Gennady said. "Is it unwrinkled?"

I gulped in air. I couldn't believe what I was hearing. Gennady winked at me.

"Are you serious, Gennady?" I bounced from one foot to the other.

"There is not guarantee for meeting, Jeff, please understand. But I have instruction to ask you be here in hotel lobby tomorrow morning at seven, dressed in suit."

I was breathless. I didn't know what to say.

"You understand?" Gennady asked.

"Yes, Gennady, I understand. I'll be there." I remembered the present I'd brought for Mr. and Mrs. Gorbachev, a copy of my school yearbook, signed by teachers and students. "I have a book for Mr. Gorbachev. Should I bring it with me?"

"Absolutely," Gennady said. It sure sounded like a guarantee.

Walking away from Gennady, I wanted to scream. I actually clenched my fists and bit my lip just to hold it in. A few feet away from the main doors, I drew in a deep breath, held it for several seconds, and then blew it out. I stepped into the dining room.

I found Mike sitting alone in the middle of the room, looking out the window. Karen was with some of the girls. She saw me and smiled, pointing to an empty seat at her table. I smiled back but motioned toward Mike.

When I reached Mike's table, he had a glass full of tea in one hand, and a big chunk of jam-covered *bliny*—Russian pancakes—on the fork he was holding, and his mouth was loaded with food. Still, he managed to ask me who I'd been talking to, with surprisingly little food falling out of his mouth.

"The guy by the front desk? He was just checking up on me. I think they're worried about my whole cancer history." I was lying flagrantly, but Mike bought it.

"Oh, okay. I was beginning to think *you* were with the KGB—you know, reporting to your boss." He slapped his thigh and laughed. I rolled my eyes. "Hey, something else happened, I just heard."

"How do you possibly have conversations with your mouth full?"

"I can totally stuff my face and listen at the same time. Anyway, Eric, the guy from Washington we had breakfast with yesterday, peeled a patch of mismatched wallpaper from his room and found a couple microphones in holes behind it. I'm telling you, man, we are totally being watched."

"I think you mean *listened to*."

"You can be so anal sometimes."

Mike tossed his napkin on the table and abruptly stood up. I thought I'd pissed him off—until he spoke. "Speaking of anal, the bathroom is calling."

"Further details are neither required nor desired," I said.

He grinned and took off.

I made my way through my porridge, a weird-tasting version of American oatmeal, before turning to my tea. Russians are really into the stuff, and it was all right with a couple of spoonfuls of sugar. I looked out onto the square, sipping away, and then it struck me that on the following day, at the same time, I might be having tea with one of the most powerful leaders in the world. What would my father say? Not *remarkable*, since that only meant something worth a remark. *Extraordinary* wouldn't be his word of choice, either, because it didn't express the degree to which something was beyond ordinary. He'd use a word I've hardly ever heard him say—"amazing"—and the most remarkable, extraordinary, amazing thing about it would be that he'd be referring to his own son.

I was lost in the feeling of that when Karen called my name. "Want to come back to Earth?" she asked.

"Sure," I said, smiling. "Sit down for a second. I want to tell you something."

She sat, squinting at me and tilting her head. "What's going on in that head of yours, Jeff?"

I couldn't keep my secret any longer.

"Remember back in Helsinki when I told you I was on this trip because I'd made a wish?"

"Of course. This is your peace mission to the Soviet Union."

"Right. So my *full* wish is to sit down with Premier Gorbachev, you know, talk about nuclear weapons and the Cold War and all that stuff. And it looks like that might happen tomorrow morning."

"No way!" she said, slapping the table. Her mouth dropped open. She slowly shook her head. "That's . . . that's just incredible," she said.

"I know. I can hardly believe it myself. I'm supposed to show up in the lobby tomorrow morning at seven o'clock in a suit."

"Did you bring one?"

"Yes, I did."

Karen had a dazed look on her face. "What are you going to say to him?"

"I'm not sure. Don't jinx it or anything. They made a point of telling me it's not guaranteed. Just that I should show up tomorrow morning in my suit."

"That sounds pretty guaranteed to me."

"I know, but I'm being cautious. Look, I had to get that off my chest. I'm not telling anyone else, except for my roommate tonight, so please keep this absolutely secret."

She touched her chest. "Thank you for choosing to share that with me, Jeff." Then she laughed and quickly shook her head again, as if she were clearing her mind. "Here we go again," she said as she stood. "Proof that you're incredible."

It took the most intense discipline not to mention my possible meeting with Mr. Gorbachev to anyone else in our group for the rest of the day. Every time I got close to telling someone, I bit my lip. It left a mark, but it did get me through the afternoon sessions, dinner, and the first half hour back in the room with Mike. It was against hotel rules to leave the room after 10:00 at night, and given that it was now 9:58, I figured I could let the cat out of the bag.

Mike's reaction was a lot like Karen's. He was dumbfounded. "Dude, why didn't you tell me about your whole wish?"

"I wasn't sure it would come true. My chances now are much better."

"Wait a sec, is that why you were talking to that guy before breakfast?"

"Yeah, I kind of fibbed. Sorry."

"Why didn't you just tell me?"

"I still don't want everyone to know, until it actually happens. Do you really think it would have been possible for you to keep your mouth shut?"

"No, but you should have told me anyway. I can't believe you're gonna meet the Gorbster!"

"Dude!" I said, putting a finger over my lips and pointing to the five-inch-square patch of mismatched wallpaper above my bed. As soon as we heard about the bug in Eric's room, we'd looked for one in ours. The mismatch seemed pretty obvious. And this was after that girl in our group found two guys searching her suitcase. I wasn't being neurotic, and Mike definitely knew it—the KGB really did have their eyes on us.

"Oh, come on. They're not going to care," Mike said.

I was wondering if I should say anything when we heard three quick knocks on the door. Both Mike and I stiffened. My stomach knotted up, so much that I keeled over for a second, but Mike's focus was squarely on the door. "Do you think that's them?" he whispered, sitting up. "What should we do?" There were more knocks. He stood next to the door and looked back at me, waiting for instructions.

"Open it," I said as my hands started to quiver.

Standing at the entrance were two girls from our group, Heidi and Kim. They were shaking. "We're in trouble," Heidi said. "Please please please let us in." Kim glanced nervously down the hallway.

"It's past curfew," I said from where I still sat on the bed. "You're supposed to be in your room."

"We don't have the key," Kim said. "We'll get busted. Can you just let us in?"

Mike looked over to me. "Come on, Jeff. They obviously need some help."

My shoulders dropped a foot, which Mike read as me conceding, and he ushered them in. He quietly closed the door.

"Thank you *so much*, guys," Heidi said, plopping down on Mike's bed. "Mind if I sit down?"

"You just did," I said, frowning. I was getting increasingly concerned, and it felt like the knot in my stomach was tightening.

"Don't you worry about Jeff," Mike said to Heidi. "He needs a chill pill. I would, too, if I were having a high-power meeting with the Gorbster tomorrow morning." I couldn't believe what I was hearing.

"*Mike*," I said sharply.

"Gorbachev?" Kim said, coming over to me. "Are you meeting with Mikhail Gorbachev?"

"I'm supposed to."

Kim seemed stunned. "Wow," she finally said. "That's incredible."

"What are you going to talk about?" Heidi asked.

"Lots of things," I said. I really didn't want to go into the details. I wanted them to leave, but they probably would get in trouble, and I couldn't just throw them to the wolves. My mind raced to find a solution, because surely, they couldn't settle in with us for the night.

"Jeff primarily wants to know if that massive wine-colored splotch on Gorby's forehead is real," Mike said before cracking up at his own stupid joke.

"Not funny," I said.

Kim was smiling. Heidi giggled. Mike pointed at their faces.

"Okay, perhaps slightly funny, but not helpful," I conceded.

I shouldn't have given Mike an inch, because he took off with it.

"Helpful," Mike said. "That's what you need to be, Jeff. When you're in there with the Gorbster, offer to polish his splotch. That could be a big first step toward world peace."

Kim tried to hold back her laugh but couldn't any longer when Heidi lost it. Mike had a huge grin on his face. He was satisfied. I, on the other hand, was fuming.

I imagined what was going on in the office where our conversation was being monitored. They were hearing jokes being cracked about their leader. We were violating hotel rules by having the girls in the room. All of this was jeopardizing something I'd worked so hard for.

I stood up, took three long steps to the door, and opened it. "Get out," I said to the girls. Their smiles turned to frowns.

"Come on, Jeff," Mike said. "We're just playing around."

I stared at him coldly. "You can leave with them," I said.

"Where are we supposed to go?" Kim asked, pouting.

"Wake up one of the coordinators. I honestly don't care. Just get out of my room—*now*." They stared at me, but I didn't budge. After a few seconds, they left.

I switched off the overhead light by the door. Both bedside lamps were on, and I could see Mike sitting there, scratching his cheek. "I didn't mean to piss you off," he finally said. I stayed silent. "Jeff, I was just playing around."

I wanted to slap him. The meeting was my only chance to do something truly meaningful with my life, and he'd put it in jeopardy. But if people were listening, and I was sure they were, getting into a huge fight with Mike might only worsen my chances. The only thing I could do was hope, and for that I needed silence.

"Good night, Michael," I said as sternly as possible, and switched off my lamp. To my surprise, he got the point.

•

I woke up early, before my alarm went off, and slipped into the bathroom, holding my suit and tie. Even though it had taken ages to calm down enough to fall asleep, I felt fully rested. In the shower, I thought about whether I should bow to Mr. Gorbachev or shake his hand, and decided that somebody would instruct me; all I had to do was get my tie on right. In the end it was good that I woke up early, since it took me seven tries.

With my suit on, my tie in place, and my ski jacket in hand—I didn't have an overcoat—I tiptoed my way through our room.

"Good luck," Mike said as I turned the knob.

"Sorry, I didn't mean to wake you up."

"If anybody's sorry, it's me, Jeff. I was a jerk last night. I hope everything goes well."

"Thanks." I appreciated the apology. "See you later—and please apologize to the girls for me. I was just freaking out."

"Will do. I'm sure they'll understand. Now go represent for us."

Ed was downstairs with Gennady and a guy I hadn't seen before. He looked very official—he was dressed in a suit—which was promising. I walked up to them and said good morning.

Gennady introduced me to Vladimir Petrov. "It is a pleasure to meet you, Jeff," he said.

"A pleasure to meet you as well, Mr. Petrov."

"I am sorry to inform you that Mikhail Sergeyevich Gorbachev is unable to meet with you today. Something important has come up."

I swallowed.

"I see." I thought quickly. "That's fine, because we'll be here for five more days, and I'm sure I could come any time he is available." I looked to Ed to back me up, and he nodded.

"Yes, Jeff. I understand," Mr. Petrov said. "I am sorry but Premier Gorbachev will be busy for as long as you are here." I felt as if I'd just gotten punched in the gut. Mr. Petrov went on. "But a very important person, Dr. Evgeny Velikhov, a scientist who is an expert on nuclear affairs, would like to meet with you. He is with his wife, Natalia, at their dacha, their home in the countryside, and they have invited you to come visit."

I didn't respond for several seconds. I couldn't. I felt completely winded, like those times when I was a kid and tried to run alongside my dad, or like in the hospital after surgery, when Dr. Egan had me stand up for the first time. I'd been given a wish, and in so many ways I'd put my whole life into it.

In a single sentence, it had evaporated.

I felt as if I'd evaporated, too.

Ed said my name, which pulled me back to the moment, and I spoke. "That is very kind, Mr. Petrov." Everyone smiled, and I followed suit, though their smiles came from relief and mine was a forgery.

"Excellent," Mr. Petrov said. "A ZiL will pick you up after breakfast." I had no idea what he meant, but I didn't bother asking. "You do not need to wear a suit. Just bring an overnight bag."

We shook hands and I went back upstairs. Mike was coming out of the bathroom with a towel wrapped around his waist. "Did you forget something?" he asked.

"The meeting has been canceled." It was painful to hear myself say that.

"Oh God. Was it because of last night? I'm so sorry, Jeff. Jeez, I can't even begin to tell you how sorry I am."

A tear started down my cheek, but I wiped it away. Mike's eyes were on the floor. I drew in a long breath and slowly blew it out.

"I'll never know, Mike. But listen"—he looked at me—"I never want to talk about it again, okay?"

"Yeah, I got it."

I started changing into regular clothes and stuffed the basics into my backpack. Mike asked where I was going, and I told him I'd be meeting a scientist and his wife somewhere in the countryside and I'd be back the next day.

Still in his towel, Mike came over to shake my hand. "I hope it's a truly satisfying trip," he said.

I could tell he was being sincere. And he obviously hadn't meant to scuttle my meeting. For all the disappointment I was feeling, I couldn't be mad at the guy.

"Look, Mike, if you don't take two hours to get ready, and if you can avoid cracking jokes about nuclear scientists, we can have breakfast together," I said.

Mike looked at me sheepishly.

"Dude, I'm kidding," I said. "Well, I guess I'm serious, since you're not supposed to leave the room naked, and I would like to grab a bite with you." I smiled at Mike, and he smiled back.

●

I assumed a ZiL was a kind of driver, but instead it was the name of a Soviet car manufacturer, so it was a guy driving a black ZiL limousine who picked me up. There was tons of traffic, but we passed all of it, racing down Moscow streets in a center lane reserved for cars with government license plates.

For a moment, I let myself pretend that I was on my way to see Mr. Gorbachev and his wife, Raisa, at his dacha. The idea was pleasant, but only fleetingly. Soon I felt the same pit in my gut that had been there when Mr. Petrov told me Gorbachev was too busy to see me.

I looked out the window. We were on the outskirts of the city, leaving it behind, along with my wish.

I inhaled deeply. As I exhaled, the window fogged over. I found myself nodding slowly.

My wish was finished.

After another forty minutes or so, we pulled into a driveway that led up to a large two-story dark wood house that wasn't quite a mansion but was definitely elegant. As we parked out front, a couple in their late forties or early fifties stepped through the front door. They smiled and waved enthusiastically when they saw me, and I waved back.

After a quick exchange of warm hellos outside in the cold, Evgeny and his wife, Natalia, ushered me into their living room. Evgeny motioned toward a comfy-looking brown leather recliner, and I sat down as he stoked the fire. Natalia had disappeared into the kitchen, but she returned a moment later with a large silver tray loaded with a teapot, cups, a bowl of sugar cubes, and a cookie plate. "Warm yourself," Natalia said, pouring me a cup of tea. I thanked her and added some sugar, also taking a small sampling from the cookie plate after she motioned toward it.

Natalia asked me about my life back home—my family and how we spent our time together, what I was currently studying, my favorite sports. Those initial questions were predictable, but soon she went deeper, asking what stimulated my mind and how I thought intellectual curiosity might be sustained throughout a lifetime. The two of them listened carefully to my answers, inquiring with more depth when I answered vaguely, which confirmed the feeling I had that their interest was completely genuine. When I'd turn a question to them, they'd respond openly, without any guardedness, in a way that made our hours-long relationship seem like it went back years.

We spoke about personal things, like the meaning of friendship and the definition of love, and international things, like borders and conflict. Evgeny asked me about my wish. When I finished talking about it, he said, "Your wish, Jeff—it really is a convergence between these two things, the personal and the international."

"It's heartwarming," Natalia said.

Evgeny nodded. "Not only heartwarming. Not just optimistic. But necessary—absolutely necessary—more than you might know."

I felt pride in that moment, like I'd passed some kind of barrier that I wasn't sure I'd ever cross. It made me think of Richard Wright and the quote I'd memorized a few years before, about the "thirst of the human spirit to conquer and transcend the implacable limitations of human life," from *Black Boy*. I shared it with Evgeny and Natalia, and it led to a long moment of quiet contemplation.

Our conversation moved to the candlelit dinner table, where we enjoyed a meaty soup with pickled cucumbers, followed by beef stroganoff, which was completely different from the microwaveable version I had back home, and a honey cake dessert. We finished in the living room, where it had all begun, with another round of tea. Close to midnight, Evgeny showed me to my bedroom, and Natalia, like a doting mother, tucked me in.

"You know something, Jeff," Natalia said, sitting next to me on the bed. "The thirst that Mr. Wright wrote about, of the human spirit to conquer life's limitations—it strikes me that this is your thirst." Evgeny, standing in the doorframe, slowly nodded.

Natalia continued. "I've reached a conclusion. Would you like to hear it?"

I smiled softly. "I would."

"In this conquering of life's limitations, something we all want for ourselves, I honestly believe you have achieved this."

My eyes flooded with tears. I didn't try to hide them. Natalia patted my head, then leaned down and kissed both of my cheeks. A moment later, Evgeny did the same.

•

The following day, I made it back to the hotel in time for lunch. A bunch of people ran over to say hello. Kim and Heather apologized for the other night, and I told them not to worry. Mike asked what the countryside was like, and I said it was absolutely beautiful. Karen gave me a hug. "I missed you, Jeff," she said. "Honestly, I think everyone missed you."

During a break in our afternoon prep session, the last one before the summit the next day, one of the coordinators, Billie, asked me what it was like to visit a major political player. "I didn't meet Mr. Gorbachev. I met with a scientist and his wife."

"I know whom you met with," Billie said. "Evgeny Velikhov is Mikhail Gorbachev's right-hand man on nuclear issues. He's the guy who led the massive cleanup after the Chernobyl disaster. I'm pretty sure he was advising Mr. Gorbachev during the nuclear summit with President Reagan at Reykjavík. The guy is huge."

At first I was stunned, but then I recalled zipping through traffic in a government limo and it made sense. "I had no idea. But I guess that doesn't surprise me, because we had maybe the best conversation I've had in my whole life."

"That's fantastic," Billie said. It truly was.

We went into the summit with enormous amounts of energy. It was massive. There were five hundred participants on the Soviet side, compared to just fifty of us, so at first we felt a little intimidated. The task they handed us seemed equally large: to draft a joint document on key global issues that would be delivered to President Reagan and Premier Gorbachev—and sent to other leaders around the world. We agreed to divide up and discuss six topics: homelessness, education, health, the environment, development, and world peace. I was assigned to the last group, because it would focus in part on bringing an end to nuclear weapons. But before we broke up into groups and started on our topics, all the kids—both the Soviets and the Americans—had to listen to hours of unimaginably boring speeches by one Soviet official after another. When our groups finally convened, a Soviet kid assigned to ours said, "Now that is finally finished, I imagine we share common feeling, which is . . . what a relief!" All of us burst out laughing.

Despite that humorous opening, our World Peace group didn't get off to a peaceful start. After introductions, a guy from the Soviet side said, "Shall we begin with discussion of how your Mr. Reagan brought end to Reykjavík peace talks?" That wasn't received very well by our team.

One of our guys, John, quickly interjected.

"I think a better start would be discussing how you Soviets seem to enjoy invading other countries, like Afghanistan."

It felt like the temperature in the room dropped twenty degrees, our own cold war.

None of the adult coordinators—Bruce on our side and two Russians, Alexy and Yanna, on theirs—stepped in. It was a girl on the Soviet side who managed to calm things down. "We are young people, yes?" she said, her eyes connecting with each person in our group. People nodded. "No one in this circle decided to invade Afghanistan. No one here ended Reykjavík talks. We can spend time, how do you say, pointing fingers?" There were more nods, and the girl continued. "Or we can talk about how we, our countries' young people, can make our leaders to support peace."

We all looked at one another. Heads starting bobbing up and down, and grins broke out. The girl, Svetlana, had instantly reset the temperature, and a constructive conversation began.

By the end of the second day, we were in full collaboration, putting together the action plan for the World Peace group. Our plan and the ones from the other groups would be compiled into *The Soviet-American Youth Summit Declaration for the Future.* I was stubbornly focused on nuclear weapons, because of the threat they posed to all of humanity, and I pressed hard not only for the inclusion of a declaration calling for their end, but for deliberate, measurable, responsible steps by our leaders to move toward that goal.

At the end of the summit, each group was asked to elect a representative to present its action plan. We chose Svetlana, the seventeen-year-old from Siberia who had put us on the right path. She ended up going last, after the five other groups, and the response to her very emotional reading was massive applause. The summit was officially pronounced closed, and there were cheers, hugs, and tears.

As I was saying goodbye to some of our Soviet counterparts, I felt a tap on my shoulder. It was Sasha, a funny kid I really liked who'd been in the environment group. He was holding two cups of Russian soda, and he handed me one. "Pretend this is vodka," he said, which made me laugh. He raised his cup. I followed and we clinked them together. *"Lyudy vezdyye adinakovyye,"* he said.

"I'm sorry, Sasha, but my Russian is pathetic."

"Of course it is. You are American," he said, smiling. "What I tell you is 'People everywhere are the same.'"

"I agree, Sasha." I honestly did. I'd come to the Soviet Union convinced they were completely different from us, a perspective almost all of us shared, and we were going home with a strong sense of brotherhood. I really wanted Sasha to come visit. "Do me a favor and get your ass to America, okay?"

"I understand you say come to America. But what means 'get your ass'?"

If it was hard saying goodbye to the Soviets, it was gut-wrenching to do it with my fellow Youth Ambassadors. In just under twenty-four hours we'd depart for Helsinki, and it killed me to think that once there, we'd part ways with the East Coast group, which included Mike and Karen. I wondered if I'd fly home feeling lonely.

I asked Karen if we could meet up after dinner, and she said yes. When we did, I told her to close her eyes and hold out her hands. In one, I placed a card. In the other, I put a small wooden box. She opened her eyes and smiled. "Which one first?" she asked.

"As you wish," I answered.

Karen opened the card. It was about the beauty of friendship, and how grateful I was to have met her. She moved on to the box and slowly opened it, pulling out two silver rings I bought for her when we were walking around the city. "Friendship rings," I said. "I'm not personally into jewelry, so you get to wear both."

She smiled and put them on. "They're beautiful, Jeff."

We talked for a bit longer, but this time I was the one who looked at my watch. Curfew was ten minutes away. I lifted my wrist and she nodded. Then she snatched me up in a hug. "Sleep tight."

•

On our first leg of the flight home, while Mike, sitting next to me, was taking a nap, I decided to sum up the trip in my diary. I couldn't find it in my backpack. I knew I'd packed it—that morning I'd written in it, itemizing all my spending, since Dad would definitely want to know exactly how I'd gone through the wad of cash Mom had given me—but it wasn't there. I was on search number three when Karen tapped me on the shoulder. "Looking for this?" she asked, holding a purple notebook. She had a devilish smile on her face.

"How'd you swing that?"

"You went to the bathroom. Mike helped. I didn't read anything, I promise. But there's something in there for you."

"You're hilarious."

"You're . . . well, you know what you are. Anyway, I'm exhausted, so I'm gonna try to copy Mike."

As she walked back to her seat, I shook the notebook, expecting something to fall out. I flipped through the pages, looking for a card. Nothing. I began a careful search. After getting to the end of all my chicken-scratch entries, I found this, in Karen's beautiful cursive.

Jeff,

I doubt I could ever express to you how deeply running my feelings for you are in my heart. We have so much in common—our love for Mother Earth, our desire to help bring peace to this disturbed world, our love for our friends.

You have made me feel so special. Thank you once again for the rings. They'll always remind me of our friendship.

I hope you can find your niche in this life. Be who you are. Do what you want to do. Keep your dream alive. You have touched the lives of millions by coming on this trip. You are loved by all.

I'm not going to say goodbye. I will see you later. You have profoundly touched my soul.

> *With love from your partner in peace,*
> *Karen*

I read her letter slowly, returning to the beginning when I finished it, doing that over and over again. I knew what was ahead for me: a battle in my mind and in my heart over whether, in this journey, I'd succeeded or failed. Karen, in addition to sharing her appreciation of our friendship, was laying down the argument for success.

So, so much, I wanted to believe her.

CHAPTER EIGHTEEN

The moment I stepped through the doors from customs along with our local coordinator and some other kids from the L.A. area, Mom hollered my name. She was at the other end of a long hallway, pressed up against the barrier, wearing her favorite black cashmere sweater over muted red pants, with people packed in on either side of her. How she could pick me out of a distant crowd so easily, I'll never know, but that lady has eyes like an eagle's. I could make out the smile on her face, it was so wide, along with her frantic waving, but not much else. I turned to our local coordinator and pointed at my mom, and he gave me a thumbs-up. I waved at the other kids and started to run.

I was exhausted, having flown (or waited for a flight) for most of a day. I was also pretty bummed to have had to say goodbye. I was all teary-eyed in the airport in Helsinki when I had to say goodbye to Karen and Mike, my closest, dearest friends on the trip, but it was probably better to get that over with abroad and have time to reflect on the way home. The Velikhovs were also

276

on my mind; they'd told me the morning I left their dacha that I would always be welcome in their home. And then there were the Russian kids we'd worked with throughout the summit. We definitely didn't see eye to eye on everything, but we shared a vision for a better world, and we realized how important it was for our countries to cooperate if we were ever going to achieve it.

As I approached Mom, she pressed her hand to her mouth and inhaled. There were tears in her eyes. I felt her love, and it warmed me.

Just then, I saw the forehead of a man standing behind her. The deep grooves across it were familiar. So was the thin brown hair. As Mom extended her arms toward me, she shifted her weight, and that was when I saw my father.

"Oh, honey!" Mom said when I reached her, grabbing me in a long, tight hug. She released me, but didn't completely let go. Her hands locked onto my shoulders and she gave me a quick shake. "Are you okay?" she asked, her eyes examining mine. I was looking past her, at Dad.

I was nervous. I wondered what Dad was going to say. But Mom needed to be reassured, so I smiled at her and told her I was fine.

"I'm just happy you're home," she said, hugging me again.

Dad extended his hand and I shook it. "Welcome home, son," he said. "How was your flight?"

"Exhausting. I couldn't sleep. I couldn't stop thinking about the trip."

I felt like I needed to share my story right then, how Leningrad was just like Paris, the interview with Nikolai Sivach, my visit to the Velikhovs in the Russian countryside, the summit in Moscow, my new friends. Maybe I wouldn't go into all the details then, but I wanted to start the story.

"Are you hungry, Jeff?" Mom asked. "We could stop for something."

"No thanks. I ate on the plane."

"If I were a good mother, I would have brought you something," she said, shaking her head.

I was waiting for a question about the trip. I looked at Dad, but he turned to Mom. "Shall I get the car and pick the two of you up here?"

I interjected. "No, let's walk together. We've got lots to talk about."

We left the terminal. Dad offered to help me carry my bags, so I handed him my suitcase. "By the way, Bob," Mom said. "Remember the accident? We might want to take the freeway."

Dad slowly thought it over. My shoulders tightened. I wondered when we were going to talk about the trip. "They've most likely cleared it by now," he said. He looked at his watch. "The freeway will certainly be congested at this time of day."

Mom frowned. "I'm not so sure, Bob."

We'd entered a massive parking garage. I saw the big red sedan with its custom plate, BOPH, for Bob and Phyllis. I couldn't believe my parents weren't asking any questions or showing any curiosity. I looked at Mom with my eyebrows raised, but she just smiled, looking perfectly content.

I exhaled sharply. "Don't you guys want to know anything about my trip?" I asked, frowning.

"I'm just so happy you're home, honey," Mom said.

Dad popped the trunk, lifting my suitcase into it. He turned to me. "I have a question," he said. I stiffened then, from my feet to the crown of my head, clenching my fists. I knew what he was going to ask.

"Did you meet with Mr. Gorbachev?"

I swallowed. Dad's eyes were fixed on mine. Mom zeroed in as well. I popped open my hands, lifting one to rub my head. "No," I finally said. "I didn't meet with him, okay? Something came up."

"I see," Dad said. He motioned toward my backpack. I shook my head. He closed the trunk, walked around to the driver's-side door, and unlocked it.

My lips were pressed together. I dropped my head and closed my eyes. I'm sure Dad didn't notice. "What's wrong, Jeff?" Mom asked.

I looked at her. "What I did over there—it doesn't matter to you, does it? It doesn't matter to either of you. Just because I didn't meet Premier Gorbachev, you think it was a failure."

"I didn't say that," Mom said. "Your father didn't say that."

"You haven't asked me a single question, Mom. And Dad obviously only cared about that one thing—look how he just walked away." I shifted toward him. "Is that it, Dad? You see my trip as one big failure?" The thought swirled around in my brain before the truth of it hit me hard. I raised my voice. "It's more than the trip, isn't it, Dad? You've reached the conclusion that *your son* is a total failure."

He spun around then, his jaw tight. "I said no such thing."

I looked him straight in the eyes. "Maybe not, Dad. But you believe it, don't you? You definitely thought my trip was one big distraction in the first place. Now it's even worse. You see me as a *loser*." I waited for him to defend himself, to tell me I'd gotten it wrong. Honestly, I wanted him to. But he was silent.

I started to sob. "People cared . . . about me . . . over there," I said as my cheeks were flooded. "People said . . . they said I actually inspired them. I wish . . ."

"What, Jeff?" Mom said, frowning.

"I wish I never came home."

Her mouth dropped open. Her hand covered her chest. "Did those Communists brainwash you? I knew we shouldn't have let you go."

I didn't respond, and Mom let out a long moan.

No one spoke on the ride home, except for my father, when we passed through the oil fields along La Cienega Boulevard. "You see, Phyllis, all that traffic you were concerned about has cleared." My sobbing had long stopped. I stared out the window, completely detached, feeling as if I'd left my true family behind.

•

On Monday afternoon, I showed up in Ms. Hamilton's English class. I didn't want to go—I told Mom I was exhausted—but she wouldn't have it. "You've been sleeping all weekend," she said. "It's time to go back to school."

I arrived in the classroom just as the bell rang. Surprisingly, Ms. Hamilton wasn't there. Cara smiled at me. "Welcome back,

Jeff," she said. "How was your trip?" That immediately prompted a question from Tim, the guy in our class I really hated.

"Oh, right, Jeff's big trip to the good ol' USSR," he said. "How was your meeting with Gorby? Have you saved the world?"

Tim was baiting me, asking his obnoxious questions with the volume of his voice cranked up. Other conversations stopped, and heads turned toward me.

"Oh, yeah," Anna said, "how was your trip?"

The room went quiet. The eyes on me felt like needles. Everyone was waiting for an answer.

I lowered my head and swallowed. "The meeting didn't happen," I finally said.

Tim snickered. Someone gasped. I kept my head down, feeling like a complete fool.

Just then Ms. Hamilton walked in. "Sorry, you guys, my stomach isn't very happy. Okay, your papers—hand 'em over." I didn't remember that we'd had a paper to write, but I thought Ms. Hamilton would have known I couldn't do it. Still, she stopped in front of me. "I just got back," I said. She frowned deliberately before continuing around the room.

After class, I walked over to my locker. I had the door open, which blocked my face, and I heard Tim's voice about ten feet away. "Henigson got dissed by the Gorbster," he said.

"Ouch" was the response. I didn't recognize the voice.

Tim continued. "Yup, the dude got burned."

I slammed my locker door. They spun around and saw me. Thomas, the guy Tim was talking to, sputtered out a hello.

"Oops," Tim said. I wanted to launch into him with my fist,

but I just glared at them both before walking off. I'd only taken a few steps when I heard them cracking up behind me.

●

That night, just like during the flight home from the Soviet Union, I had trouble sleeping. It had been hard enough saying goodbye to my new friends, both the Americans and the Soviets. But my dad's reaction, along with the comments of those jerks at school, made me feel like my whole trip was a failure. Before I'd gone overseas, I'd had my wish to hope for, to look forward to. All those times when Dad was angry at me, or when he was distant, I told myself—and Mom told me, too—how proud he'd be when I came home from Moscow.

Now I had nothing.

●

I managed to make it through the third quarter of my junior year. Toward the end, I still had a couple of papers to turn in to Ms. Hamilton. She'd given me a warning, but I figured she'd hold out until I finished everything. I just needed a few days. I'd definitely have everything to her by the following week, the last of the quarter.

On Saturday, I finished the papers. I went over to Paul's place and hung out for a few hours. It was good to catch up. When I got home, after stepping out of my car, I saw Mom and Dad sitting at the dinner table. Mom wasn't in her usual position, looking out toward the hills. She and Dad were both facing the entrance. I got this fluttery feeling, butterflies in my stomach.

Amiga met me at the door, and I leaned down to pet her, glancing into the dining room. There was a stack of mail in front of my parents. Dad had a letter in his hand. I was pretty sure I knew what he was holding.

"Could you come here, Jeff?" Mom said. Her tone was formal.

I stood up and walked in. "What's up?" I said unnecessarily. On the table, in front of Dad, was an open envelope with *Polytechnic School* in the top left corner. He was looking at my grades—or grade, as it turned out.

His eyes fixed on mine. "Did you know about this?" he asked, drawing in a breath and controlling his exhale.

"I knew I'd get a grade," I said, "but I haven't seen it."

He passed it to Mom. She handed it to me.

COURSE: English
INSTRUCTOR: Hamilton
GRADE: F
NOTE: Jeff did not turn in required homework this quarter despite multiple requests. I am concerned about him, as this is his only class. I would be happy to discuss his performance and what can be done to improve it.—Grace.

I gave it back to Mom. She held it in front of Dad, but he waved it away. I could see his nostrils flaring.

"You had a *single* class, Jeff," he said.

"Yes. That and treatment for brain cancer."

"That is beside the point."

"Is it, Dad? Have you ever received chemotherapy?"

"I do not dispute the intensity of the treatment you've undergone, but it certainly didn't stop you from traveling halfway around the world."

"Maybe that's because the trip meant something to me, Dad."

"Well, that distraction—"

"Distraction? Is that what my wish was to you?" I was steaming now.

"Not to me. To you. That is precisely why I opposed your pursuing it in the first place."

"If you knew me at all, you'd know it wasn't a distraction. It gave me something to live for." My anger muted my fear. I looked straight into his eyes. "But you don't care about that, do you? That would require you to actually give a shit about me."

Mom's jaw dropped. "Jeff," she gasped.

Dad shoved back from the table and stood. His fists were clenched. It reminded me of a trip in the family camper when I was eight, when Dad, already in an awful mood, saw my brother punch me. Dad responded by slamming Ted in the gut so hard he couldn't breathe. It was the only time he ever hit one of us.

"What are you going to do, Dad, beat me?"

He wouldn't have, but Mom wasn't going to give him the option. She jumped to her feet.

"Stop!" she shouted. "Both of you, stop!" She wiped away tears.

"I'm sure I won't be a problem for you much longer." I stepped back, then turned toward the door.

"Where are you going?" Mom asked.

"For a ride, Mom, okay? I'm going to explode if I don't get out of this house."

Dad stood there, but I didn't look at him. Mom threw up her hands. I don't think either of them saw me start to cry, but the tears were pouring by the time I reached my car.

I drove to the hills across from ours, parking my car in a spot where I could look back at my own house. The stream of tears slowed, then stopped. When I cracked the windows open for some air, the breeze dried my face.

In the distance, I heard howling, coyotes that had probably succeeded in their hunt. I often listened to them from our back deck. The sounds freaked some people out, but they settled me. The only difficult part was when other sharp pitches pierced through, intermittent yelps and screams from the coyotes' prey. Sometimes that would send a chill through me.

Not far from where I was parked was a dirt path. I'd heard about people walking it, but I never had. It threaded through the hill above the houses behind me, back to the area where the coyotes roamed in packs.

There was pain in me, so much of it that I felt like stepping out of the car, finding that path, walking along it, offering myself. I imagined my father watching his news program while the coyotes encircled me, sipping his glass of wine as the pack moved in. Their teeth would tear into me, and I'd shriek in pain. Mom would hurry to the back deck, wondering what she'd heard. Dad would grab the remote and turn up the volume. For me, the coyotes would release more pain than they induced.

I stayed in the hills until the howling stopped.

•

The outside lights were on when I pulled into the driveway. I walked down the steps to find Mom and Amiga waiting by the front door. "Would you like me to warm up a plate for you?" she asked.

I shook my head. "I'm not hungry." I slipped past her, heading toward the stairs.

"Jeff . . . ," she said. There was neediness in her voice.

I froze in place. "What, Mom?"

"I'm sorry. I almost forgot to tell you that Monique called."

I couldn't believe what I'd just heard.

"Seriously?"

"Yes. She said you can call until eleven tonight. She really wants to hear from you."

I felt like a dirty sheet instantly washed clean.

"Thanks, Mom. Like, really."

•

It was so bizarre to be drowning in despair one moment and then, after an interruption, to be flooded with an emotion that felt more like hope. My heart was beating fast when I made it to my couch. It wasn't just from hurrying downstairs. It was anticipation and nervousness, exactly what I'd felt the first time I called Monique.

She answered on the second ring. "Hey, Mo," I said.

"I'm so happy you called me back." Her voice was full of eagerness. "Listen, I owe you a *huge* apology. I'm so, so sorry for making you feel like you made the wrong wish. That was me imposing my stuff on you. I really feel—"

"May I interrupt?"

She paused. "Yes."

"You were absolutely right. I mean, I ultimately loved my wish, but I made it for the wrong reasons. I was trying to impress my father. You know, get him to love me, which is crazy. It's just a really shitty way of living."

"But I shouldn't have—"

"Mo, I ain't done yet." She drew in a breath. "I owe *you* an apology, not just for getting angry at you, but for disappearing. Believe it or not, I missed you."

"I missed you, too, Jeff, for real. Now will you do something for me?"

"Absolutely."

"Tell me about the trip!"

I gave her a quick summary, considering how late it was, but she barraged me with questions. She wasn't very different from that journalist back in Leningrad, Mr. Sivach, who had interviewed me. Monique was equally thorough. I felt a little anxious before letting her know that the meeting with Mr. Gorbachev fell through, but she was completely unfazed. We talked about my visit with the Velikhovs and the peace summit. When I was done, I could hear Monique exhale, like she'd been holding her breath. "Your trip sounds absolutely amazing. I'm so proud of you."

It was like she'd just wrapped me in a blanket and kissed my forehead—*instant* calm. I decided then to tell her what had happened when I got home, how my dad had asked me the one question and nothing else. "I honestly don't think that man could care less about me as a person," I said.

"Well, he frankly does sound like—and I'm going to need to request an absolution from the Pope for this—a total pain in the ass."

I snorted out a laugh. "I'd say that's a fair description."

"But can I tell you something without you freaking out on me?"

"Yes. I mean, like, really you can."

"Well, I'm pretty sure your dad loves you."

I felt my whole face tighten. That sounded pretty far-fetched.

"Sure," I said, rolling my eyes.

Monique heard the sarcasm in my voice. "I'm serious. I think he loves you. Not only that, I think he wants the best for you. Wanna know how I know that?"

"Enlighten me."

"Because your dad is basically my dad's long-lost twin brother."

I definitely wasn't expecting that. It was funny, but she wasn't making a joke. I was instantly curious. "Tell me more."

"Our dads love us. If they didn't, do you really think they'd show up at the hospital, or come to our big medical appointments, or ask about school or simply how we're doing? They wouldn't care one bit. But my dad does all those things, and from everything you've ever told me, your dad does, too. Is that right?"

I was dumbfounded. I blinked several times. "Well, yeah."

"Right. But that doesn't mean they *get* us—you know, and understand what we're really feeling, or what we love, or what scares us. Like, I would give my dad a hundred dollars if he could name a single band I'm into. And that's to say nothing about the million priorities he's got for me that might not jibe with mine. Anyway, I love him, and I know he loves me, but I live for myself."

I was silent. Could something that felt so complicated—my relationship with my dad—be as simple as Monique was making it sound? And that last thing she'd said, about living for herself, was that some kind of prescription I could fill for my own life?

"Jeff, are you still there?"

"I'm here. I think you pretty much instantaneously vaporized three gazillion tons of my stress. Do you take credit cards or would you prefer cash?"

Monique laughed. "Adulation and praise will suffice. And chocolate."

CHAPTER NINETEEN

Monique's words sank in deep. I realized that if I was going to live my own life, I needed to get out of my father's house. That meant clearing things up with Ms. Hamilton, my only teacher, and then, as quickly as possible, getting caught up on all the classes I'd missed.

After stopping by the college advisor's office, where I picked up an information package about a summer program at Boston College, I walked over to the English building. Ms. Hamilton was chatting with a fellow teacher, but she waved me in when she saw me. "Hi, Jeff," she said. "What's up?"

"Well, um," I started sheepishly. Luckily, her colleague picked up on it and said she had to run. When we had the room to ourselves, I continued. "Look, Ms. Hamilton, I want to apologize to you for being a complete moron last quarter."

"You weren't a moron. Maybe just a little stubborn about not asking for help."

"I was an idiot. I just want you to know I'm going to make it up to you. I was going through some hard stuff, but I promise you I'm really going to focus this quarter."

"I've never seen a student face challenges like yours. And I felt awful about failing you. But I can't treat you any differently, and I don't think you'd want me to."

"You're exactly right, Ms. Hamilton. I wouldn't want to be treated differently. And I don't want you feeling bad, either. You're a really good teacher."

She smiled at that, and for the first time since I entered the room, she seemed to relax. "Thanks, Jeff."

"I mean it. I hated English until you showed up. Now it's my favorite class."

"Come on, it's your *only* class."

"Fair enough. But I could hate my only class, right?"

Ms. Hamilton laughed.

"By the way, I realized I made the wrong conclusion about *East of Eden*."

"Tell me."

"Well, you know that part where the Chinese philosophers are debating the meaning of the Hebrew word *timshel*?"

"Of course."

"I totally got it was related to the whole fate-versus-free-will thing. We discussed that last year in Mrs. McKendrick's class, after reading *Macbeth*."

"So what did you misunderstand?"

"More the application of it in my actual life. You know my whole wish and trip to the Soviet Union? I definitely chose that.

But the actual reason I chose it was to please my dad, the same way Cal in *East of Eden* is always trying to impress his dad."

"Very interesting. So what's the lesson?"

"Maybe that we're not truly living freely if the choices we make are to please someone else. We've got to live for ourselves."

"Wow, it sounds like my dear friend Mr. Steinbeck has had an effect on you."

"I can't give all the credit to Steinbeck. This girl—she's just a friend of mine—gave me that last part. But it was definitely a good book. Thanks for recommending it."

"You're welcome."

I put my backpack on and moved toward the door. She waved her fingers, but then I had a quick thought. "One last thing, Ms. Hamilton."

"Sure, what's that?"

"If you want me to get the rest of my work in on time, please don't give me another extra thick, super-compelling book!"

She snorted out a laugh and I left her office.

On my way to the parking lot, I ran into Paul. He had a huge smile on his face. He usually did, but it was bigger than normal. "What's up with you?"

"Truth you won't say anything?"

"Truth."

"I asked Esther to prom."

I'd completely forgotten about prom.

"And she said yes!"

"Dude, that's awesome."

"I know. I'm a stud," he said, smiling broadly and tucking his thumbs under his belt. He tipped his head toward me. "Who are you asking?"

"I don't know. I wasn't even thinking about it."

"Dude, you have to come. I know Lucia is available. At least Cara said that's what Michelle told her."

"Nah, not Lucia. She totally sees me as cancer boy."

"Well, invite somebody. We'll have a blast."

"I'll think about it."

So much for instant clarity.

•

Ms. Hamilton definitely didn't go easy on us with homework. I had so much reading to do that evening. Still, I finished surprisingly early, before dinner even, so I decided to give Monique a call.

"Hey, Jeff!" she said with a ton of enthusiasm.

I loved the way she answered my calls.

"How are you?" I asked.

"I'm doing well. Really well. I'm going to Hawaii." She almost sang the state's name.

"Seriously? That's awesome. When?"

"I'm not sure yet, but I'm really looking forward to it. It's gonna be my girlfriends, Mom, and me. Sorry to make you jealous."

"Hardly. I'm psyched for you."

"Thanks. How are you? Are things better with your dad?"

"I'm not depressed about it anymore, which is a major improvement." I thought for a second. "Yes, things are definitely better."

"That's wonderful, Jeff. I'm really happy for you."

"Well, thanks a ton for that amazing talk the other day."

"You're welcome."

"Now my big worry is just prom—whether to go, who to invite."

"Oh," she said. There was surprise in her voice. "Have you, um, got someone in mind?"

"I was thinking of this American girl I met on the trip to the Soviet Union. She had a boyfriend but said things were shaky. I guess I could try calling her. Anyway, I don't mean to bore you. How are things going with Edward?" She didn't say anything. "Mo, you there?"

She cleared her throat. "We broke up."

"Seriously?" I couldn't believe it.

"Yeah."

"Why? I mean, if I can ask that."

"He thought being in the cancer world was just a little too heavy."

"So what you're saying is he's basically an asshole."

"In technical terms." We both cracked up. A thought popped into my head—maybe Monique would join me for prom? I knew I'd like her to come.

I was just about to ask when her mom called out her name.

"Hey, I've gotta run—we're going out to dinner tonight. And we're out of town this weekend. But I'll be back Sunday, if you want to talk about . . . prom. I mean, if you want to talk about anything. Anyway, call me, 'kay?"

I started to say "I will," but she'd already hung up.

•

That night, I had a dream. Monique and I were at the beach. The prom was happening there—she was my date—and we'd slipped away from everyone else. We were holding hands, walking along a mostly empty pier.

I wanted to kiss her. I kept trying to build up enough courage, but I just couldn't do it. She'd glance up at me from time to time and smile, and I'd nervously look away.

We reached the end of the pier, and there was nowhere else to go. She turned to me then, putting her hand on my shoulder, smiling broadly, and slightly tilting her head back. It was an invitation, and my anxiety gave way to excitement.

The moonlight fell on her lips, and there, just beneath the surface of her skin, I could see thousands of tiny cancer cells swarming. I gasped. Monique opened her eyes, which showed a mixture of confusion and disappointment. But then she saw the fear in me as I stared at her pulsating lips. Her eyes crossed as she tried to see them, she touched them with a finger, and they burst open. I woke suddenly, my face soaked in sweat.

•

I ended up going to prom with Karen. I called her the weekend Monique was away, and she was really happy to hear from me, and she ultimately got around to saying that she found out her boyfriend had cheated on her while we were in the Soviet Union. "I wish I'd kissed you, Jeff," she said.

That reminded me of the nightmare I'd had about kissing Monique. I quickly pushed her out of my head.

"Well, how about you come to prom with me?"

"Seriously?"

"I'm always serious," I said.

"I'd love to!"

I was really busy Sunday and forgot to call Monique. She called a few days later, when I was out, and left a message. I meant to call her back but never got around to it. Then prom was just ahead, and something felt weird about calling her with it so near, so I didn't.

Karen and I had a good time. Mom was thrilled I was going, and she immediately took a liking to Karen. From the moment she arrived, Mom was right there, almost to the point where I had to remind her that Karen was *my* date. Even Dad hung around more, telling us to wait for just a second when our limo arrived because he wanted to take a photo. It felt like I was in an alternate universe.

Our night out together ended up being pretty fun. Things only got weird when we came home, after my parents went to sleep. I slipped into the room where Karen was staying, and we started making out, and things got pretty intense. So did my worry. When she unzipped my pants, I suddenly blurted out, "I'm a virgin."

Her hands flew out of my pants. She sat up. Her voice, which had sounded really sexy up until that point, suddenly changed. "I see," she said.

"I know I may have given you the impression during our call—"

"May?" she said, flipping on the light. Her eyebrows were raised.

We'd talked about sex once. I told her how much I liked it. "Okay, I *did* give you the impression I wasn't. I didn't want you to think I was a loser."

"It's not that, Jeff. I don't think you're a loser. I just obviously didn't think you were a virgin, and I feel majorly uncomfortable about the idea of being your first."

Just what I needed—two stressed people. I didn't know what to say to that. We lay back down and snuggled for a while, and finally she let out a long yawn. I asked her if she wanted to go to sleep.

"I think so," she said.

I kissed her forehead. "Good night, Karen."

You'd think I'd be depressed about how my junior prom came to an end, but I wasn't. In a way, I felt relieved. I felt like I'd kind of betrayed someone. At some point, I was going to have to make amends.

●

The week before I left for the summer program at Boston College—I was very happy to be saying goodbye to my junior year—I had two important phone calls to make. The first was to Monique. I'd left a message on her answering machine a while ago, but that was it, and she hadn't called me back. It'd been weeks since we'd talked about the dance, and I owed her an apology. I really should've invited her to the prom.

When her father answered, I worried something might've happened, sort of the norm when you're calling people who've had cancer in their lives. But no. "If you're looking for Monique, she's in Hawaii," her dad said. "She'll be back in just over a week. I can take a message if you like."

I covered the mouthpiece and sighed. My heart fell—we'd probably miss each other, which meant I might not get to speak with her for a whole month.

I asked him to say hi for me and hung up. I felt awful.

The next day, while I was going through my stuff and deciding what I needed for Boston College, the phone rang. Mom picked it up. Ten seconds passed, followed by a quick pitter-patter of feet crossing the floor above me and Mom shouting my name from the staircase. She sounded extremely excited.

I ran to the stairs. "What's up?"

"Somebody is calling you from Moscow! I think it's a big deal!"

I gave her a thumbs-up and raced back to my room. After sucking in a breath and exhaling, I picked up the phone.

"Hello?"

"Is this Jeffrey Henigson?"

"It sure is."

"Hello, Jeff. My name's Jack Matlock. I'm the US—"

"You're our ambassador—to the Soviet Union! You were with President Reagan and Premier Gorbachev at the Reykjavík talks. It's an absolute honor to hear from you." I couldn't believe he was calling.

"Why, thank you, son. I have to say it's an honor to speak to you. Now would you tell me something? What the heck did you do out here, exactly?"

I told him the whole story, the bullet-point version, from my cancer to my wish, the trip with Youth Ambassadors of America, the interview in Leningrad, and the summit and my visit with the Velikhovs.

"That is very impressive, young man. I've got some news for you. That man who interviewed you is a popular journalist, and his article about you seems to have hit quite a nerve over here. At the end of it, he invited people to write you letters. The embassy has been flooded with them. Stacks and stacks, I'm telling you. You made quite an impression on the folks over here, young man."

"I—I find that hard to believe."

"You don't need to believe anything, because I'm sending you the evidence. We're not the US Postal Service, so we can't possibly get all of these letters to you, but I asked my folks to find your phone number and your address, which your mother kindly provided. We'll fill up a pouch and ship it out your way. You should have the letters in just a few days."

"Thank you, sir. That's very kind of you."

"How's your health, son?"

"Things are looking pretty good. My last brain scan was clear, so I'm good for a few months. Just have to keep at it."

"Well, that's very good to hear. Jeff, I'm afraid I've got to run now, but thank you for representing our country over here. It looks like you've done a very good job."

•

The pouch came two days later. I happened to be the one to get the mail, and like I did when I was a little kid being handed a new model rocket kit by the postman, I ran it down to the house.

"Did it come?" Mom asked at the door, equally excited. I held it up.

I tore open one end over the dining room table and dumped out the letters. I couldn't believe how many there were. Ambassador Matlock had told me he'd be forwarding just a small portion of the letters the embassy had received, which made it even more remarkable that this *huge* bag represented just a handful.

All of them had been opened, I noticed, a metal clip holding each to its respective envelope. The Soviets probably read everything going to the United States. I wondered if any had been censored and withheld. It would have been very Soviet Union–like.

Mom and I pored over the letters. "Do you understand any of them?" she asked.

"The only thing I nailed in Dr. Dillon's class was the Cyrillic alphabet. So I can pronounce the words, but I don't know what they mean." All the letters so far were in Russian, handwritten in Cyrillic cursive.

"Here's one in English," Mom said. We read it together.

Hallo, Jaffe!

I'm sorry, I know English badly very. My name is Irina. My house in the Leningrad.
  I and my friends want your life!

I'm glad to have the opportunity said this your, Jaffe!
You will be to live!
Soviet people do not want war!
Long live the cause of world peace and you!
Write! Good bye!"

"It's beautiful," Mom said, scratching her head. "Maybe those Soviets aren't so bad after all."

"Oh, Mom," I said, "you crack me up."

She looked at her watch and her eyebrows rose. "Oh gosh," she said. "I've got an appointment."

She hurried to get her keys. Just before stepping out the door, she said, "Show the letters to your father tonight—he'll be impressed."

As she stepped out, I gathered the letters, grabbed the pouch, and headed downstairs, where I laid everything across my bed. My eyes landed on one letter with beautiful cursive. I unclipped it from its envelope, and a photograph, black-and-white, with the name *Natalia Pozemova* handwritten on the back, fell out.

Natalia, if she was the person in the photograph, was a young woman. She stood in light snow in front of a row of apartments. There was a thick wool scarf wrapped around her head, and her body was covered in a heavy fur coat. Her dark brown eyes had a gentle feel, and her nose and lips were soft and full. She wasn't smiling, but she didn't need to—her warmth, despite the wintry backdrop, came through.

For a moment I thought about what I'd write to her if I spoke her language. I'd thank her for reaching out to me. I'd tell her how heartwarming it was to know that a step I'd taken toward creating peace in the world had positively affected a human being on the other side of it.

I smiled as I set down Natalia's picture.

Methodically, I went through dozens more letters. Several included photos or drawings; one had a booklet. There was a bunch of postcards, some with pictures of buildings I recognized from our tours in Leningrad and Moscow. I flipped over one of them to find WORLD PEASE handwritten in multiple colors along the back.

There was one typed letter. It came in an envelope that was different from the others—not the airmail kind with a watermark image of some famous Soviet building or leader, but a heavier, plain white stock with nothing other than my name, typed in English, on the front.

I pulled out a bundle of folded yellowish-brown paper. There were thirty numbered questions spanning three pages. I flipped to the last page and found the typed name of the author—Nikolai Sivach, the journalist who'd interviewed me in Leningrad.

Tucked between that page and a blank one was a folded-up newspaper clipping. The article took up about half a page, and there was a picture of me in the top-right corner. The title appeared in big block letters toward the center. I could make out the letters, even the pronunciation—*Oohodya, Oostaiyoos*—but I had no idea what it meant.

I sat there for a second thinking about what to do. There was only one person I knew who spoke Russian.

I picked up the phone and dialed 411. I prayed that Information would have Dr. Dillon's number.

They connected me, and Dr. Dillon answered on the second ring. I recognized her voice, always deep and elegant. "This is Jeff from Poly," I said. "You know, the guy who dropped out of your class last year." I thought she might be upset, but instead she asked me how I was feeling. We'd spoken before about the trip, but I told her about the article and the letters it seemed to spawn. She got excited and said she'd love to see them. I told her that would be great and everything, but I was leaving for the whole summer in just two days, and I was really curious about the article's title.

"You remember the Cyrillic letters I taught you, yes?" she asked.

"Yup, I think so," I said.

"Great. Just read them out to me, one by one, and include any punctuation." I did. She pronounced the two words out loud, not far from what I'd come up with. I was dying to hear what it meant.

"The literal translation is, 'In leaving, I will stay.'"

That didn't make much sense. "What do you think Mr. Sivach meant by that?"

"Well, Russians are famous for nuance in language, and I imagine he is no different. I can only take a guess, based on your medical condition when you went there."

I clutched the phone. "What's that?" I asked.

"I think he's saying—and I'm sorry if this is difficult to hear—that while you're likely going to die, you'll live on in the hearts of Russians. It's quite poetic. Beautiful, actually."

I found myself needing to get off the phone. I told Dr. Dillon another call was coming, thanked her, and hung up.

Deep in my chest, I could feel my heart pounding. I closed my eyes, breathing deeply and trying to calm myself, but it didn't seem to help. An image formed. It was the same icy backdrop as the one in Natalia's photo. I was in the center of it.

What flooded my mind then was death, death in a dozen forms. It was the cancer cells that had inundated my brain, the potential for my surgery to go the wrong way, the possibility of radiation and chemotherapy destroying too much of me, or killing me down the line by not having destroyed enough. There was my wish, which I learned about from people who were dying, and its incomplete realization, which, for that moment up in the hills with the coyotes, brought me close to dying by my own hand.

I grabbed the pouch, filling it with Mr. Sivach's article and letter and the many other letters his article had sparked. I stood there for a moment, nervous and unsure what to do, until I caught a glimpse of my desk. I knew what was in the large bottom-right drawer: three old photo albums that had been sitting there, untouched, for years. I pulled them out, setting them on top of the cabinets behind me. In their place I put the pouch and quickly closed the drawer.

I opened my eyes. It was warm outside, and I'm sure my room was warm as well, but I found myself shivering.

CHAPTER TWENTY

All through the three-course dinner Mom had prepared to mark my return home from the intensive summer program at Boston College, she kept looking at me strangely. She and Dad seemed genuinely interested in hearing about the whole experience—in total contrast to when I came back from my trip to the Soviet Union—but there was something else on Mom's mind. Her eyes kept examining me, her head would tilt to the side, and no matter where I was in my story, she had a contemplative look on her face. I was seconds away from asking her what she was thinking about when she yanked her napkin from her lap and tossed it onto the table. Amiga was startled. She jumped out of her bed and rushed over to Mom, who, while petting her, said, "I do believe you're taller than your father."

I groaned. "Did you hear *any* of what I just told you?" It was a little irritating. She was the one who asked the question I was in the middle of answering.

"I was listening. And I'm very happy you enjoyed your classes.

I was just puzzling over what looked different." The smile on her face grew, and then she snapped her fingers. "Shall we measure?" I looked over to Dad. He shrugged. I shrugged. Mom interpreted that as an enthusiastic yes from both of us. "Great," she said, hopping to her feet. "Let's go to the playroom." Amiga barked.

She brought us to the section of wall where Ted and I had been measured throughout our childhoods, the marks still there, at the top of the stairs leading to our old bedrooms. "You first," she said to Dad. It was kind of awkward to see that exchange, with Mom telling Dad what to do, which was rare in our family. He obeyed and moved into place. She looked at his feet and frowned.

While he was removing his shoes, she grabbed a tape measure and unfolded a step stool. She balanced a book on his head to get a level recording and marked his height on the wall, then measured. "Six feet even," she said to Dad as he stepped away. She motioned to me. "Your turn."

The moment she had the book positioned on my head, a smile broke across her face. She shook her head slowly.

"What is it, Phyl?" Dad said. She stayed quiet as she stretched out the tape.

"Six foot one, Bob," she said when she was finished. "Your son has finally got you beat."

For me, there was something kind of nice about hearing that, considering for my whole life I'd only heard about my father's superiority. Mom had him on a pedestal, and in a way she was taking him down. I hadn't matched his brain—I doubted I ever would—but something about it was still satisfying.

Mom was putting the tape measure away and Dad was sitting down on the couch to watch *NewsHour* when the phone rang. I picked up. "Ted!" I said. We hadn't spoken in ages.

"Hey, bro, how was Boston University?" I wasn't expecting a question from him, even if he did get it wrong.

"Boston College. A total pain in the butt. That said, unless I somehow screw things up senior year, I'll actually graduate with my classmates."

"Good job."

"How's Penn?"

"Fine. I mean, nothing much is going on. The semester is just starting." I would have stayed on with him, just the two of us, but eventually Mom demanded I put him on speakerphone.

When the call was over, Mom took in a satisfied breath. "So nice for us to talk together like that," she said, touching her chest. It was definitely rare for us as a family.

I thought Dad would switch on his news program, but the conversation with Ted seemed to trigger a question I'd expected him to ask at the dinner table. "Speaking of classes, Jeff," Dad said, "how did you perform in yours at Boston College?"

Just a few years before—perhaps even a few months before— I would've been drooling over the opportunity to present the results. It would have popped in and out of my mind the whole flight home, with me envisioning his question, practicing my response, and imagining the look on his face. Now things felt very different. I wasn't eagerly awaiting his question. And now that he'd asked it, I wasn't contemplating his reaction to my answer.

I glanced at my watch. Ted's call had reminded me that there was another call I needed to make myself. I looked at Dad and said, "I did just fine."

He nodded. I think he might've even left it there. Mom couldn't, because she'd gotten the details when she picked me up at the airport. "Your son earned three A's," she said, crossing her arms.

Dad looked at me, an eyebrow raised. "I thought you took four classes."

"I did. Mom's just being particular. Pre-calc was an A-plus."

•

Monique's mom answered the phone after hardly one full ring. "Hi, Mrs. Anstead, it's Jeff Henigson."

"You call me Hugette, remember? Are you back from your trip? Monique will *luh-ove* to speak with you." Monique's mom was so animated.

Over some noise on the line, I heard Monique ask her mom to close the door. A couple of seconds passed. "Hi, Jeff," Monique said. She didn't sound nearly as energetic as her mother.

"How's it going, Mo?"

"All right. How was Boston?"

"Amazing. I mean, boring in the sense that all I did was study my butt off, but I'm going to graduate with my classmates now, thank God."

"That's wonderful. I'm really happy for you." Her voice was in monotone. I was pretty sure she was angry at me for ditching her, but I didn't want to bring it up.

"How was Hawaii? You went, right?"

"Yeah, with my mom and some girlfriends. It was pretty wonderful." She sounded sincere. "I kind of wish we could've stayed there." That was more wistful, like she really regretted having come home.

"Well, I'd take Hawaii over Tarzana, too—no offense to your hometown or anything." I was trying to be funny, but she didn't laugh a bit.

I felt the need to confess. "Look, Monique, I'm kind of dodging saying something that I need to say."

"Tell me."

"I owe you a huge apology. I should've invited you to my prom."

"You don't have to apologize for that."

"No, I really do. I wanted to invite you. Seriously. I was planning on it. But then I had this awful nightmare in which your cancer came back and it completely freaked me out. So I kind of ran away."

"Wow."

"Yeah, I know, totally uncool, and stupid. And I've been a jerk twice over—first for not inviting you, and then avoiding you, because I've been feeling all guilty and everything. Anyway, I'm really sorry, Monique. I hope you'll forgive me."

"I just—"

"Are you angry with me?" That was a stupid question. She had to be. "Look, I completely understand if you are. I deserve it."

"I'm not angry with you. Not at all. You got scared. The whole thing is just . . . weird."

"How so? I mean, yes, I was acting weird, no doubt, but like what specifically are you talking about?"

"I . . . I don't want to freak you out."

I drew in a breath and let it out quietly.

"What's up?" I said, trying to sound calm. She stayed silent for several more seconds. I could hear her breathing. "Please, Monique, tell me."

"My leukemia came back."

I felt as if a stone had struck me in my stomach, knocking the wind out of me. I snatched a pillow from my bed and held it against my chest.

"When?"

"A month ago." My whole body tightened. I spun around and looked at the calendar on the wall behind my couch. I was switching into action mode.

"So you've got a bone marrow transplant scheduled, right?" I needed her reassurance. She told me once that her last transplant had been so excruciatingly painful that she didn't think she could ever do it again. They stuck her in an ICU, loaded her veins with high-dose chemotherapy—a form that was much more intense than anything I'd ever been through—and then, for several hours, they irradiated her entire body. The point of all of that was to kill every cancer cell in her body. The transplant came after that hellish eradication, its purpose to generate new, cancer-free blood cells from the freshly injected bone marrow. She was in intensive care for weeks. I understood her fear of going through all of that again, but she'd already made the consequence of avoiding it clear: she would die.

For several seconds, she stayed quiet. I clenched the receiver. As calmly as possible, I repeated myself. "When are you doing the transplant, Mo?"

She let out a quick burst of air, then spoke quietly. "I'm holding off for a bit."

I moaned. "What the heck is 'holding off' supposed to mean?"

"This is my *third* relapse, Jeff. Why would it work this time if it failed twice before?"

"I know it's awful, Mo. But you can't give up." My mind went to Steinbeck. "You remember the whole fate-versus-free-will thing in *East of Eden*, right?"

"Of course. You deluged my ears with talk about that."

"Well, I really think it's where you are right now, Mo. You're feeling like your fate has been written for you, but the truth is you've got a choice. Don't give up. Please, please, please do the transplant."

"Look, I'll think about it. But can we talk about something else now?"

I sighed. "Like what?"

"Do you like the Beach Boys song 'Kokomo'?"

"Seriously, Mo?"

"Yes, seriously." It was obviously a diversion, but I let her get away with it. She needed to talk about something else. "Kokomo" was on a mixtape I'd listened to a lot in Boston, and I really liked the song. It had been her absolute favorite in Hawaii. She told me all about the trip, how she would stay there forever if she could, just relaxing on the beach and swimming in the ocean with her friends. After sharing a story about a sunset dance party, she yawned. I knew she needed some sleep.

"Promise me you'll think about the transplant?" I said, squeezing that in after saying my goodbye.

"I promise," she said, and hung up. For several minutes, I lay on my couch and cried.

Just like in the weeks and months after her dance party, Monique and I talked a lot after that. Even though she'd forgiven me for disappearing, I still felt guilty. And that just made me commit myself more to convincing her to get the transplant, because I knew if she didn't, she'd be the one to disappear. We'd spend the first half of our conversation on that, with her listening to my latest arguments, after which we'd move on to school and family and friends. She was still cheerful, and I think happy to talk to me, but her optimism was missing, as if she didn't believe things were going to come around her way. Over and over again, I kept telling her to trust me.

At the same time cancer returned to Monique, I concluded it was done with me. My MRI came out clear, and Dr. Gourevik told me I could drop down to just two scans a year instead of one every three months. "I'll do that for one more year," I said. "But if the next two are clear, I'm only going to swing by here once a year."

"We'll cross that bridge when we come to it," Dr. Gourevik said. I was pretty sure I already had.

At the end of August, Monique and I were having one of our evening chats. "You haven't harassed me yet about getting a bone marrow transplant," she said.

"I thought I'd let you tell me in excruciating detail all about your mani-pedi first."

"Ask me about the transplant."

"Are you gonna friggin' get one?"

"Yes!" she shouted into the phone. I jumped to my feet and screamed.

"Everything okay down there?" Dad hollered from the staircase. He was watching *NewsHour*.

"Yes!" I shouted back. I couldn't believe what I'd just heard. "When are you going to do it?"

"As soon as my doc says I'm ready."

"Oh, Monique, thank you so much!" I screamed again.

She laughed.

I heard a pitter-patter of steps upstairs. "Are you okay?" Mom called.

"Fine!" I shouted.

"Don't freak out your poor mom," Monique said.

"Oh, Mo, I'm so happy to hear this. I know it's going to work this time." I so hoped it would.

•

I visited Monique in the hospital whenever I could, though all the school-related stuff made it challenging. I put together a mixtape for her, just like the ones Paul had made for me, and of course I added "Kokomo" to it. We played it in the hospital room.

"It's a damn good song," I said, and Monique nodded. Her mom, who had been sitting in a chair reading a book, looked over at me with one eyebrow raised. I caught my mistake. "*Darn* good, I believe I was saying."

"Yes, Jeffrey," Hugette said with her French accent. "I believe you were."

Monique giggled.

Norman, Monique's dad, showed up a few minutes later. The polio he'd had as a kid might have weakened his legs, but boy, did he ever have a strong grip. "Jeff!" he said as he vigorously shook my hand. "So good to see you!" There was so much enthusiasm in his voice it felt like he was saying hello to his son. "How are things?"

"Well, your wife nearly shot me a minute ago," I said, "but somehow I made it through."

Norman smiled. "Hugette knows a good man when she sees one," he said, and patted me on the back. It felt in that moment like the four of us were a family, with the only confusing part being whether Monique was my sister or my wife. Which one, I couldn't exactly say.

On Monique's second day of "high-dose" chemotherapy, I flew to the East Coast for a round of college interviews. It had been so unsettling a few days before to learn that the schedule for my trip conflicted with the one her doctors put together for her transplant. I told my parents I wasn't going to go, but when I visited Monique in the hospital that afternoon, she practically threatened me.

"Don't you dare think of missing a college interview because of me," she said sternly.

I was worried about her—something that must have shown up in my face.

She smiled confidently back at me. "I'll be fine, Jeff. Just swing by when you return, and we can listen to our favorite song."

I reached down and hugged her then. I wanted to do more, say more, but both her parents were in the room, a few feet away from us. The moment just didn't seem right. "Okay," I said, grasping her hand. "I'll see you the second I get back."

The whole flight out, I was thinking about Monique. It was a lot like coming home from the Soviet Union, when my mind was focused on my new friends and everything we'd done together. The moment I arrived in New York, I called the hospital. It took ages for them to get Monique's mother on the line. "How is she?" I asked.

"She's hanging in there," Hugette said. There was some hesitation in her voice, which concerned me. "They have her in isolation."

I quietly groaned. "I'm so sorry I went on this trip."

"She absolutely wanted you to, Jeff. I heard her make you promise."

"I know. It's just—"

"She's going to be fine, Jeff."

"Well, please tell her I called, Hugette." That wasn't the whole of what I wanted to communicate. I think Hugette sensed that, because she stayed quiet. I bit down on my lip. "Okay, I guess what I'd really like you to tell her, if you wouldn't mind, is . . . that I love her."

"She knows, Jeff. But I'll tell her anyway."

My college trip was a whirlwind tour of four schools. I didn't do a very good job of "being present" during the interviews — which Mrs. Cobb, our college advisor, had told us to do. At Princeton, an assistant dean interviewed me in a group setting with three other prospective students. I completely checked out in the middle of it, wondering when Monique's transplant was going to happen. "So . . . Jeffrey," the lady said.

I looked up at her and she smiled curtly.

"How would you respond to a situation like that?"

I had no idea what she was talking about.

That evening, back in my hotel room, I had a very brief conversation with Hugette. She said the transplant would take place the following day. The second we hung up, I did something that wasn't normal for me: I got down on my knees to pray. I'd prayed before, like at Sylvia's gravesite, but not like that, on the floor. It took me a while to feel comfortable, but finally I closed my eyes and clasped my hands together.

"Dear God, I'm going to ask you for something really, really important. Could you please completely heal Monique? Take all the cancer cells out of her body and don't let them come back — not those ones or any other kind of cancer. And give her a long, healthy, happy life. Amen." I forgot something. "Oh, one more thing: also give her love. Or let her know she's loved."

With my eyes still shut, I thought about how much I wanted Monique and me to be on the same track, squarely on the road to recovery. I didn't say it out loud; I just let it float through my head. Monique and I had been through so much suffering, though hers was obviously worse than mine. Once she got through this, maybe we could go through life together. We could graduate high school, go to colleges not far away from each other, and maybe, if it felt right for both of us, we could let ourselves fall in love.

I checked in with myself. I decided I'd covered everything. "Amen."

I opened my eyes then. My prayer felt finished. I took a deep, satisfied breath. Something somewhere was telling me Monique was going to be fine.

●

When I arrived at LAX two days later, Mom was waiting for me. I could immediately tell something was wrong. The way she waved at me when I got off the plane seemed almost frantic.

I was nervous myself, and had been for the whole flight. I'd called the hospital twice but couldn't reach Hugette or Norman. Neither the guy I'd spoken with the day before nor the woman I'd talked to that morning would give me any information. The lady at least sensed my desperation. When I blurted out "Can you at least tell me if Monique is alive?" she said she was. She also took a message from me, which she promised she'd get to Hugette.

As Mom and I hugged each other, I asked if Hugette had called. "She did. And she got your message. Monique's having a rough time. Hugette wants you to call when we get home."

I left my suitcase in the trunk when we pulled into the driveway and I raced down to the house. Amiga darted to the front door, greeting me with a wagging tail and a red rubber chew toy.

I ignored her and rushed to the nearest phone. Mom wasn't far behind me.

"*Jeff*," Hugette said, sounding relieved.

"Is Monique okay?"

"Can you come down to the hospital?" Hugette asked.

My heart sank. She would've told me if she had good news.

●

The plastic barrier that normally separated visitors from a transplant recipient in the ICU had been taken down, and when I saw that, I felt like I was going to collapse. A bunch of Monique's friends and family were scattered in small groups around the room. Hugette saw me and hurried over, burying me in one of her hugs, and then she started to cry. Norman came over and put his hand on my shoulder, and when Hugette pulled back, he hugged me himself.

"What . . . happened?" I asked. I was doing everything I could to maintain my composure.

"They're not exactly sure," Norman said. "She went into shock from the toxicity of the treatment, something they'd told us was a risk, and now her whole body has been overwhelmed with a terrible infection."

Hugette touched my shoulder. "Would you like to say good-bye to her?"

I closed my eyes, trying to grasp the situation. After several seconds, I nodded.

Hugette walked me over to Monique's bed, patted my back,

and stepped away. Others cleared the immediate area as well, so it was just the two of us. Monique was alive, but barely. She labored through each breath. Her face was badly swollen, to the point where it was hard to even recognize her. She had rashes all over, and her lips were severely chapped. Everywhere I looked I saw a tube protruding from her—God only knows how many. For several minutes I said nothing, but finally I drew close and stroked her fingertips.

"Monique, it's Jeff. I don't know if you can hear me, but I want you to know what I feel for you."

I leaned down. With our heads inches apart, I whispered into her ear. "I love you, Monique. I love you with all my heart. And you'll always be with me. I swear that—I'll never let you go." Gently, I kissed her cheek and her forehead. Then I stood. For several seconds, I cried, trying without success to clear the tears from my face. I turned then to Hugette, who quickly walked over and wrapped me in another hug, handing me a tissue when I let go.

Monique hung on for another few hours, until her best friend, who got the message late, arrived and said goodbye. All of us gathered around the bed and held one another's hands, with Monique's parents holding hers. Her pulse steadily declined, and she died.

We stayed in the room for an hour or more, with most people, at least at first, weeping. Some people were praying. Conversations began after a while, people chatting about this and that, the road they'd take home, how life was so delicate, if only they had the next day off from work. One person approached me—Beverly,

Monique's friend who came with her to the inaugural meeting of our cancer support group. She said a few words and I think she hugged me, but I wasn't there for any of it. It was like I had died, too.

To the extent that I was thinking, it was all about the fact that there was a corpse lying a few feet away from us, the dead body of a person I loved, my *partner* on a shared path to recovery and being normal and living the way everyone else does. There was anger building inside me, first toward the people in that room who had the nerve to start up some godforsakenly stupid conversation about how at least there wouldn't be any traffic on the road at this time of night, and then my anger went internal, at myself, for running away from Monique because of my selfish fear of losing her, and finally to God, whom I'd knelt before and begged—pleaded with the full force of my soul—to let Monique live. The anger was smoldering, consuming me from the inside, while on the outside I was motionless, like a corpse myself, with my body slowly stiffening.

The tapping I felt on my forearm brought me back to consciousness. Hugette was standing in front of me, her face full of worry. "Jeff, are you okay?"

I blinked several times. "Me? Why? I'm fine." She was the one who had just lost her daughter.

"Listen, you drove alone, no? All the way from Pasadena? We don't want you driving by yourself. You come home tonight with us."

I needed to be alone. "Thank you, Hugette. I'm fine, though. Real good. I'll get home. No problem."

"Are you sure, Jeff?" Hugette had so much concern in her eyes, like my mom the night before my surgery. I was close to losing it, but I hated breaking down in front of people, so I looked straight at Hugette and lied.

"I'm really fine. But I should get going." I gave her and Norman a hug, said goodbye to the other people I knew, and left.

Sitting in my car a few minutes later, my hands tightened. I formed a fist and slammed it into the steering wheel, screaming at God. "Why did you take her?" I cried out. Then I hit the steering wheel again before slamming my fist into the passenger seat. I started to weep, softly at first, but soon I was sobbing. The pain and anger in me built, along with a sense of abandonment, and the certainty that I would always feel alone. If God didn't exist, then what was the point of life in the first place? If he did, then I *hated* him. He'd taken Monique away. If this was the fate he'd chosen for me, giving me a taste of love and then ripping it away, then I'd make my own choice: ending my life.

I started the engine. It was nighttime. I raced down the freeway on-ramp and accelerated until my car maxed out at 120 miles an hour. I contemplated where and how to die. After a few minutes, I settled on the concrete wall near the exit to Dodger Stadium.

Then I yelled at God.

"If you even exist, then fuck you!" There was rage inside me. It was in my hands, gripping the steering wheel, and in my foot, pressing the accelerator hard into the floor. I'd never been so angry, not at my brother when he beat me up, not at the English teacher who hated me so, or at my father who thought his Jeep was more important than his son. But there was a deeper emotion inside me, a powerful yearning that Monique be more than just the memory of her I held in my head.

I saw Monique then, on the beach in Hawaii, scrunching her toes in the sand and smiling and listening to "Kokomo." "Put that song on the radio," I said to God. My foot was still pressed to the floor, and the stadium exit was close. The freeway began to curve, and I skidded across two lanes. The exit was in sight. With total conviction, I said, "Put 'Kokomo' on the radio or I swear to you I'll kill myself."

I started singing the song, just like I had for Monique in her hospital room, as I hit the button on my radio. The Beach Boys, in perfect synchrony, were backing me up.

I jammed on the brakes, slowing to 55. A smile burst across my face. I looked at the moonlit sky and started laughing.

CHAPTER TWENTY-ONE

A month after Monique's death, I showed up in a Pasadena court-room to testify against the guy who'd shoved the machine gun in my stomach and stolen my father's Jeep. His name was Harold Woods, I found out, and the circumstances of this meeting were pretty different from our first. He sat next to a public defender as I answered questions from the witness stand. He didn't once look at me, and he spoke only when he had to. Otherwise, he was dead to the world, seemingly resigned to his fate, which one of the assistant attorneys told me was likely to be many, many years in prison.

"How'd it go?" Mom asked when I got home from the trial. She had wanted to come, but her father needed a favor, and I insisted she help him. Now she was in the kitchen, with three cookbooks open and every inch of counter space taken up with ingredients and mixing bowls and utensils.

"It was intense. Turns out I wasn't the only victim. Four other people testified against him—all pretty much the same story as mine. He's gonna get locked up for a long time."

"Well, that's good, isn't it?" she said.

I wasn't all that comfortable with it. Mom could tell from the expression on my face.

"Honestly, Mom, it's depressing. I'm glad they caught him and all, but that's like the end of his life. And nobody cares what got him into that kind of world in the first place. You think he had some nice, nurturing dad? Not a chance."

Mom smiled. "You're very thoughtful, Jeff. But he did point a gun at you—and others. Thank God none of you were hurt. It could've been a very different outcome."

"It doesn't make it any less dreary."

She looked away for a second, then turned back.

"Well, perhaps a Caesar salad, followed by garlic roasted chicken and creamy white rice, and finishing, perhaps, with apple pie, might put you in a better mood?"

My mouth fell open. I couldn't believe what I was hearing. With the exception of someone's birthday, Mom hardly ever made real desserts.

"What the heck got into you?" I said with an eyebrow raised. "Weren't you busy helping your dad anyway?"

She put her hands on my shoulders.

"I was, but I looked at my calendar this morning. I don't have you that much longer. Can you believe you're heading to college in eight months? Then this place becomes an empty nest."

I smiled at her. I honestly couldn't imagine how she could stand living here with Dad, but that was her thing. I gave her a big hug, took a step back, and, after putting a serious look on my face, pointed a finger at her.

"There'd better be vanilla ice cream next to that apple pie. And that frozen yogurt crap doesn't count."

"*Jeff*," she said, faking offense.

"You heard me," I said, winking at her, and walked to the stairs.

•

The first time I'd stepped into my bedroom after returning home from the summer program at Boston College, I felt as if I'd gone back in time. On my bookshelf, fluorescent orange light was beaming out of a glass bottle filled with rhodamine 6G, an organic dye I'd acquired for my failed laser project. There were kids' books all over the place, like *The Swiss Family Robinson* and *Island of the Blue Dolphins*, and everything Mark Twain ever wrote. There were stacks and stacks of notebooks, one for every class I'd ever taken, and every crazy project I'd come up with, and blank ones waiting for the next great idea.

My intention right when I came home from Boston was to go through everything, get rid of the stuff I no longer needed, and save the things I never wanted to lose. I got into it right away, boxing up and storing every part of the laser project that had owned the space in front of one of the windows for the previous three years.

I soon came upon the letters from the USSR, tucked into a desk drawer. The deep chill I felt when I learned the title of the article that had triggered them hadn't left me. My own mortality, intertwined with those letters, had kept me from returning to them.

And that was where cleaning out my room had stalled, months ago.

When I went downstairs after Mr. Woods's trial, still thinking about his dismal future and also incredulous that Mom was making an actual dessert, my eyes went directly to a model rocket that had been sitting in the same place on a shelf, collecting dust, for several years. I didn't know what drew me to it, but I picked it up nevertheless, examining it in the light. There were two parts to it, the main rocket and the booster unit. Of all the rockets I'd ever constructed, this one was the most special, and not just because of its build.

Early one morning in the summer of 1983, at the beach condo my parents had rented in Marina del Rey, I woke to the alarm on my wristwatch. I quickly shut it off before Ted was disturbed. I'd gone to sleep fully dressed the night before—I had a plan—and after slipping out of bed I reached under it to grab that same rocket, along with my launch kit, and quietly snuck out of the room. I tiptoed to the front door, and as I opened it and stepped outside, I practically ran into my father.

"You're up early," Dad said. He was tying the laces on his running shoes.

"Yeah," I said, sounding as grumpy as possible.

"Where are you headed?" I couldn't believe he was asking me that. In one hand I was holding my Porta-Pad and launch controller, and in the other, inches away from him, I was gripping the rocket he'd promised to build with me six months before. I was deeply irritated. At least he figured out which rocket it was. "Ah, you're going to launch your special rocket today?"

"Yeah," I grunted.

"I see," he said. He paused for a second. "I thought we were going to do that together."

"We were going to launch it together *after* we built it together, something you gave me your word we would do *six months ago*, and which I reminded you of *four times* since then. So *I* built it," I said, tapping my chest, "and *I'm* gonna launch it."

"I was really hoping to do that with you, Jeff. I just got caught up in a case. I'd certainly like to join you now, if you'd be willing." I stared him down for a full five seconds. Part of me wanted to punish him for breaking his promise, but I figured it might be pretty cool for him to see what I'd accomplished without any of his help.

"Okay," I finally said.

The deep blue sky had a smear of pink along the horizon line, and the cool air moved in a gentle breeze. Perfect conditions. The beach was mostly empty, save for a few runners at the water's edge and a guy with a bunch of bags stacked around him who seemed to be asleep. Otherwise, we had our own version of Cape Canaveral.

We rigged up the rocket on the launch pad, inserted an ignitor into the engine, and rolled out ten feet of ignition wire.

"Are you ready?" I asked Dad. I couldn't keep myself from grinning. This was my favorite part, and I was just dying for him to see this thing fly.

"I most certainly am," he said. His grin was twice the size of mine, like a kid's.

I pulled the safety key out of my pocket, inserted it into the launch controller, counted down from ten, and pressed the button. The engine lit instantly and the rocket raced skyward, a perfect takeoff.

Dad's jaw dropped, which I'd hardly ever seen before. And the amazing part hadn't even happened yet. When the rocket reached a thousand feet, it jettisoned a rear assembly that tumbled back to Earth, and a pair of hidden wings popped out. The rocket became a glider, slowly circling back to us.

"Yes!" I shouted, making a fist and pulling my elbow downward to my waist.

Dad tried to respond, but his mouth just hung open as he shook his head and clapped. He was blown away.

During the rocket glider's second loop on its way back to Earth, Dad and I realized the same thing: we hadn't compensated for the ocean-bound wind when we set up the launch pad. My glider was going to touch down at sea.

That was when Dad took off, as if he were a rocket himself. He raced toward the water and didn't stop when he got there, kicking up ten-foot-high saltwater splashes with his brand-new running shoes. The rocket was still ahead of him, certain to be swallowed by the waves, but he stretched his body, extending one arm as far in front of him as he could, and caught it just before it splashed. He came back toward the sand and started jumping when he reached it, up and down, up and down, only stopping when I finally got there. He gave me a hug, something he practically never did, and handed me my rocket. I looked up at him and smiled. "Well done, my son," he said, patting my shoulder. "Very well done."

While dust-covered now, the rocket was intact. With some new rubber bands to pop out the glider wings, I was sure it could be made to work again. But did I want to fix it and fly it once more? Not really. I hadn't launched a rocket in years. In fact, I'd gotten rid of the other ones. So why did this one still occupy a space on my shelf? How much longer would it stay there? What was I waiting for?

The answer to that question was simple: I was waiting, as I had my entire life, for the father I'd wished for. He would spend time with me. He'd listen to my worries. He'd help me explore my interests. To the extent that a father could, he'd help guide me on my own path through life.

What struck me in that moment, as I slowly turned the rocket glider in my hand, was that the father I actually had would never become the father I longed for.

Dad didn't deny me everything. He gave me the things he thought were necessary. And there were moments, difficult if not impossible to anticipate, when I'd receive a snippet of something I deeply desired from him. But the satisfaction would be fleeting. What he gave me—what he chose to give me—was never enough. It would never be enough.

I contemplated that for a while longer. Then I walked over to the couch and set the rocket on the floor in front of it.

I walked down the hallway to the basement and found a pile of broken-down U-Haul boxes. In a nearby closet, I grabbed some extra-sturdy trash bags and a roll of packing tape. I came back to my room and divided it into three areas—Toss, Keep, and Give Away—and quickly got to work sorting my stuff.

All my notebooks went straight to the Toss pile. I didn't even open them. The last thing I needed was to read about how to become an astronaut. Some kid would want my rocket kits, and maybe *his* dad would take him out to launch one, so they, along with the rocket glider, went to the Give Away pile. The coins Dad had given me when I was much younger were definitely going to Keep, but I resolved—if I ever had a kid who was interested in coins—that we'd collect them together, even if it meant we had to travel all the way around the world to find them.

I was deep into arranging the room's contents when a shadow appeared on the wall in front of me. "Impressive," Dad said, just as I spun around. The Toss and the Give Away piles were knee-high by now. "I should undertake a similar endeavor in my office downtown."

"Thanks," I said, wishing that I hadn't labeled the piles, because now his eyes were going through their contents. Of course he saw the rocket glider, which he leaned down to pick up off the floor.

"I remember this," he said, slowly nodding. "You're not getting rid of it, are you?"

"Rockets are for kids, Dad. I haven't launched one in years."

"We sure enjoyed launching *this* one, though," he said. He turned it in his hands, just like I had moments before, with an expression more nostalgic than the one that had probably shown up on mine. It was obviously a sweet memory for him, too, and I found myself annoyed by the satisfaction he was feeling from seeing the rocket again. Sweet memories for me—at least ones that involved my father—were few and fleeting.

A few months before, in response to his comment, I would have said something sarcastic. I was inclined to at first, but just as quickly I realized the need wasn't there. Somehow, I'd managed to let it go.

"Look, I'd like to get back to this. I'll meet you upstairs, okay?" I glanced toward the door. He got the point, placing the rocket on the bed and looking at his watch.

"Your mother asked me to inform you that dinner will be served at seven o'clock."

"Sounds good."

The second Dad left, I glanced at the clock. It was a little past 6:30. If I focused, I could get everything cleared out before heading upstairs.

I filled one of the U-Haul boxes with my Keep pile—a framed photo of the Mercury astronauts, a picture of Monique that her mother had given me, a handmade card Loretta had delivered to me in the hospital, and a few other things that were close to my heart. I turned to my desk next, emptying all the drawers and distributing their contents among the piles across the room.

I saved the letters for last. I sat at my desk, breathing for a moment, deep and slow, before opening the drawer.

The pouch felt different, as if there was some distance now.

I checked the clock. Ten minutes. I could set the pouch aside, deciding what to do with the letters down the line, but something about that idea bothered me. I wanted to finish what I'd started.

There was no thought of getting rid of the letters—I was definitely keeping them. The question was whether I'd place them in that box, which meant relegating them to the past, along with other things from my childhood that brought me warmth or meaning, or do something with them in my life now, or in the near future. I sat there, with the clock ticking away on the wall across from me. No answer came.

I thought about my first conversation with Monique, when we were talking about what my wish would be and she told me to close my eyes and just let it come. So that's what I did, still breathing slowly, but nothing about the letters emerged.

Instead, Monique showed up. She appeared in quick flashes—the two of us at her party, burning up the patio dance floor; then a telephone call with her laughter warming me; then the pier in Santa Monica, where I'd kissed her in my dream.

The last flash was of her death—my rushing out to the hospital, seeing her in the ICU, saying goodbye, and then, by way of a miracle, understanding that she'd moved on.

I realized I needed to move on, too.

I opened my eyes. They landed on the pouch in my lap. Lifting it, I pressed it close to my chest, and mouthed *spasibo*—"thank you" in Russian—to the writers. I carried it over to the box.

I was about to close everything up when I remembered a copy of the *Pasadena Star News* that had been sitting on my bookshelf. Dated February 7, 1988, it had a story about my experience with brain cancer and my wish for world peace: *Poly Student Fights the Big Fight*. For a while I'd contemplated having it framed, to mark the whole crazy experience. But I knew seeing it would just return me to the past. I pulled it from the shelf, folded it in half, and placed it on top of the letters.

After sealing the box shut with packing tape, I grabbed a Sharpie and wrote "NOSTALGIA" in block letters along the top. Satisfied, I picked it up, carried it to the far corner of the walk-in closet, and tucked it away.

Just as I stepped back into the room, I heard Mom call down from the staircase. "Dinner's ready," she said. "And no ice cream if you're late!"

"Got it," I called, smiling. I was heading toward the door when I saw my old rocket glider sitting on the edge of the bed where Dad had left it. I picked it up, gave it a kiss, and assigned it to its fate.

AFTERWORD

The process of writing a memoir is at first one of collection—recollection is probably more accurate, as memories are not perfect facts—and then, when too much presents itself (and it invariably does), synthesis and elimination.

A number of memories didn't make the cut. Some were painful, like the phone conversation a well-intentioned social worker set up between me and another brain cancer survivor whose tumor, I learned in the course of our chat, had recently returned. Others were considerably warmer, among them an appearance my mother and I made on *Good Morning America* in San Francisco. Mom was so nervous, they had to redo her makeup.

There is one I thought worthy of sharing: an extraordinary trip I embarked on with the Starlight Children's Foundation in the beginning of 1988, before I left for the Soviet Union. Emma Samms, the *Dynasty* soap opera star and cofounder of Starlight, asked if I would be interested in joining her at the Winter Olympics in

Calgary, Canada, as the organization's world peace envoy. I could bring a guest, she said, so of course I invited my mom.

Accompanied by Carol Brown, the then-director of Starlight, Mom and I flew first-class to Calgary. We were met by two producers from ABC Sports: Noubar Stone, our point man, and Geoffrey Mason, who managed all the behind-the-scenes miracles. Soon after, we had the delight of meeting Emma Samms, and in her company watched a number of extraordinary competitions, met athletes from around the world, and enjoyed five-star treatment by the ABC Sports team.

Noubar, well aware of my wish, made arrangements for me to meet with a number of Soviet athletes. The first was Irina Rodnina, who'd won three successive Olympic gold medals for the Soviet Union in figure skating. She was hardly five feet tall, but her presence was commanding.

Ms. Rodnina was stunned by my wish. She asked what had inspired it. I said it didn't make much sense for our countries to spend so much money trying to come up with more effective ways of killing each other.

Ms. Rodnina's face broke out into a broad smile. She nodded. When Noubar told her we had to leave for an ABC Sports appointment, she said, "Jeff must first meet a great man." We followed her through an adjacent building, where she found a man my height but built like a tank. "Vladislav Tretiak," Ms. Rodnina called out to the captain of the Soviet ice hockey team, "let me introduce you to an American hero."

In Russian, she shared with him my wish and what I was

hoping to achieve during my trip to their country. When she finished, Mr. Tretiak turned to me and said, "It is truly an honor to meet you."

That evening, Mom and I, accompanied by Emma and Carol, watched the Soviet ice hockey team trounce Norway 5–0. I waved to Mr. Tretiak when the game was over—we were just a few feet back from the ice—and he motioned for me to come down. He called his team together and introduced me, I think briefly relaying my story.

"*Prosty. Moy roosky ochen ploha,*" I said. *I'm sorry. My Russian is very bad.*

Mr. Tretiak smiled. "I say to them you will bring us peace."

"*Spasibo bolshoi,*" I said. *Thank you very much.*

A LETTER

Hey Jeff!

Should I even write that the story about you really shook me up?

    I'm sure you will receive tons of letters. I know English pretty good, but right now I'm too excited to search the shelf for a dictionary and try to explain myself to you in your language.

    I'm Natasha. I'm a sophomore in Shipbuilding Leningrad University. I'm completely in love with theater! Especially the student theater I'm a part of. It's the best in the whole university.

    During New Year's Eve we performed on Nevsky Prospect. You know, it truly is amazing here on New Year's! In the fall we went on tour.

    I really want for you and your friends to understand that

we have such lovely, beautiful and kind people. They really know how to love, believe and sacrifice themselves!

You know, Jeff, I was always able to get everything I wanted in life. All I wanted to do was want really really bad. I want for you to live! This is why I'm writing to you.

Jeff, in July I'm going into the mountains, Pamir, it's in Central Asia. I know now that while I'm there, on the ice, fighting to keep going, fighting not to throw away the heavy backpack and send everyone to hell, I will be thinking about you.

And you will help me, I know it!

When the night comes and we will be sitting by the fire, when next to me will be those closest people, my wonderful friends, when we will be remembering our beloved Leningrad, when we will be singing our songs about sea to the sounds of a guitar in someone's hands, and when everyone gets quiet, thinking about those who are in sea at that moment, and when only the thousands of lonely stars and the outline of the mountains surrounds us that night, I will also remember a young boy in USA who wants peace and happiness for all the people.

It's great that you came to us Jeff, believe me, you don't have to think about it, but you found a lot of people who think like you do, a lot of truthful, smart and kind people who would really want to be your friends!

You know, I have grand plans for the future. I want to do a lot of acting in theater, I want to conquer Seventhousand in Pamir, I want to ply the seas on a yacht, to travel the entire country, swim in Lake Baikal, walk with geologists through tundra, travel abroad. And I believe that all of these will come true! I believe that there will no longer be wars because there are such wonderful people like you. And there are a lot of them and they can do anything! Thank you, Jeff!

Until we meet, you hear!

> *Natalia Pozemova 24.06.88*
> *Leningrad*
> *Union of Soviet Socialist Republics*

UNDERSTANDING THE COLD WAR

Throughout *Warhead*, there are references to the Soviet Union and the Cold War. Because both are essential components of the story—and of history—here's some background information you might find helpful.

WHAT IS THE SOVIET UNION?

While Russia shows up frequently in the news, you've probably heard less about the Soviet Union. From 1922 until 1991, Russia was part of the Union of Soviet Socialist Republics (USSR), also known as the Soviet Union, a communist country and a rival of the United States. The Soviet Union was composed of fifteen republics: Armenia, Azerbaijan, Belarus, Estonia, Georgia, Kazakhstan, Kyrgyzstan, Latvia, Lithuania, Moldavia, Russia, Tajikistan, Turkmenistan, Ukraine, and Uzbekistan. Today, each of the former Soviet republics exists as an independent country.

WHAT IS THE COLD WAR?

A conventional war is carried out through armed conflict. A cold war, on the other hand, involves economic, political, and military rivalry *without* direct combat. When we speak of the Cold War, we are referring to a period of geopolitical rivalry between the Soviet Union, with its allies in Eastern Europe (together known as the Eastern Bloc), and the United States and its allies (known as the Western Bloc) that began after World War II.

Eastern Bloc countries were united by communism, an economic, political, and social ideology under which businesses, goods, and property are publicly owned and controlled, and separate socioeconomic classes—like the rich, the middle class, and the poor—cease to exist. Communist Eastern Bloc governments were repressive and often brutal, limiting free speech, controlling the media, and imprisoning people who opposed their policies and practices. Western Bloc countries were political democracies, where the civil and political rights of the people are protected by constitutional law, and they had capitalist economies, which allow for private ownership of businesses, goods, and property. Many political theorists considered these two systems incompatible and believed that the survival of one required the destruction of the other.

The Cold War was a fierce conflict between capitalist and communist forces, represented by the superpowers: the United States and the Soviet Union, respectively. Each superpower labored, directly and indirectly, to expand its influence. They also invested in new technologies, some of which were ultimately good for the world. But among them were increasingly sophisticated arms, including nuclear weapons systems powerful enough to threaten human existence. The fast-paced competition to develop ever more destructive weapons systems is known as the arms race; at its peak, the U.S. and the Soviet Union had stockpiled as many as seventy thousand nuclear warheads. The danger nuclear weapons represents to humanity prompted public outcries around the world. Nearly two hundred thousand people participated in an antinuclear protest in Spain in 1977; 100,000 people marched in Hamburg, Germany, four years later; and in the summer of 1982, one million people demonstrated in Central Park in New York City.

Growing public unease in the West, pressure from antinuclear groups, and concerns expressed by national security experts helped galvanize support for nuclear disarmament. The Soviet Union, in the middle of a massive economic downturn, couldn't afford to continue in an arms race that threatened to bankrupt the country. The result was increased support on both sides for arms control. Agreements reached between the United States and the Soviet Union in the 1970s were substantially expanded in the 1980s.

HOW DID THE COLD WAR END?

When Mikhail Gorbachev became general secretary of the Communist Party of the Soviet Union in 1985, the country's economy was stagnant. He introduced radical reforms to open political discussion and reignite the economy and reached out to U.S. President Ronald Reagan to reduce East-West tensions. But the Soviet economy did not recover, and the new political openness only magnified Soviet citizens' growing dissatisfaction with communist rule. The country's influence across Eastern Europe declined. In 1991, the Soviet Union collapsed, and the fifteen nations that comprised it ultimately became independent countries. The end of the Soviet Union brought an end to the Cold War.

HOW HAS THE COLD WAR IMPACTED THE WORLD TODAY?

After the Cold War ended, Russia and the United States agreed that the fourteen other countries that were previously part of the Soviet Union would hand over their nuclear arsenals to Russia. Arms control agreements reached between the United States and the Soviet Union have largely been upheld, and the number of nuclear warheads has been reduced to about 15,000 today.

Still, in the wake of the Cold War, several countries have acquired nuclear weapons, and some are investing in ever more powerful systems. Key arms control treaties are at risk of being terminated. An important lesson from the Cold War is that the voices of everyday people matter—and that politicians are listening. The safety of the world, for this generation and those to come, depends on all of us—politicians and citizens alike—engaging, listening, and working together.

ACKNOWLEDGMENTS

No one these days, or, I imagine, any days ever, writes a book alone. I had *tons* of help. Here are the folks who fill my List of Serious Gratitude:

Paul Rhim. Yup, *that* Paul, the one who shows up in the first chapter, my awesome friend of three-plus decades. For the past five years, I read to him *every work day,* and he gave me invaluable feedback, inspiration, and first-class pep talks. Thank you, my dear friend and wonderful human being!

Daniel Lazar, my extraordinary agent at Writers House, has expertly worn every imaginable hat in this project, from advocate to cheerleader to whip cracker to deeply insightful editor. Helping him—and me—was his superb assistant, Victoria Doherty-Munro. It's been a pleasure working with you, Dan.

•

Kate Sullivan, my editor at Delacorte Press, artfully steered me through *four* rewrites of the manuscript, holding my hand throughout as she helped me refine the story. She works with a thoughtful, dedicated team at Random House Children's Books: Beverly Horowitz, Alexandra Hightower, Colleen Fellingham, John Simko, Ray Shappell, and many others played a part in the production of this book. My thanks to all of you.

A number of folks—aspiring writers, published authors, teachers, and avid readers—provided crucial editorial input throughout the project. Early feedback came from Lenore Appelhans, Elaine Attias, Katie Cunningham, Elisabeth Diaz, Cara DiMassa (the same Cara who pops up in the book), Lisa Gossels, Sharon Grobeisen, Jennifer Hoffman, Laura Sidoti, and Tori Ulrich.

Members of my writers' circle offered many useful critiques: Frantzie Bazile, Nick Broad, Cara O'Flynn, Jenine Holmes, Lisa Kirchner, Sheila McClear, Dorri Olds, Eddie Sarfaty, Court Stroud, Lavanya Sunkara, Wendy Toth, and Dean Wrzeszcz. One of them, Piper Hoffman, added inspiration, encouragement, and a key lesson in self-discipline.

Three pros in the writing world, author extraordinaire and editor David Ebershoff, literary agent Bonnie Nadell, and writer and teacher Sue Shapiro, gave me critical direction.

Brian Gresko and Xeni Fragakis helped me package my manuscript, drawing together its many elements and persuading me to let go of a few that didn't quite belong.

•

My memories of the events covered in this book, and of the period, one during which my brain was under fairly regular assault, weren't completely intact. I was fortunate enough to have my old journals to refer to, but I also had help. My mom, Phyllis Henigson, and her assistant, Debbie Post, pored over calendars, notebooks, and records from the period. My cousin, Loretta Clark, told me stories of when I was in the hospital. Hugette Anstead, Monique's mom, recounted my visits with her daughter, and what she heard of our phone calls. Poly classmates Paul Rhim, Cara DiMassa, and Bianca Medici, along with Grace Hamilton, my favorite teacher and very dear friend, shared their memories of those days at school. Joni Ashworth recounted my volunteering in her classroom at Monterey Hills School. Billie Hopkins and Chace Warmington walked me through the trip we took together to the Soviet Union. Irina Titova, Svetlana Krylova, Dina Rayzman, and Eugenia Zhurbinskaya helped with translation and made sure I portrayed their country of origin accurately.

The enablers of my story are the citizens of the former Soviet Union who, after reading Nikolai Sivach's article about me in the Leningrad newspaper, *Smena*, decided to sit down with pen and paper and share their thoughts, fears, hope, and love with a teen, now on the other side of the world, who had come to visit their country. In the end, I received only a sampling of their letters — both Mr. Sivach and U.S. ambassador Jack F. Matlock Jr. told me there were thousands — but my gratitude to those who wrote, and to Mr. Sivach, for his article, is limitless.

•

You've probably figured out how much I love my mother. She's my best friend, my greatest inspiration, and the first example that pops into my head, effortlessly, when I'm visualizing gratitude.

What might've been difficult to pull from the story is my love for my father. My whole life, I respected him deeply, and I'm grateful for the values he and my mother instilled in me. We had our battles, many of them, but ultimately, we found our peace. Dad, I miss you deeply.

And Ted, my big brother, I'm grateful to you for having put up with so much. I love you, bro.

My last expression of gratitude is to those of you who read this book. Especially young adults. We've been busy mucking up this world for you, whether through our disregard for the environment, or the belligerence we tolerate in our politics, or the many conflicts in this world that we've incited, or perpetuated, or failed to end.

It's *your* turn. Create the world you want to live in. Get involved in politics. Advocate for peace, tolerance, and fairness. Spread love.

Thank you.

ABOUT THE AUTHOR

Jeff Henigson grew up in South Pasadena, California. After a teenage bout with brain cancer, he attended university at the London School of Economics and graduate school at Columbia University's School of International and Political Affairs. He has worked for UNICEF and the United Nations in humanitarian emergencies, and for a nonprofit in human rights. He has lived in London, Seoul, Rome, Beijing, New York, St. Petersburg (Russia, not Florida), and Ko Samui, a beautiful island in the Gulf of Thailand. Today he calls Seattle home. You can find him paddling on Lake Washington or, alternatively, on Twitter at @jeffhenigson or on his website at jeffhenigson.com.